Life Medicine

Ten Prescriptions from The Great Physician

Bart Barrett, MD

PRESS

Life Medicine
Ten Prescriptions from The Great Physician
by Bart Barrett, MD

Printed in the United States of America

ISBN 9781622304448

www.xulonpress.com

Contents

Dedication

To Lisa, who believed in me from the beginning.

Acknowledgments

*L*ife takes interesting turns, and we frequently end up in unexpected places. I started my college studies planning on being a youth pastor and nine years later had an MD after my name. This book began as an outline for a series of lessons for children. Five years and a few hundred pages later, here it is. As with my medical degree, this book is the direct result of the support and encouragement of many different people, without whom this book would have remained an idea. I owe them many thanks.

My mother-in-law, Shirley Rehm, has been a source of continuous encouragement, wisdom, prayer, and support. Linda McGlynn, who in 1993 first identified my ability to teach and communicate God's word, and then cajoled me to join her in ministry to children, has supported my ministry efforts in unwavering fashion. Brian Howard, pastor and friend, was the first to invite me into the pulpit to preach. That opportunity opened doors for ministry and expanded my understanding of what I could accomplish, and gave me confidence that I could make a difference. Joe Aguirre took time from his family to edit the book, and his willingness to challenge my reasoning and correct my grammar extended beyond the realm of editor and into that of friend.

Most of all I thank my family, who tolerated the ongoing noise of my three-fingered pounding of the keyboard and the hours of inattention to their needs this work required. No man has ever been more blessed.

Bart Barrett, MD 2012

Introduction

*M*edicine tastes bad. Well, almost all medicine tastes bad. The bubble gum stuff kids take for ear infections is actually pretty good. Most of the rest of it is bitter-tasting and foul. Woe to the child who lets a pill sit on his tongue too long before swallowing it! I have observed the grimaces, frowns, and expectorating in my own children when they make that mistake. Mary Poppins was right: a spoonful of sugar would help the medicine go down!

In spite of the terrible taste of oral medications, to children there is something far worse than having to swallow a pill, a fate that for many seems worse than death. Shots. The word alone strikes fear in the hearts of children everywhere.

Over and over again in practice, almost on a daily basis, I enter an exam room in which I find a child quivering in fear of a potential shot. Tears often roll down their cheeks as they cling to their parents in terror. Frequently there is nothing I can do or say to calm this fear, and my repeated assurances fall on deaf ears. For some, the dread begins in the parking lot, gathering in strength as they approach my office door. Some of the frightened children aren't even there to see me; they are merely accompanying a parent in for the parent's visit! It doesn't matter. They are in the "shot place" and shots could happen. It is only when they safely traverse the threshold of the waiting room door on their way out that they relax and accept the reality of their escape. For the ten minutes I am in the exam room with them they squirm and thrash and scream, certain that excruciating pain is just a needle away.

Will the Treatment Hurt?

Many of us are no different from the terrified children I see in the office. When it comes to living spiritually healthy lives, we are afraid the treatment will hurt, and we pull away and hide. Even when told that God's medicine can make us better, though we try and believe that to be true, we fear that accepting God's help will bring pain that is too great to bear.

In reality God's prescription for our lives is anything but painful. On the contrary, following God's instructions allows us to avoid much of the suffering that would otherwise consume and define our existence. Our lives, burdened and broken by the disease of sin are destined for pain and sorrow, much of which can be alleviated by allowing Jesus, the Great Physician, to perform His healing and transforming work.

This purposeful work of God is accomplished through His Word, His truth. In His Word God has laid out for people a treatment plan for those who would live healthy lives. Thousands of years ago He first proclaimed the cure for the wrong thinking that plagued human-kind. As with a contagious disease, the Israelites of Old Testament times had caught many of their unhealthy thoughts from those around them, from the unbelieving cultures in which they lived. Just like them, we also frequently find ourselves infected with the sinful ideas and habits that dominate the world around us.

God had compassion on the Israelites thousands of years ago, and He has compassion on people suffering the consequences of their sin today. He gave them His Ten Commandments, ten "prescriptions" that could protect them from lapsing into ungodly, unhealthy lives. Fortunately for us, the ancient medication has no expiration date, and the truths of God's commandments still contain all of their power.

Like bubblegum-flavored antibiotics that are easy to swallow but ineffective if not taken as directed, God's commandments are neither burdensome nor painful. They are instead a way for a society to experience blessing, success, and joy, a way to avoid so much of the pain that characterizes human life. As a practicing physician who sees this pain on a daily basis, it is my prayer that you will allow God's prescriptions for living to transform your thinking and heal your hearts.

Called in for a Talk

*C*hildren are afraid of getting a shot, but for most adult patients there seems to be another deeply held fear—receiving bad news. For many, every blood test, x-ray and physical exam is just another opportunity for a disastrous result. It is as if they expect me to find something terribly wrong every time I see them.

I sense the anxiety when I call people on the phone. Most doctors have their office staff call with normal test results, so when patients hear my voice they are convinced that something must be wrong. I frequently hear sighs of relief through the phone when patients realize that everything is okay and that I am calling with good news. Experience has taught them that doctors don't usually make such calls.

There are certain situations in which doctors are especially unlikely to call. When news is really bad, as in "you've got cancer" bad, most doctors don't tell the patient anything over the phone at all. The patient is simply told, "You need to come in." These are scary words for a patient to hear. To patients, "no information" never means good news.

My nurse's husband was the recipient of one of these "You need to come in" phone calls not too long ago. He had gone to his doctor for a routine checkup and the doctor had ordered routine blood work. A few days later the doctor's assistant called and told my nurse that her husband needed to come in to see the doctor. My nurse was immediately concerned, and tried to get more information from the medical assistant. "Is it serious?" "Is he okay?" "Can it wait until

Monday when he is off?" All of her questions were met with the same response. "Just have him schedule an appointment."

For the next few days my nurse was distracted with worry about her husband. Her experience working in doctors' offices convinced her that something had to be seriously wrong. When that Monday came she anxiously waited for the appointment time and for her husband to call her with the news. When the call came, she hurried into my office to tell me—it was not serious at all, he just had high cholesterol! She was both relieved and annoyed. She couldn't believe that her husband had been called in to see the doctor over high cholesterol. Didn't the doctor know that "You need to come in" phone calls were only for important things? You didn't call someone in for a talk unless you had something serious to talk about!

While not everyone has been called in to a doctor's office for a talk, at some time or another almost everyone has had a "talk" about something important. Our mother or father took us aside and told us that we needed "to talk." We have all experienced it, the "this is completely serious, you better pay attention because this is really important" kind of talk. I have had a few of these talks with my kids over the years. These talks come in different sizes and shapes. There is THE talk, the "where babies come from talk" (which is dreaded by parents everywhere) and then there are other talks such as the "you had better get your grades up talk," the delivery of bad news talk, and the "we are going to have to move to a new town" talk. Regardless of the content, when a mom or dad wants to make sure they are heard clearly they sit their children down for a "talk".

Some "Talks" Are Bigger Than Others

I particularly remember THE talk with my son. He was only eleven years old. I wasn't sure he was ready for it, but the fifth graders were going to be having the reproductive health class (which included watching "the video") in school in a few weeks. I figured I had two choices. I could either tell him the facts of life right then, or I could delegate the responsibility to some prepubescent self-anointed procreative expert who decided it was his job to tell the facts of life to all of the younger children on the playground. I decided it was my job, and rather awkwardly tried to explain things to my son. I can still remember the look of disgust on his face when he realized exactly what I was saying. For his little-boy mind it was WAY too much information. It was a talk neither of us will forget.

I can recall being on the receiving end of parental talks as well, including "a talk" I had with my dad when I was eighteen years old. It stands out in my memory in large part because my father and I did not have very many meaningful conversations over the years. When we did talk it was mostly him doing all the talking; I was expected to nod and make appropriate grunting sounds of understanding while he told me what he wanted me to know. On this particular occasion, in the garage at his home in San Diego, he gave me a brief but intense lecture on my career goals.

I had dropped out of college several months earlier and been working in a grocery store. I thought I was doing rather well—as a union produce clerk I had reached the point where I was making almost $12 an hour. It was 1980, and to me that was a whole lot of money. My father's pointed objective in his talk was to show me that $12 an hour wasn't as much as I thought it was.

I watched as he scribbled numbers on a chalkboard he had on the wall over his workbench. (Looking back on it now the thought occurs to me—who has a chalkboard in their garage?) He wrote down for me the typical monthly expenses for a family of four. The list was not comprehensive, but it was long enough to make his point. When you added up mortgage, food, car payments, insurance, gas, utilities, and savings, a $12 an hour job would not come close to making ends meet. My plans of stacking apples for a living suddenly didn't seem so wise, and pursuing a college degree became a worthwhile objective.

That conversation had a profound impact on me. It was one of the few positive lessons I learned from my father. As I look back on it I realize that it wasn't just the words spoken and logical arguments that stuck with me. What mattered was that my father actually was expressing concern for my future. He shared his thoughts with me because he truly believed he was teaching me a lesson that was crucial for success in life. The conviction in his words had as much impact as the content. As a result of his conviction and concern the talk was a lesson that stuck, a conversation that was remembered.

Moses' Big Talk

As impactful as that "talk" with my father was and as vital as the "talks" (including THE talk) with my own children have been over the years, they are nothing compared to the talk Moses had with the people of Israel thousands of years ago in the desert of Moab. Moses had gathered the children of Israel together for a *talk like no other*. It was the most important talk these people would ever hear, the most significant words Moses would ever speak to them, and Moses knew it.

When Moses called the people together he did so with a memory of the time he had called their parents together for a similar talk forty years earlier. The talk that time had come mostly from God Himself, for only a few weeks after leaving Egypt God had personally and powerfully spoken His law to the newly freed Israelites. Sadly, the people of that generation did not listen to God's words and, as a result, paid a grave price. The adults of that time were told they would never enter the Promised Land. At the time of this gathering, that generation of disobedient adults had all passed on, leaving only their leader Moses and two others (Joshua and Caleb) as the living adult links to the past.

It was the adult children of those long-gone disobedient ones who were now gathered to hear what Moses had to say. They had surely been told the story of how, forty years earlier, their parents and families had been gathered together for a talk at the foot of Mount Horeb. They had been told of the miraculous events of that day. They knew their ancestors had watched in amazement as the mountain was engulfed in smoke and fire. Their forefathers had stood in awe and listened as the voice of God proclaimed the Ten Commandments to His people. The voice of God had been terrifying, so frightening that the Israelites of that day had fearfully begged God to speak no more.

Moses knew that in spite of the manner in which that message had been delivered, the talk had not achieved its desired purpose. Even though they had recently experienced remarkable deliverance from Egypt, even though they had seen firsthand the power of their Divine Rescuer, they failed to heed the words God spoke through Moses.

Moses had to wonder how the people who had seen such great things could be so deaf to the words that were spoken. On that frightful day when the people of Israel had first stood at the foot of Mount Horeb and heard God speak they had been free from Egyptian bondage for less than three months. The memories of slavery were vivid, fresh in their minds. For their entire lives they had been slaves in the land of Egypt—battered, bruised, and abused by a ruthless Pharaoh. No one alive among them had ever known freedom or could remember a time when their lives were their own. In the midst of their suffering, God heard their cries. As a result of God's miraculous intervention through the man Moses, they became the last generation of their people to live in captivity. When God spoke the law to the people for the first time, Moses must have thought that gratitude for their recent rescue would have improved their hearing and ensured their obedience, but it did not.

Forgetting God's Deliverance

The freed Israelites should have been grateful, for they had seen God do incredibly great works as He delivered them. They saw Him strike the Egyptians with terrible plagues and eventually kill all of their firstborn children. In response to God's power they saw the once-proud and mighty Pharaoh humble himself and set them free. In the middle of the night they had fled, over a million refugees taking only what they could quickly gather and carry. Under cover of darkness they streamed triumphantly into the desert, years of bondage undone in a single night.

God continued to reveal His power as they began their journey out of Egypt. Their freedom was threatened almost immediately, and God miraculously saved them. Shortly after fleeing Egypt the Pharaoh changed his mind about losing his slave labor force and soon the people had the massive Egyptian army at their backs. With the army closing in on them they found themselves trapped against the Red Sea.

One can only imagine the fear the Israelites must have felt. Surely many of them were thinking that the whole freedom "thing" didn't seem like such a good idea after all. Life in Egypt had been bad, but it was life! One can almost hear the grumblings: "I knew this was a bad idea! Why did we open our big mouths? Why did we follow this Moses guy in the first place? How do we know God isn't going to kill us like He did the Egyptians? They at least got killed in their sleep by an angel of death, we're going to die with chariot wheel tread marks across our foreheads!"

The people soon saw they had no reason to fear. Seemingly hopeless and doomed to destruction at the hands of the pursuing army and with nowhere to turn, the Israelites watched in awe as God divided the waters before them. The massive sea parted and in amazement they walked on dry land where the waters had earlier stood. Once safely through, they turned and watched as the waters crashed down on the Egyptian army, removing forever the threat of a return to bondage and slavery. They were free!

As glorious as their newfound freedom was, their subsequent lack of gratitude revealed another. It was not only physical freedom they needed. The people of Israel were also spiritually destitute; they had been deeply influenced by the pagan culture of which they had been a part. They were in desperate need of spiritual freedom and awakening. They needed to learn the nature and purposes of the God who had saved them.

Thus, just a few short days after the victory at the Red Sea, at the base of Mount Horeb, with the knowledge and understanding of their time in Egypt, God spoke to them and communicated His law, the way they could be totally and completely free. He revealed the cure for the sinful thinking with which they had been afflicted. God gave them a "talk" like no other.

For 400 years the Israelites had been exposed to and infected by Egyptian religion, idolatry, and immorality. Egyptian thinking was deeply engraved on their psyche. So deeply woven into the fabric of their minds was Egyptian culture, so natural to them were Egyptian ways, that many could not even recognize its influence or impact. For a great number of them their values, beliefs, and thought processes were more Egyptian than Israelite. They had much to learn and to unlearn if they were to live as God intended and desired. They desperately needed to be taught about God.

God, in His wisdom and grace did not delay His instruction. Only three months after leaving Egypt He provided a way to be set free from the sinful mindset to which they had been accustomed. He called them together for a profound "talk." He gave them His law, delivered directly from His lips, as a means of guarding their lives and healing their minds. The principles contained in His law would lead them in the way they should go and could transform them into the chosen people that they were destined to be.

And yet, even though the commandments were directly spoken to them by God, they did not listen. They did not believe. When put to the test the Israelites failed miserably, acting as if they had never experienced God at all. Only a few short months after their deliverance at the Red Sea, they returned to an Egyptian way of thinking and crafted an idol of gold, forming a golden calf and worshipping it. As a result of this grievous sin God punished all of the adults then alive and condemned them to wander in the desert for the rest of their days. They would never enter the Promised Land. Gradually those unbelieving Israelites all passed on, leaving only Moses, Joshua, Caleb, and the next generation, their children, alive.

Gathering for a God-Talk

Forty years later the doubters and unbelievers—the faithless ones who had rebelled against their Redeemer—were dead and it was their children who now stood before Moses. It was this second generation of free people that Moses gathered together for this "talk." There can be no doubting the seriousness and passion with which Moses addressed the people. I am certain that the conviction in my father's "don't be a produce clerk forever" talk paled in comparison to the intensity with which Moses spoke on that day. Moses had been with the people for forty years. He knew what they needed to hear, and at 120 years old, he knew he wouldn't have too many more chances to tell them.

The content of the talk wasn't new. Moses repeated to them the same words of the law that had been delivered to their parents forty years earlier. The exact same law was given, but it was now given to a different people. While the audience had changed, the law had a similar purpose.

When the law was first spoken it was given to a people who lacked personal experience with godly living. They had a religious heritage that came down from Abraham, Isaac, and Jacob, but had been without a God-appointed leader for 400 years. Those Israelites who had escaped Egypt needed to unlearn what they had learned about deity, morality, and humanity. They had come out of a polytheistic culture that worshipped frivolous "gods" who were endowed with human and animal qualities. Everything they had known was wrong. Their thinking was diseased and broken.

How could the newly rescued Israelites rid themselves of such deep-seated erroneous thinking? How could they break free from the pagan mindset? What could cure the sickness that threatened to destroy their culture? God's Ten Commandments, His Divine prescriptions, were given as the way to properly understand exactly who God was and how human life should be lived. They were the key to right living and right thinking, the only hope the people had if they desired to live and think for God. They held the key to freedom from the sinful patterns learned in Egypt and from the sinful tendencies ingrained in all of their hearts. This was the purpose of God and Moses' first talk. The words the people had to hear were the words of God's law.

For both the original Israelites who heard God speak His law and the second generation who heard the law spoken by Moses the talks had a similar purpose. *They were intended to help the people break free from lifestyles of sin.*

While the original hearers needed to escape from their past, the Israelites who heard the law forty years later were in a totally different circumstance. For a generation they had lived in the wilderness in isolation from other people and nations. Those alive at the second giving of the commandments had not grown up in a culture of idolatry or worship of other gods. They had known only one God and had worshipped only Him. His sacrifices were the only religious rituals they had ever known, and His priests had been their only religious guides.

Moses knew that this insulation from erroneous thought was all going to change in a matter of days when they entered the Promised Land. They would soon meet barbaric people of pagan faith and customs. They would encounter polytheism for the first time in their lives. What was hardwired in their ancestors would be new to them, but no less dangerous. What their parents had needed to set aside they would have to avoid.

And in His infinite love, wisdom, and grace, God had Moses give to them again the means of accomplishing the task; He gave them His law, His prescriptions for healthy living. It could guard them and protect them from lapsing into the disease of sin, both the sin in the culture around them and the sinful desires in their own nature. Moses understood this and desired to tell it to the people he loved and led.

Christians as Modern Israelites

It is with this historical context in mind that we see these commandments are relevant today. Those who call themselves Christian can be divided into two classes of people, each similar to the two generations of Israelites. There are those who have grown up in homes and families with no knowledge of the Savior and no experience with His ways and commands. Worldly thoughts, values, and attitudes are their natural way of thinking and acting. If they are to live for God today they must unlearn the secular philosophies and erroneous reasoning that have characterized their previous lives. In the same way as the Israelites who had first emerged from bondage in Egypt, they have much to learn and unlearn if they are to live for God.

The second group consists of those who came to faith as children and grew up in homes where the Savior was known. For all of their lives they have been fed and sustained by God, free from true challenges to their thinking and beliefs. But they live in a world that does not share their faith. Like the second generation of Israelites to receive the law, in the world in which they must live they will encounter pagan people who worship false gods. They will be confronted with gods of humanism and evolution, of sensuality and relativity. If they are going to live for God, they will need to know with certainty what and in Whom they believe. The What and the Whom they need to know are contained in and explained by God's law.

In addition to the cultural influences that challenge and divert attention from God's path, both groups have a common enemy dwelling within. Isolation from an ungodly world does not provide freedom from temptation or removal of sin. Every person is plagued by a sinful heart. As the prophet Jeremiah said, "the heart is deceitful above all things and beyond cure. Who can understand it?" (Jer. 17:9). For all of us who are burdened by our sinful nature, the truth of God's law provides a way out.

Just like the children of Israel so long ago, we all could use a good talking to. We need to be told about the sin that can infect us, to hear about the God who wants to heal us. Just like the people of Israel so long ago, we don't do a very good job of living right. The Great Physician is calling us in for a talk. He knows the condition of our hearts and lives, and He has the prescription for what ails us.

Finding Motivation

I love baseball. I love the game with an unhealthy passion and a shameful devotion. If I was given back all of the hours I have spent watching baseball, playing baseball, coaching baseball, talking about baseball, reading about baseball, and thinking about baseball, I would be twelve again. As a baseball lover, one of the greatest joys I have had in life has been sharing my love for baseball with my son. We go to games together, watch games on TV together, and are even in the same Fantasy Baseball league. (If you have no idea what a Fantasy Baseball league is, my wife will tell you that you don't want to know.) For five years, from the time he was six until the time he was eleven, I coached my son's little league teams. For the six following, he kept playing and we continued to practice together on a regular basis. Looking back on our time practicing I am pretty sure I had more fun than he did!

One practice together stands out in my memory. When he was eleven years old it became clear to me that if he wanted to succeed as a ball player he was going to need to learn how to hit a curveball. For an eleven-year-old boy, hitting a curveball is not an easy task. Curveballs are scary. When thrown correctly, especially from a certain arm angle, the ball starts off looking as if it is going to hit the child squarely in the head. At the last moment, as the ball approaches, it breaks away from the batter and over the plate. Most young players are so fearful of getting hit that they simply cannot keep from ducking as the pitch comes in.

For a young boy the fear level is exponentially increased by the fact that baseballs are hard. *Really* hard. When a baseball hits you, it hurts. When a very hard baseball seems to be heading straight for your left ear it is tough not to flinch. Unfortunately for kids, success as a hitter demands that the batter not flinch, but instead dig in, wait for the pitch to break and then hit it. Only those players who overcome their fear can truly succeed.

I had a large bucket of baseballs on the ground next to me and was throwing him pitch after pitch. About halfway through the session I started throwing curveballs. I had learned that if I aimed at his front shoulder the ball would end up right over the plate, never coming close to hitting him. Sadly, comically, he never saw the ball go over the plate. He would see the ball coming straight for his shoulder, then duck and turn away. Over and over again I threw curveballs, and over and over again he flinched and sometimes completely backed away. He just could not summon the courage to hang in there. Fear of pain outpaced desire for success.

I explained to him that it was important to hang in there, that if he could learn to do this he would be one of the best hitters on his team. Although he said he believed me, he could not muster the courage to stand firm in the batter's box. He kept backing away.

Desperate, I turned to another approach. I shifted my tactics to the age-old parental tool handed down from generation to generation. I bribed him. I promised him that I would give him fifty cents for every curveball he made contact with. I told him I would take away twenty-five cents every time he backed out. To further bolster his confidence, I promised him twenty dollars if I hit him with a pitch. Eleven pitches later, he walked away with five dollars and the ability to hit a curveball. He had found his motivation.

It is a truth of human nature that people need motivation to succeed. As much as we would like to say we do the right thing simply because it is the right thing, if we are honest we all do better if we know there is a reward waiting. The promise of tangible benefits helps as we try to do the things we know we should.

Rewards as Incentive

The God who made us knows that simply telling us what to do, without any promise or hope of benefit, won't always be enough to motivate people. I believe that it was with this in mind that He spoke through Moses and told the people of the blessings that awaited an obedient people, the blessings that would come if they followed God's commandments. He didn't simply write a prescription, tell the people to swallow the medicine, and send them on their way. He made sure the people understood how their lives would be better if they followed His instructions.

As with the children of Israel, when we look at each of the commandments it is helpful to remember that there are benefits promised to those who keep God's commands. Simply stated, life is better when we obey! The commandments are not a cosmic billboard declaring "No Fun Allowed!", nor are they God's way of getting our attention by removing all pleasure from our existence.

The commandments of God are not punitive, but freeing. They are both curative and preventative medicine. Scripture makes it clear that the blessings of God associated with the keeping of His law are truly remarkable. When we truly understand what awaits those who are obedient, we can only wonder why anyone with even a pittance of faith would want to disobey! With a full understanding of how motivating the promises of blessing are, God packaged the presentation of His law with promises of blessing. Moses outlined these blessings of keeping God's law just before and after he shared God's law with the people of Israel.

Moses didn't just remind them of the blessings that would come in the future. He reminded them of blessings in the past as well. In the first few chapters of Deuteronomy Moses began the second telling of the law by reviewing the events that had brought the people of Israel to that place and time. He reviewed the Exodus and the disobedience that led them to wander in the desert. He recalled Joshua and Caleb's obedience, and reminded the people that those two faithful men were the only surviving members of the preceding generation. All of the disobedient adults of forty years earlier were dead, but Joshua and Caleb were alive and vibrant.

As an additional reminder of the powerful God they served and of His ability to defeat all of the foes they would face, Moses recounted to the people their recent victories in battle. These skirmishes were a preview of that which would come. "You have seen with your own eyes all that the LORD your God has done to these two kings. The LORD will do the same to all the kingdoms over there where you are going. Do not be afraid of them; the LORD your God himself will fight for you" (Deut. 3:21–22).

Moses went on to recount how the territories just conquered were the promised inheritance of the Reubenites, Gadites, and the half-tribe of Manasseh. In the same way, the soon-to-be-conquered territories across the Jordan would become the inheritance of the remaining tribes of Israel. In the context of these achieved and promised victories Moses proclaimed to the people the blessings of obeying God's law. Moses reminded the people of past blessings as a way of building the Israelites' confidence in the future blessings God promised.

It was upon this foundation of challenge and encouragement, and with an understanding of their transcendent purpose, that Moses read the Ten Commandments to the people. We will be spending the bulk of our time reviewing each of the commandments and their significance both then and now. But before moving on we would be wise to give attention to the words of Moses upon completing this second giving of God's law. Just as he spent some time laying a philosophical and practical foundation for God's law, he spent even more time emphasizing the tangible benefits of obedience to God's law. He did this in combination with a summary of the law, all of which is found in Deuteronomy chapter 6.

1 "Now this is the commandment, the statutes, and the judgments which the LORD your God has commanded *me* to teach you, that you might do *them* in the land where you are going over to possess it,

2 so that you and your son and your grandson might fear the LORD your God, to keep all His statutes and His commandments, which I command you, all the days of your life, and that your days may be prolonged.

3 "O Israel, you should listen and be careful to do *it* that it may be well with you and that you may multiply greatly, just as the LORD, the God of your fathers, has promised you, *in* a land flowing with milk and honey.

4 "Hear, O Israel! The LORD is our God, the LORD is one!

5 "You shall love the LORD your God with all your heart and with all your soul and with all your might.

6 "These words, which I am commanding you today, shall be on your heart.

7 You shall teach them diligently to your sons and shall talk of them when you sit in your house and when you walk by the way and when you lie down and when you rise up.

8 You shall bind them as a sign on your hand and they shall be as frontals on your forehead.

9 You shall write them on the doorposts of your house and on your gates.

10 Then it shall come about when the LORD your God brings you into the land which He swore to your fathers, Abraham, Isaac, and Jacob, to give you, great and splendid cities which you did not build,

11 and houses full of all good things which you did not fill, and hewn cisterns which you did not dig, vineyards, and olive trees which you did not plant, and you shall eat and be satisfied,

12 then watch yourself, that you do not forget the LORD who brought you from the land of Egypt, out of the house of slavery.

13 You shall fear *only* the LORD your God; and you shall worship Him, and swear by His name.

14 You shall not follow other gods, any of the gods of the peoples who surround you,

15 for the LORD your God in the midst of you is a jealous God; otherwise the anger of the LORD your God will be kindled against you, and He will wipe you off the face of the earth" (Deut 6:1–15, *New American Standard Bible*).

As we review the passage we can see that Moses first gave a reason for the commandments being given and then followed that with four tangible results that come from obedience to the commands.

The basis for the commands is stated in verse one. Although simple, it is important: "...God has commanded *me* to teach you, that you might do *them*." God told Moses to teach the people the commandments so they might DO them.

Barriers to Wellness

It reminds me of conversations I have had with patients. All too often patients come to the office for a follow-up visit for an illness, only to admit that they hadn't done any of the things I had recommended the last time they were in! Patients with infections have said they weren't feeling any better but hadn't taken any of the antibiotics. Others have come in complaining of persistent back pain but then tell me they had not gone to see the physical therapist as I had ordered. It is hard for me to remain kind and gracious as I am forced to explain again and again that medications only work when they are taken, and that physical therapy recommendations are useless unless they are followed!

It seems that there may be something inherent in human nature that keeps people from following instructions. I have mistakenly assumed on too many occasions that my treatments had failed, only to discover that the remedies had never even been attempted! I have learned that I need to remind patients that good health requires effort. Knowing what to do is useless unless you actually do what you should!

The same can be said for God's commandments. They were given to the people specifically that they might *do* them. They were not given for mere head knowledge and meditation. The giving of the commandments was designed to bring about desired behavior in the people of Israel, and the commandments are intended to bring about behavioral changes and effects in us as well. Moses was understandably concerned that after all he had done and the people had heard they would not end up doing as God intended.

We are no different in this way than were the children of Israel. We need to be careful lest we end up with heads filled with biblical knowledge but lives devoid of change. Believers need to encourage each other to not just hear but do those things that God commands. In my experience I have seen that when I hear the word of God taught it is very easy to simply nod my head in agreement with the content without putting into practice that which I have learned. James the brother of Christ addressed this tendency in his epistle, "Do not merely listen to the word, and so deceive yourselves. Do what it says" (James 1:22).

It is important to note here, and wherever else in Scripture we see a command or instruction, that when God tells us to do something it is invariably because, if left to our own devices we would either: a) not do it, or b) do otherwise. Another way of saying this is that our natural inclination, that which would come to us as a result of our sin nature, is to act in direct violation to the will of God. Effort is required if we are to follow God. Obedience requires intentional action on our part. As any parent will attest, obedience doesn't "just happen," it takes work! So when James tells us to not be merely hearers, but also doers of the word, it is because "just listening" is what we are most likely to do!

With a similar understanding of human nature in mind, Moses made it clear that there was effort involved in obeying the commandments. The people of Israel needed to *do* them, it would take work. The concept of work being the response to the grace of God is not novel in Scripture, as the passage in James affirms. Scripture is clear—grace alone saves, and salvation is followed by works. Listening and *not* doing are not what God has in mind. Jesus Himself addressed this innate tendency to listen and not follow-through. Note what He said in His story about the wise and foolish men who built their homes on the rock and on the sand. He speaks to both mere hearers and true doers in His illustration.

> Therefore everyone who hears these words of mine and puts them into practice is like a wise man who built his house on the rock. The rain came down, the streams rose, and the winds blew and beat against that house; yet it did not fall, because it had its foundation on the rock. But everyone who hears these words of mine and does not put them into practice is like a foolish man who built his house on sand. The rain came down, the streams rose, and the winds blew and beat against that house, and it fell with a great crash. (Matt 7:24–27)

It was implied that some would do the words of Jesus, and some wouldn't. The wise would put God's word into practice and the foolish would not. It is up to each of us to make sure we are wise doers and not foolish disobeyers of Jesus' teaching. It was up to the people of Israel to similarly act in obedience to God's law.

So right from the start of reading the law, Moses purposely reminded the people ("that you might do them") of their need to intentionally follow God's commandments. Simply hearing it was not enough. Paul the Apostle gave a similar instruction to the Philippians when he encouraged them to "work out their salvation with fear and trembling" (Phil 2:12).

After Moses told the people what to do—obey the commands— he then told them where they were to do it. Moses said they were to do this work of obedience "in the land they are going to possess" (Deut 6:1). Remember what's been said before about the nature of this land they were about to enter. It was not a land filled with God-loving people. It was a land of terrible idolatry and immorality. When Moses told them to "do" the law in the "land they were going to possess." They were being instructed to live godly lives in the midst of a pagan, unbelieving culture. The Israelites were not going to be surrounded by only like-minded people as they had been in the wilderness. They were moving into a land filled with idolatrous, polytheistic people who had warped views on deity, humanity, marriage, sex, and family. The land they were being given was a place where fornication was a common part of worship, where fickle gods could be influenced and controlled by the whims of men. Here human life was devalued and even sacrificed in worship, and the One true God was completely unknown. It was into this philosophically and physically hostile environment that they were to go and demonstrate the reality of God by the way in which they lived.

Living in a Contemporary Pagan Culture

Can we not relate? Our commission is the same. We are to do God's law in the "land He has given to us." We are all living in the midst of a pagan and unbelieving world, where tolerance of all beliefs and ideas is held up as the standard for "truth" (even though absolute truth is not thought possible!). It is amazing that Moses' words still ring true thousands of years after they were first spoken. What was true then is true now. We must strive for godliness in an ungodly world!

It was encouraging to the Israelites then (and to us now) to see that Moses did not stop by simply reminding the people of their need to live out the commands God had given. He followed up the admonition of why the law was given with promises of tangible benefits that would come from obedience. These blessings can all be found in the words he spoke in Deuteronomy 6, and served to motivate the Israelites to follow God.

Before enumerating these benefits, it is important to note the people to whom these promises were made. They were made to the *nation* of Israel. That is, to a gathering of all of the people together. These guarantees were not made to, or intended for, individuals. This is not to say that individuals would not receive benefit, only that no particular person could consider these promises to be uniquely his or her own.

It may not be the best analogy, but in a similar fashion there are group benefits received from the keeping of worldly laws. For example, if everyone in a society strives to obey traffic laws, the accident rate declines and people in the society will live longer on average. In the same way, if I alone obey traffic laws there is no guarantee that I will live longer. I *might* live longer, but long life would by no means be assured to me. Someone else's bad driving habits could nullify all of my safe driving practices. Even the best of drivers could be injured by another poor driver, so individual effort doesn't guarantee individual benefit.

The same is true of God's law and the promises elucidated by Moses. It was guaranteed that the nation that obeyed God's law would prosper, but a specific individual could not claim a similar promise.

There was also no assurance that the keeping of the law by the children of Israel would result in the elimination of all negative life events for all people. Even in an obedient nation people would continue to become ill and die. Soldiers would still fall in battle. Children would still quarrel and disobey. None of these problems, or any number of other bad things, would completely disappear from society. Nevertheless the nation as a whole would be blessed: the people as a group would prosper and thrive as they followed God's commandments.

We see a similar truth in the earthly blessings that come with faith in Christ. Although centuries of testimony attest that the quality of earthly existence is greatly improved by godly living, even the most devout lives can be marked by pain, suffering, and loss. Nevertheless, when we look at the overall pattern of blessing manifested in the lives of all believers we see that the benefits of godly lifestyles are in fact significant. We do well to bear this in mind as we consider the promises that Moses laid out for a nation that would obey God's commandments. The nation as a whole was guaranteed blessings that might elude an individual faithful Israelite. Even so, the blessings promised were profound.

The first promise given to the nation that would follow God's law is found in the first part of the second verse of Deuteronomy 6, where Moses said, "so that you and your son and your grandson might fear the LORD your God." God's law, specifically God's commandments, were given to help people fear (revere) God. They are, and were given to develop in the hearts and minds of God's people right thinking and appropriate attitudes about the God who gave the commandments. Another way of expressing this is that the regular, consistent obedience to the law of God produces, as a natural consequence, a healthy reverence for God Himself. Not only do we obey God because we love Him; love grows as people obey!

Generational Blessings from Obedience

It is a profound truth that, as people worship God by obeying His commandments, they grow in fear and respect. Personal reverence for God fills our hearts and flows out of our lives. Amazingly, this attitude isn't limited just to the people who obey! Moses says that the law and commandments were given that "you, your son, and your grandson" might obey. It is clear from this statement that obedience to God actually outlives the one who obeys. This passed-on obedience, this contagious fear of God, is essentially a societal benefit of a transgenerational fear of God. It is as if Moses was saying that, at least to a degree, godliness is hereditary! It can be passed on to children and grandchildren!

How can this be? It happens because godly living impacts the lives of those around us. Although we are all individually saved and individually accountable, there can be no doubt that a life of godliness and obedience to the word of God impacts families. Respect for God is a behavior that can be taught and instilled in one's children and grandchildren.

We should not be taken aback at the idea that attitudes about God can be passed on. Thoughts and views are easily transmitted to our kids. We see this evident in ways not related to faith and accept it without question. We teach our children to fear all kinds of things beside God, and they learn from us. We teach them to be afraid of strangers, and they run when approached. We tell them it isn't safe to be alone in a dangerous place, and they avoid going to such places without someone else going along with them. Some of us even teach our children to be afraid of the dentist, and they demonstrate their learning every time they get their teeth cleaned!

Though passing on the truth of worldly lessons is significant, the impact upon our children of a God-fearing life is far more profound. Our attitudes and respect for our Creator establish a pattern of thought in our children that is passed on for generations. It is truly a humbling thought to realize that we can be such powerful spiritual role models.

As we consider the value of passing on the fear of God to our families, it is important to begin with a basic understanding of what it means to "fear God." The word translated "fear" is the Hebrew word "yare'." Language scholar W. E. Vine states that when used of "a person in an exalted position, yare' connotes 'standing in awe.' This is not simple fear, but reverence, whereby an individual recognizes the power and position of the individual revered and renders him proper respect. In this sense, the word may imply submission to a proper ethical relationship to God."[1] It is this sense of respect and awe that is transmitted to future generations. If we truly believe Moses' words, this attitude is transmitted even if those future generations do not fully embrace faith!

A look at the history of the United States lends credence to this principle. The initial colonists were exceptionally devout men and women for whom faith was an integral part of their lives. A reverence for God was embedded in their culture. The initial settlers arrived with a desire to worship God in freedom and in truth. As a result, God's commandments and law were the foundation of pilgrim society. The people feared God. This reverence continued through the founding fathers, and is seen in the language of our Declaration of Independence and the writings of presidents and influential men. "In God we trust" was not meaningless when it was first inscribed on our currency. A fear of God was an integral part of early American life. In ensuing generations this legacy was passed on. America's Christian heritage shone forth through the 1800s and into the early 1900s.

At the end of the nineteenth century and the beginning of the twentieth the influences of Darwinism and intellectualism began to take hold, becoming pervasive in American universities. Higher criticism attacked the Bible, the historicity of Jesus, and the foundations of the faith. Many denominations saw an increasing trend toward faith in a nonspecific God and moved away from a belief in absolute truth. In the minds of many Americans God was no longer an Almighty Being worthy of awe. Instead He was an abstract concept to be relegated to the nonintellectual realm of faith, mostly irrelevant to everyday life.

Yet even as the culture became more secularized, the influence of previous generations' reverence remained. Although the seeds of secularism were planted around the turn of the last century, it was not until 1962 that prayer was removed from public schools. It is still considered inappropriate to say God d—on broadcast television. Unbelievers, those with little or no knowledge of Christian doctrine or even those vehemently opposed to Christian belief, will frequently proclaim their belief that Jesus was a good man or a prophet.

Many other examples can be given to illustrate the lasting impact of God-fearing people upon their progeny. For most people in our culture, the Bible is respected over other works of literature. Defacing a Bible is more egregious than defacing the phone book.

Graffiti on a church is more offensive than graffiti on a liquor store. Even in our increasingly secular culture there are remnants of a respect for God. These vestiges are a direct result of our faith origins. They were passed on.

I have seen evidence of this in my own life. Although I was not raised in what would typically be described as a Christian home, my childhood was not devoid of godly influences. My maternal grandparents came to faith in Christ when I was a very young boy, and my mother for a time taught me Bible stories. Even though my total amount of church attendance amounted to less than a year by the time I was fourteen years old, I still possessed a sense that certain things were right and certain things were wrong.

This respect for God influenced my behavior even though I did not have a well-formed or mature faith. I remember (vividly) a situation and conversation with a friend my freshman year in high school. We had been close friends in elementary school but gradually had drifted apart. During that year we shared one class together and on occasion casually talked. One day we were yapping in the library when he invited me to go with him to a popular hangout to meet girls. In hushed but excited tones he told me that he was sure there would be an opportunity for me to have a sexual encounter. To him, this was the ultimate pursuit, the best thing going. In spite of his passionate assertions that it would be a great experience, I remember a profound sense of fear at the thought of going with him. I was completely appalled, and I told him no. When he asked me why, I said because it was wrong. When he asked me why it was wrong, all I could think of in response was, "It just is!" I could not explain my reasons, yet something deep inside told me I just could not go with him.

As I look back on that time now, I realize that the angst I was feeling was a result of a fear of God that had been taught to me by my grandparents and my parents. I could not fully explain it and didn't truly understand it, but it was a part of who I was and it influenced my behavior. I could not knowingly and intentionally go against God in that way. Unwittingly, I had inherited a fear of God!

This small example demonstrates how the fear of God can be passed on. Our children are undeniably affected by the lessons we teach them from God's law. This is what was promised to the nation of Israel, and it is clearly true. This first promise of God regarding the keeping of His law as spoken through Moses has been validated in our culture, in our history, and in our personal lives. When we fear God, others will as well.

Obedience Leads to Longer Life Spans

The second promise Moses put forth as a result of keeping God's law also entailed a tangible earthly benefit. The second verse in Deuteronomy 6 says "so that you may enjoy long life." Wow! Moses was actually saying that the children of Israel would live longer if they followed the law of God! What a remarkable promise!

It bears repeating that the promises were to the nation of Israel as a whole, and are therefore not individually claimable. Not all Israelites who obeyed God's law lived to a ripe old age. But there was a promise that the people *as a whole* would live longer ("enjoy long life") if they followed the commandments.

The question then arises: Is there any evidence outside of Scripture that people live longer if they walk with God? Author Denise Mann, in an article written for WebMD, cites the conclusions of more than forty scientific studies that addressed the issue.[2] The answer is a resounding YES!

She writes, "Overall, the people who were most involved in their religions were 29% more likely to be alive when the various studies were completed than were their nonreligious counterparts." Another way of expressing this is to say if 70% of non-religious people were alive at the end of the study, 90% of religious people would be. In the studies cited, religious people didn't die as early as faithless people. Research showed a profound difference in survival.

The various study authors cited such things as improved social support and avoidance of unhealthy practices as reasons for the difference in longevity. While this is undoubtedly true, I do find it interesting that it took a few thousand years for scientists to recognize the truth of God's promises! If people obey His law, they will (on average) live longer!

If one stops to think about it, it is not too difficult to come up with more potential reasons for increased survival. Among them:

- Avoidance of sexually transmitted diseases. The Israelites had no knowledge of germ theory and they didn't need it to avoid sexual diseases. By faithfully obeying God's law they would avoid gonorrhea and syphilis, diseases which are deadly without antibiotic therapy. Other sexually transmitted infectious diseases such as chlamydia and herpes would be nonexistent. As a result of living chaste lives they would see a dramatic decrease in birth defects such as blindness, deafness, and brain damage.
- Stable marriages. The prevention of adultery would lead to strong marriages. Studies have shown that married people live longer. A study in Australia published in the journal *Stroke* found that married people over the age of sixty-five had a 30% lower risk of stroke when compared to unmarried people!
- A lower murder rate. I think this one speaks for itself!

Obedience Leads to Prosperity

All of these examples, which are by no means all of the possible benefits one could list, are real and measurable evidence of the life-prolonging blessings upon a nation of people living in obedience to God's law. Yet the benefits of obedience are not just limited to longer life spans and having children that also fear God. Moses gave another benefit of following the law, which can be seen in Deuteronomy 6:3. Moses told the people that they should be careful to obey God's law in order "that it may be well" with them. This suggests that life as a whole would be better as a result of following God's law.

Moses was saying that the quality of Israelite life would be noticeably better than the lives of the godless people around them. The phrase "be well" contains within it a sense of doing good, being glad, and being well. Implied in the phrase is a measurable degree of success and satisfaction. The nation would be more content, successful, and satisfied as a result of adhering to the law of God. This principle runs throughout Scripture and multiple passages support this conclusion. Here are two that accurately sum up the rest:

> Be strong and very courageous. Be careful to obey all the law my servant Moses gave you; do not turn from it to the right or to the left, that you may be successful wherever you go. Do not let this Book of the Law depart from your mouth; meditate on it day and night, so that you may be careful to do everything written in it. Then you will be prosperous and successful. (Josh 1:7–8)

> All these blessings will come upon you and accompany you if you obey the LORD your God: You will be blessed in the city and blessed in the country. The fruit of your womb will be blessed, and the crops of your land and the young of your livestock—the calves of your herds and the lambs of your flocks. Your basket and your kneading trough will be blessed. You will be blessed when you come in and blessed when you go out. The LORD will grant that the enemies who rise up against you will be defeated before you. They will come at you from one direction but flee from you in seven. The LORD will send a blessing on your barns and on everything you put your hand to. The LORD your God will bless you in the land he is giving you. The LORD will establish you as his holy people, as he promised you on oath, if you keep the commands of the LORD your God and walk in his ways. Then all the peoples on earth will see that you are called by the name of the LORD, and they will fear you. The LORD will grant you abundant prosperity—in the fruit of your womb, the young of your livestock and the crops of your ground—in the land he swore to your forefathers to give you. The LORD will open the heavens, the storehouse of his bounty, to send rain on your land in season and to bless all the work of your hands. You will lend to many nations but will borrow from none. (Deut 28:2–12)

In these passages God is promising material success to His people. Although we are discouraged from seeking financial gain as a motive for our behavior (and contrary to the teachings of those preaching a prosperity gospel there is no such guarantee of individual success), a nation that strives to follow God can expect a greater level of prosperity.

We again need look no further than the history of the United States as evidence of this truth. Although it is easy to attack America's shortcomings, there has scarcely been a nation whose roots were more completely implanted in biblical soil. Consequently, perhaps no modern nation has been more blessed. The fact that both of these realities apply to America is not a result of random chance. Research supports the fact that godly people are, on average, more successful than nongodly people. Simple mathematics allows us to conclude that a nation full of godly people would be more successful than a nation of those without God!

The prosperity that results from godly living is described in an article by David Francis on the *Christian Science Monitor*'s website.[4] Francis cites the work of MIT professor Jonathan Gruber and summarizes his findings: "On average, his paper notes, a household with double the rate of religious attendance as another household has 9.1 percent more income. That extra participation in religious activity decreases welfare participation by 16 percent from the usual rate."

The reasons for this benefit are less easily explained than those associated with long life, yet they are no less certain. Although one may postulate that the blessing may be a result of a greater work ethic or diligence in religious people, the foundational truth remains—godliness is profitable for a culture! God blesses godly nations in this life! As David said in Psalm 23, "Surely goodness and mercy will follow me all the days of my life."

Obedience Leads to Healthy Populations

A final benefit enunciated by Moses to the people on that day in the desert is also found in verse 3 of Deuteronomy chapter 6. Moses told the people they should keep the Law "that you may multiply greatly." Simply put, he told the people that if they kept God's law, there would be more of them! God actually promised population growth as a consequence of obedience. There would be more Israelites, and a greater growth rate relative to other nations. What an amazing promise!

This did not just mean that the children of Israel would have more children. It was not just a promise of fertility. Many factors contribute to the population growth of a society in addition to the number of children per family. These factors include infant mortality, age at which a first child is born, duration of fertility, and life expectancy. An understanding of health and reproductive physiology supports the truth that many of these variables are positively impacted by godly living.

A decline in infant mortality would be impacted directly as a result of decreased infant illnesses and congenital abnormalities. There are a number of sexually transmitted diseases (from herpes to syphilis and gonorrhea) that impact infant survival. People who follow God's law completely never get these diseases, as monogamy is guaranteed protection against such infections. A godly people would be devoid of these illnesses and would see a significant rise in infant survival.

When we remember that in ancient times people got married at a very young age, we can understand that if fertility arises earlier the potential for more children is greater. A woman who begins having periods at age eleven has two more years of fertility than a woman who starts at age thirteen. The age at which a first child is born is directly related to the age at which menarche (onset of menses) occurs. Multiple studies have confirmed that the more healthy and nourished a girl is the sooner she will begin her monthly cycles. It is not a stretch to believe that following God's dietary laws, when combined with the prosperity resulting from obedience to God's law, would result in a better-nourished society. Good overall health also impacts the age of menopause, or the age at which fertility ceases, providing for additional years of fertility. It is easy to see how following God's law directly leads to the fulfillment of God's promise to the people. They would have more children!

When our understanding of improved fertility and infant survival is put together with the increased life expectancy that was also promised, we cannot help but be amazed at how God's promises align with modern medical knowledge! God knew exactly what He was talking about!

All of these blessings laid out by Moses represent a remarkable compilation of promises. The nation would live longer, better, more successful, more fertile, and God-fearing lives if they would only heed and obey the law of God! Although these assurances were made thousands of years ago, God's word is eternal, and I believe that societies that follow God's law in the present day will see similar blessings.

It is important here to stop and remind ourselves again that the temporal benefits promised by God were given to the nation of Israel, not to individual Israelites. These promises were not made to each person separately, but to an entire group of people. In other words, for a culture as a whole the results of striving to obey God's law are certain, for an individual they are not.

The lack of individual, personal assurance in this instance is different from the personal assurances guaranteed in eternity to each person who is a child of God. There are clearly specific blessings promised to each one who is faithful to God's calling. The Apostle Paul speaks of eternal rewards in his letter to the church at Corinth (1 Cor 3:11–16). Although the gift of salvation is entirely that, a gift, Scripture states that when we arrive in heaven each of us will be rewarded in some fashion: "If what he has built survives, he will receive his reward" (1 Cor 3:14).

Although we must never feel ourselves entitled, Moses made it clear that it is wrong to think there is no benefit at all in this life to obeying God's law. The promises of God served as motivation to the people of Israel long ago and serve as motivation to us today. Just as money helped my son hit a curveball, and prescriptions are easier to take when we know they will make us well, these promises can help entire nations. The blessings are significant and the promises great for the people who will just obey!

A Matter of Desire

"We have to do something about my knee pain!"

*D*ave was frustrated. He had been coming to me for several months with nagging pain in both knees. The pain made it hard to walk and nearly impossible to exercise. The anti-inflammatory medications I had prescribed had barely put a dent in the discomfort, and physical therapy hadn't helped much either. From his perspective he had done all he could. From my perspective he was ignoring the obvious cause of his continued suffering.

I knew there was one thing he hadn't tried, and I decided to address the root of the problem head-on. I resisted the urge to tap my knuckles on his forehead and say, "Hello, McFly! You're FAT!" I instead softened my approach and said, "Honestly—don't you think your weight has something to do with it? You weigh 334 pounds! You are at least 100 pounds overweight! Your knees can't take it! It makes no sense to try all of these other therapies if we don't address the obvious problem. You have to lose weight!"

I could tell by the look on his face that this wasn't what he wanted to hear. He had been overweight for years and his knee pain had only been present for the last several months. It was easy for him to wonder why, if weight was the issue, he hadn't had pain earlier. I explained to him that things can add up over time and that perhaps he did have a mild and newer injury. Nevertheless, even if there was a recent injury that had triggered his problem, his obesity now made it impossible for his knees to heal. I explained further that the obesity didn't just hurt his knees, it hurt all of him. Obesity would not only cause him pain but also shorten his life. To help him with his problem I recommended that he see a colleague of mine who was a weight-loss specialist.

He told me he couldn't afford to see the weight-loss doctor. The $500 monthly fees were out of his price range. For the next few minutes I reviewed with him how much he spent on food and other luxuries. I told him further that when we factored in the thirteen years of life the average overweight person loses due to obesity, $500 a month was actually a bargain. I was offering him the chance to buy thirteen years for three to four thousand dollars! Reluctantly, he took my colleague's card.

I saw him again about six months later for a mild respiratory complaint. He had lost over sixty pounds and looked great. Although he wasn't in to talk about his knees, I asked him how they were doing. A sheepish grin spread across his face as he replied, "You were right! They don't hurt at all!"

Looking back on his story I am reminded how difficult it is to encourage people to do what they need to do. People like Dave remind me that motivation isn't only a matter of knowing what should be done. There is much more. Knowledge needs to be combined with a desire to change. In Dave's case, until he understood that weight loss was the only way to relieve his suffering and that he had no other options, he wasn't likely to do what he needed to do and go on a diet. To perform the seemingly external act of going on a diet and losing weight, something had to happen deep inside of him. Simply understanding that change was necessary was not enough to improve his life, he needed to have a deep desire to change before that change was possible. Although it was brutally and immediately obvious to me that he needed to change his lifestyle and lose weight, it took him time to come to grips with that reality.

What was true with Dave was true for the people of Israel. They needed encouragement to do what they knew was expected of them. Moses had spent considerable time laying out for them the wonderful blessings they would receive as a people if they obeyed the law of God, yet in order for the people to change their thinking and behavior something more was required. They needed to understand they had no other choices, and they needed a deep desire to change if they were going to live the lives God desired.

Moses, divinely inspired of God, appears to have understood this predicament. Moses knew that the promises given, great as they were, were insufficient to bring about obedience in the nation. There was something else required. Simply hearing what God had said would not be enough. Something would have to happen in the hearts and minds of the people if they were to follow God's law.

Honoring God and His Way

Moses related to the people what would be required, and his words are also found in Deuteronomy 6. He laid the foundation upon which faith and obedience were to be built, and he then described the effort that would be required to achieve the obedience God wanted:

> Hear, O Israel: The LORD our God, the LORD is one. Love the LORD your God with all your heart and with all your soul and with all your strength. These commandments that I give you today are to be upon your hearts. Impress them on your children. Talk about them when you sit at home and when you walk along the road, when you lie down and when you get up. Tie them as symbols on your hands and bind them on your foreheads. Write them on the doorframes of your houses and on your gates. (Deut 6:4–9)

The section of Moses' discourse stating the foundation of the law begins with words that are simple, yet whose impact has spanned generations of Jewish culture, history, and practice. Moses declared "Hear, O Israel: The LORD our God, the LORD is one." The first words of the verse, "Hear O Israel" ("shema Yisrael" in Hebrew) are sacred in Jewish culture. The passage in Deuteronomy introduced by these words is considered the most important Scripture passage in the Jewish faith, more important even than the Ten Commandments themselves. The Jews understood that what the passage says about the person of God was the very foundation of their faith.

The beliefs of the Jewish people in this regard are beautifully articulated on the website aish.com,[1] a site focused on Jewish teaching and tradition. The site says of the Shema Yisrael (the name given to Deuteronomy 6:4 by the Jews):

"Hear O Israel, the Lord our God, the Lord is One" is perhaps the most famous of all Jewish sayings. The Shema is a declaration of faith, a pledge of allegiance to One God. It is said upon arising in the morning and upon going to sleep at night. It is said when praising God and when beseeching Him. It is the first prayer that a Jewish child is taught to say. It is the last words a Jew says prior to death.

We recite Shema when preparing to read the Torah on Sabbaths and festivals. And we recite Shema at the end of the holiest day of Yom Kippur when we reach the level of angels.

Shema is contained in the mezuzah we affix to the doorpost of our home, and in the tefillin that we bind to our arm and head.

Throughout the ages, the cry of Shema has always symbolized the ultimate manifestation of faith in the gravest situations. With the Shema on their lips, Jews accepted martyrdom at the Inquisitor's stake and in the Nazi gas chambers.

The Shema was and is incredibly important to the people of Israel. The Jewish religious leaders got it exactly right when they assigned supreme importance to the words of Deuteronomy 6:4. This verse is indeed the very foundation of the law and thus of Jewish faith. The singular nature, the Oneness of God, is at the center of all correct belief. In acknowledging this truth one also accepts that there is no other truth. There are no other options. The Shema is a declaration that there is no other way besides God's. His way is the One and only way, just as He is the One and only God.

The Shema declares that God is One, and that He is united, distinct, holy, unmatched, unequaled, and unapproached. God is not one among many—He is all there is. There is no other alternative. He is the only Hope, the only Savior, the only Name upon which people may call to be saved.

Implied in this Oneness of God is a lack of otherness. There are no other options for those who would consider faith. People do not get to pick and choose their gods. Contrary to what our culture seems to believe, there is no heavenly catalog from which people can select the god of their liking. It is unfortunate that there are many people who do not understand and accept this truth and who think that they are the final arbiters of what and who God is.

I encountered this thinking many years ago when I was an employed physician. During a down time in the office I was discussing faith in Christ with a group of medical assistants. Most of them were receptive to a degree, but there was one young lady who was clearly uncomfortable with the conversation. In an attempt to end her involvement in the dialogue she said, "I believe in God, I just believe in him in my own way." It was apparent that she felt that by declaring her belief in *something* she had displayed appropriate religiosity. In her thinking, people were free to choose what they believed in and she had made her personal choice. She obviously believed that her statement would end the discussion, as her beliefs were equal to anyone else's. She was wrong!

"You can't do that," I replied. "You can't decide for yourself what you believe in. Once you acknowledge the existence of God you forfeit the right to define Him. Because He is God, He defines Himself. And He will decide how He is to be worshipped. We do not get to decide what we want Him to be like. He is who He is, and we have no option but to accept that."

She was clearly taken aback by this thought. At some point in time she had been taught that faith was a personal thing subject to individual understanding. Like so many in our postmodern world, she believed that truth was individual, not universal. I explained that her statement revealed an attitude in which she placed herself above God. She made herself out to be the final judge of what was true, and had determined that she was the one who could decide who and what God was.

I shared that if God existed, then it would be impossible for Him to be fully defined by man. By definition God is beyond complete human understanding. If finite man could fully understand Him, He wouldn't really be an infinite God! He would be equal to man. I shared that our journey of faith is not one of definition but of discovery. As we pursue the one God, He reveals Himself to us and we learn who He is. And He is who He is, not who we determine Him to be. When it comes to faith there are really no options. We simply have to accept the fact that God is.

I am not sure she understood what I was saying, but the others did, and the Jews of Moses' day did. God is One!

The Apostle Simon Peter also understood the Oneness of God and that God's way was the only way, even when many others did not. In John 6, as Jesus' teaching proved more challenging, the majority of His "disciples" grew uncomfortable with His instruction and left. In response to the many who forsook his teaching Jesus turned to those few that remained and asked them, "You do not want to leave too, do you?" (6:67). Simon Peter replied, "Lord, to whom shall we go? You have the words of eternal life. We believe and know that you are the Holy One of God" (6:68). In the phrase "Holy One" Peter revealed his understanding that there was no other option, no other way to go. Peter grasped that he didn't get to choose for himself what truth was. Truth was whatever God declared it to be, and he had no choice but to accept it.

Peter's declaration expressed the core of all faith—the realization that God is truly all there is and that there is no other place to go. It requires a supreme surrender of the will and a complete bending of the knee in submission to embrace the truth that "He is One." There can be no true obedience to God if people believe that faith in God is optional, or that there are other reasonable alternatives. As Dave demonstrated with his weight loss, only when people accept the fact that there is only one way to go will they actually move in that direction!

Believing and Acting

The people of Israel needed to adopt this mindset if they were to follow God. By understanding and receiving in faith the truth that God is One, they would be motivated to respond and act as they should. Acknowledging truth has consequences; it changes the hearer. True faith has consequences as well. True faith is characterized by a change in the heart and life of a believer. This faith response, the visible outflow of belief, is the second half of the foundation laid down by Moses in his challenge to the nation of Israel. Moses told the people that a right understanding of who God is results in right action toward Him—that people who believe act differently than people who don't.

When people grasp the truth of God's supreme value, His holiness, majesty, and mercy, behavior changes. There is only one possible response to accepting truth about God. When people realize that God is their only hope, when they consider His total perfection, recognize His complete transcendence, and contemplate His absolute holiness, their hearts cannot help but cry out, "God, you are GOD!" When confronted with these truths, no one can do anything other than bow before Almighty God and declare, "You are ONE!"

As people of faith, when we understand that it is THAT God who has chosen us, it is THAT God who has saved us, and it is THAT God who sent His Son to die for us, there is a natural response. The recognition and acceptance of this truth brings about in us an ever-growing love for God. It is this love of God that completes the foundation of obedience. It is this love that forms the basis for the deep-down change that completes our motivation. This love was described by Moses:

> Love the LORD your God with all your heart and with all your soul and with all your strength. (Deut 6:5)

If I correctly understand what Moses was saying, it seems that more than simple awareness of God's promised blessings, more than an acknowledgement of God's person, was required to bring about change in the people of God. Although there is a natural response and action that results from faith, that response does not come without effort. Moses made it clear that the people could not be obedient to God's law unless they loved the God of that law with an all-consuming and all-encompassing love. People needed to be possessed with a consuming passion for Him that rendered everything else irrelevant. This type of love for God creates in the faithful a desire for Him and to please Him. It is out of this consuming, complete, heart-soul-mind love that obedience to His law arises.

On these two pillars—the knowledge of who God is and a consuming love for Him—were the foundations of obedience set. The foundation of the law as described by Moses can be summarized in just a few words: know Him and love Him. Know Him, that He is One, and love Him with all of your being. Although this truth can be simply and concisely stated, living it out is not an easy task. I believe that it was with this in mind that Moses went on to challenge the people to incorporate a love of God and allow His law into every aspect of their lives.

We are not different from the children of Israel. If we desire to follow God's law, we need to be changed deep in our hearts. Like Dave with his weight loss, we must acknowledge that God is our only hope, and we need to pursue Him with intense effort. It is the understanding of who God is and acceptance of His Oneness that brings about the love that will guide and transform us.

Maximum Effort Required

Several years ago I volunteered to help coach the junior high baseball team at my son's school. It was a very small school and my son was one of only twelve boys who tried out for the squad. With such a small group, no one was cut from the team and everyone who signed up was assured of a chance to play.

Unfortunately for the head coach and me, what we lacked in numbers was not made up in talent. That team was without a doubt one of the worst collections of baseball players ever assembled. The Bad News Bears were all-stars compared to these kids. Fly balls went under gloves, over heads, and—on one especially painfully comic occasion—off a player's head. In spite of the certain futility we faced, the head coach and I determined to do the best we could to teach these boys the game of baseball.

What made the coaching especially difficult was that even though the players were incredibly bad, they were surprisingly hard to coach and teach. Despite a lack of the most basic understanding of the game and with poor physical skills and mechanics, they persistently talked back to us when we tried to explain how to play correctly.

Looking back on it, I vividly recall one instant that epitomized the struggles we had with the team. I was doing a one-on-one hitting drill with one of the players. I had him hitting baseballs off of a tee so I could closely watch his hitting technique and provide immediate feedback. It did not take long for me to recognize a serious flaw in his swing. (The fact that he frequently hit the tee instead of the ball was a dead giveaway!)

With every swing he would stride forward with his front foot and transfer his weight forward. As a result he would pull away from the ball as he swung. This common mistake meant that if a pitcher threw a pitch over the outside part of the plate he would never be able to reach it. Any curveball would spell certain doom as he would be unable to adjust to the break (the last-moment "bend" or curve) and would not come within a foot of hitting the ball.

I stopped the drill and explained to him what was going on and carefully demonstrated why the way he was swinging would lead to failure. I then put the ball on the tee and watched as he repeated the exact same mistake again and again. After a series of painful misses I stopped the drill and again demonstrated for him the proper technique. I showed him how his weight was transferring, and how it would make it difficult to hit certain pitches. I explained to him that because he played golf, he was swinging the bat like it was a golf club. Although the swing felt natural to him, it wasn't correct, and it needed to change.

He took the bat from me, shook his head, went back to the drill and proceeded to repeat the same bad habits. When I attempted to correct him again, he stopped, glared at me and yelled, "This is how I do it!" He had always done it that way, and he saw no need to change. At the age of twelve he apparently believed he had learned all he needed to know about baseball.

He never changed his swing and he was seldom successful. He failed to see that success depended on his learning to be comfortable with something that at the start would feel unnatural. Success required intentional effort and constant practice. It did not come easily. It took sacrifice and commitment.

If we are honest, we must admit that in our natural inclination to remain in dysfunctional comfort we are very much like that young baseball player. We have a natural tendency to resist improvement that requires commitment and effort. Loving and obeying God is as unnatural for us as a baseball swing was for that boy. As sinful people we are by nature rebellious, not obedient. God has given us a prescription, but it won't work if we don't take it as prescribed! Diligence and effort are required if we hope to succeed in following

God's law, and if we hope to succeed in training children to follow Him as well.

Moses understood this principle of effort and commitment. As we look at the verses in the first part of Deuteronomy 6 we see Moses outlining for the people just what would be required of them if they were to truly follow God's law. It is clear that Moses realized that it would not be easy. He knew obedience wasn't a natural act. We see this as we consider what Moses told the people:

> These commandments that I give you today are to be upon your hearts. Impress them on your children. Talk about them when you sit at home and when you walk along the road, when you lie down and when you get up. Tie them as symbols on your hands and bind them on your foreheads. Write them on the doorframes of your houses and on your gates. (Deut 6:6–9)

It Doesn't Come Naturally

By beginning with "these commandments are to be on your heart" Moses intended to communicate that the words of the law were to be seared on their minds, ingrained in their psyche, cherished at the very core of their being. They were to be so firmly implanted in their souls that there was no room for any other law or any other purpose. Their commitment to obedience needed to be so strong so as to crowd out any thoughts to the contrary.

How could this happen? How would such a level of commitment arise? It certainly would not happen by chance! Relentless effort would be required. No one could say a quick, simple prayer at the altar and suddenly become a rich depository of God's truth. It is clear that putting God's commandments on one's heart would happen only as a result of intentional effort.

This truth that work is required was confirmed later by the Psalmist who wrote, "I have hidden your word in my heart that I might not sin against you" Ps 119:11. The key words in the verse are "I have hidden." Clearly, words don't just hide themselves, someone has to put them there! It takes personal effort to learn and memorize

God's word. The effort required is greater because learning God's word is an unnatural act. As unnatural as it was and is to know God's law, the Psalmist and Moses agreed that it must be done.

Moses made it plain—if the people were to live lives of obedience, they would need to know God's word and His law. The same is true for us. We cannot obey God's law without a knowledge of it. This won't and can't happen by accident. For us to know God's word we have to want to know it and purposefully learn and study it.

Though the fact that knowledge of God's word requires obedience to God's word seems inherently obvious, it is a truth that seems to have been lost in the church today. Ignorance of Scripture is epidemic in the modern church. The overwhelming majority of people who describe themselves as "born-again" or "bible-believing" Christians cannot even recite half of the Ten Commandments.

A sadly comical example of such biblical ignorance was watched by millions of people a few years ago on cable television. A congressman who had introduced legislation supporting displays of the Ten Commandments in public buildings was a guest on Comedy Central's *The Colbert Report*. He proudly proclaimed to the host the importance of the Ten Commandments and his commitment to the legislation. The host, Steven Colbert, then asked him if he could name the Ten Commandments. The congressman hemmed, hawed, and stumbled over the question before admitting he could name only a few of them. Apparently he believed the commandments were important enough to post on a wall, but not important enough to commit to memory!

The bumbling congressman is an accurate representation of most people I meet. Like him they are truly unaware of how important it is to know God's word in general terms, and even less aware of the significance of knowing God's commandments specifically. Not too long ago I heard of another example of such ignorance from a pastor friend of mine. He told me a story of a couple that came to him for relationship counseling. They had been attending church for quite some time and had been dating for a while. He nearly fell out of his chair when in the course of the conversation they asked him whether the Bible said anything about having sex outside of marriage. They thought it was okay for them to have sex, but wanted to be sure! It was clear to him that they did not know the law of God! The ignorance of this couple serves as a real life example of the fact that you cannot follow what you do not know, and that you can't know without some effort to learn.

At the risk of being redundant—if we want to live as God intends, we will need to know what it is that God intended! We must take to heart the words of John the Apostle, "This is love for God: to obey his commands. And his commands are not burdensome" (1 John 5:3). We saw this truth in the previous chapters. Not only are the commands of God not burdensome, they bring great blessing! As believers, we must strive to know them and write them on our hearts.

You Can't Teach What You Don't Know

Besides the personal benefits of knowing the law of God, there is another reason we should know God's law and His commandments; if we don't know it, we can't teach it! In the section of Deuteronomy above, Moses stressed the importance of teaching the law of God to children. Moses commanded the people of Israel in regards to God's laws to "impress them to their children." Implied in the challenge to the people is that they knew what it was they were going to teach. A deep understanding and commitment to God's law was essential if they were to impart it to their children.

Almost everyone who has ever attended high school has seen what happens when someone tries to teach something they don't really know. My son's senior year physics class was a perfect example. Time and again the teacher would write a physics problem on the board, work through it step-by-step and come up with the wrong answer. The kids in the class would correct the error, and the teacher would have to go back to the text to discover where he went wrong. The teacher's lack of commitment to knowing the material rendered him all but useless as an instructor. What is true for high school physics is true for the commandments of God. We are ineffective teachers of that which we do not know well.

Not only is a deep commitment to knowing God's law essential to teaching children but also it is part of the means by which children are taught. The imparting of God's word to children naturally occurs when adults have filled their hearts with it. This seems to be what Jesus meant when He said "out of the overflow of the heart the mouth speaks" (Matt 12:34). And it resonates with what Moses was telling the nation of Israel. The truth of God's law was to flow out from parents' lives into the lives of their children.

This principle is crucial for parents expecting to train children well. God's truth is to "spill out" onto one's kids. According to Moses, parents are to impress, or as the NASB reads, "diligently teach" God's law to their kids. Lest they misunderstand what that meant, or overlook the required effort, Moses spelled it out for them: "Talk about them when you sit at home and when you walk along the road, when you lie down and when you get up." There isn't much time of the day left out here! They were to talk about God's law all the time! It was to be a common topic of discussion, something that occurred every day and in every circumstance.

In one sense, the implications of this verse were not missed by the Jews. Remember, it was a part of the Shema. However, although the words of the verse were held dear and memorized for generations, it seems the Jews actually missed the point of the verse by taking things too literally. We know they recited the Shema at the specific times mentioned in the verse, but history tells us they did not take the law to heart. They recited Deuteronomy 6 when they lay down and when they got up, and when they walked along the way, but for many it seems it became a rote obligation instead of the overflow of an obedient and devoted heart.

I do not believe rote recitation is what God desired for the Israelites then, nor is it what He desires for us now. What the verse suggests is that He expects His law and His word to be normal and persistent topics of everyday conversation. This is not an unreasonable expectation, for His Word and Law apply to every area of life! Moses' challenge to incorporate Scripture into daily life arose from this expectation.

I have tried to meet the challenge in my own family. Although I have not done a great job over the years of having family devotion times and have struggled to set aside specific times for focusing on God's law, I have been able to make God's word a part of everyday life. I can recall unplanned spiritual conversations with my children in many different places, during many different activities. Opportunities to teach and apply God's law spontaneously arose while taking walks on the Huntington Beach pier, sitting in the outfield at Anaheim Angels baseball games, eating dinner at the kitchen table, playing catch in the park, and even while painting ceramics at Color Me Mine. In each of the circumstances I was able to point out a Scripture or Bible story that directly applied to the situation my son or daughter was experiencing at that moment. None of these conversations were planned, but all of them were valuable. On each occasion I was grateful that I had studied God's word to the point where I could recognize its application and share it with my child. The words that filled my heart spilled over into the lives of my children.

I am convinced that each of these unplanned lessons was far more valuable than any intentional, sit-down discussion I have ever had with my children. This is not to say that in those moments of opportunity I was not purposeful. I have made it a point and intention of my parenting to apply God's word to life whenever possible. It is because of this intent that I have been able to spontaneously share with my children. These opportunities to teach God's truth did not "just happen." They occurred because I had prepared for them.

Over the years I have seen that God's word does not just spring de novo out of human hearts. It comes out only after it has been put in. It is because we can have full confidence that God's word applies to everyday life that we can joyfully put it in our hearts. Its future usefulness is guaranteed! There is nothing more valuable than God's word and His law in guiding us and our children through life.

The value in the law of God springs forth from the fact that embodied in each of God's commandments are eternal principles that apply today. The Ten Commandments are not just ancient laws given to an ancient people for life in an ancient time. An obvious example of the commandments' enduring significance is in the seventh commandment: "You shall not commit adultery." In our current culture there are daily opportunities to teach the truth of this command. The nonstop media bombardment of immorality constantly challenges God's plan for a lasting relationship between one man and one woman. God's word gives us a way to respond to the attacks of our culture—a way to protect our children from the damage that such immorality brings.

Knowing and following God's law in this everyday, applicable-to-life fashion is a key to successful living. It is my desire that readers of this book will grow in knowledge of God's commandments, and go on to develop and strengthen a personal desire to better know God's commandments and pass them on to their children. It is my prayer that as a result of learning the eternal principles and meaning contained in each of the Ten Commandments others will be motivated to incorporate them into everyday life.

You Can't Teach What You Don't Embrace

Daily effort is required. If we are not diligent in teaching our children about God's law, they will almost certainly reject it. A conversation I had some years ago with a young female patient and her mother brought this truth to life in a powerful way. The young woman and her mother had come in to the office for a routine visit. During the course of the visit with the young teenager it became clear to me that she was a girl with faith. Desiring to encourage her and let her know that I shared her faith, I asked where she went to church. She named a solid evangelical church in town with which I was quite familiar. We chatted a little about church and what it meant to follow Jesus Christ. I noticed that her mother was very proud of her. As the conversation continued I was somewhat surprised to discover that although the daughter was devout, her mother was not. The mom was proud of her, but did not share her commitment to faith.

A few minutes into the discussion with the daughter her mother, apparently thinking I might be doubting her daughter's faith, interrupted me. "It's not her I worry about. She's fine. It's her older sister that concerns me. She's turning Mormon!" This surprised me. With a typical "Barrett-style" lack of tact I replied, almost without thinking, "Of course she is!"

A look of surprise came over the woman's face. "Why would you say that?" she asked.

I explained to the mother that she had already made it clear to me that she did not attend church herself. Her lack of seriousness about her own faith had made it less attractive to her other daughter. "If your faith doesn't mean enough to you to get you out of bed on a Sunday morning, why would she embrace it?" I said. "She sees Mormon friends who are dedicated and devout. Their faith appears to be far more real to them than yours is to you. Their faith is more attractive to her!" My blunt words took her aback, but she did not challenge them. She realized the truth of what I was saying. Why would anyone embrace a meaningless faith? If a parent shows no serious commitment to God's truth, why would their child?

The futility of shallow faith was a major theme underlying Moses' admonition to the people of Israel. Casual, pointless faith cannot be transmitted to subsequent generations. Weak faith cannot last. If we do not truly believe, we cannot expect our families to believe either. In fact, if we do not take faith seriously, if we do not make it an integral part of our lives, it is almost guaranteed that our children will reject our beliefs. If we want a legacy of godliness we must practice and apply our faith on a daily basis.

Moses clearly wanted the people of Israel to understand this principle and go on to establish a legacy of faith. To aid the people in their efforts, after telling them to teach God's law to their children, Moses gave them additional counsel as to how to achieve generational faith. The people were told they needed to do more than just make obedience to God's law a part of their everyday conversation. God's law was not to be a space holder in their lives, it required a prominent place. Note how Moses described it to the people: "Tie them (God's commandments) as symbols on your hands and bind them on your foreheads. Write them on the doorframes of your houses and on your gates" (Deut 6:8–9).

The seriousness of Moses' words was not lost on the Jews. Out of these words sprang traditions that continued on even in Jesus' day. The Pharisees in the time of Christ, as did many Jews before them, took this command literally. The words of Moses were placed inside of phylacteries, specially designed little leather boxes. The boxes were affixed with a strap to the Pharisees' foreheads and wrists. These religious leaders did not adhere to merely symbolic interpretation of this passage; they had the actual words of Moses, the commands of God, physically attached to their foreheads and wrists! (Most readers of the law would recognize that the instruction of Moses was symbolic, but many Jews piously took them literally.)

As externally impressive a display as the phylacteries were, Jesus was obviously not impressed with the Pharisees' piety. The disciple Matthew gives an account of Jesus' critique of the Pharisees in Matthew 23. In the passage Jesus specifically attacks the superficial religiosity that was practiced so fervently by the hypocritical Jewish leaders. Jesus knew that God's words in a box on a forehead were no guarantee a person would walk with God. (Although they do guarantee a person will look silly!) Similarly ineffective were words written over a doorway. Although they could be seen whenever someone entered or exited a home, simply writing them on the wood did not assure obedience. Mere externals are never enough.

One may ask—if he did not want literal obedience (phylacteries and such) why did Moses say the words should be on foreheads, wrists, and doorposts? I believe Moses was using symbolic language to emphasize the need to keep God's word at the forefront of our daily lives. We must intentionally take measures to tangibly remind ourselves of God's word. When we put 3x5 cards with Scripture on our bathroom mirrors or on our dashboards to aid memorization (if we actually refer to and apply them!) we are fulfilling Moses' instruction. Anytime we intentionally put our hearts and minds to God's commandments, we are living out Moses' advice.

Find Your Way to Be Intentional

There are many ways to do this. Some families have devotion times each night. Some families read a passage of Scripture together nightly after dinner. Others have nightly or daily prayer times. Still others have the Ten Commandments as framed artwork in their home. Regardless of the manner in which it is done, the point is that it should be done! We need to learn God's law.

Although the principle of intentional learning applies to all Scripture, it is specifically to the law and in particular the Ten Commandments to which Moses referred. We must intentionally apply Moses' advice to the commandments of God if we desire to have lives and families that honor God. There is a special significance to the commandments. Moses understood this and passionately believed it.

It is the intentional learning, understanding, and application of God's commandments that motivated me to write this book. As we go through each commandment we will see why God took the time to single it out as crucial to understanding Him and His ways. Just as a good doctor doesn't prescribe medications at random but instead selects the right drug for each patient's condition, God, the Great Physician, gave specific prescriptions for our sin and impaired thinking. Good patients listen to their doctor's advice and work hard to follow it. May we all be such patients as we see the prescriptions God has given us so that we may live healthy lives, God's way!

Prescription #1

Follow the One Road

You shall have no other gods before me.
Deuteronomy 5:7

*D*iabetes is an interesting disease. In many ways it is very simple—the levels of glucose (sugar) are too high in the bloodstream. The treatment objectives are simple as well. The goal is to get blood sugars down. The simplest way to achieve the goal of lower blood sugars is to have the patient eat less. In particular, it helps if the patient eats less sugar. As straightforward as this seems, it is a concept not grasped by everyone.

Several years ago I had a 65-year-old diabetic in my office. He had been a patient for years and, in spite of my best efforts I had not been able to get his blood sugars under control. I had tried many different medications, sent him to diabetic education classes and recommended exercise, yet nothing seemed to work. The most challenging aspect of his care was my inability to get his fasting (before breakfast) blood sugars into an acceptable range. Visit after visit we reviewed his blood sugar logs, and the cause remained elusive. After several months of wondering, it all became clear one afternoon.

We were in the process of reviewing his blood sugars when he asked me, "Do you think it could be the cereal I eat at night?"

Caught off guard I asked, "Cereal?"

"Well, I get hungry at night lots of the time, so I get up and have a bowl of cereal and then go back to bed," he replied.

After several months of medical care and several hundred dollars of medications to treat his disease it had suddenly occurred to him that maybe eating a bowl of sugar-coated cereal in the middle of the night might somehow contribute to his high morning blood sugars! What was remarkable to me was that he had not been intentionally hiding from me his night-time snack habit; he just had never thought that it mattered. That diabetic patient (and many others since) taught me that things aren't always as obvious as they would seem, and that some people seemingly overlook the obvious.

Overlooked Violations

There are aspects of God's commandments that are obvious, and there are other aspects that are easily overlooked. As I am sure many others have done before me, when I was much younger I viewed the Ten Commandments as the Basic List of rules that everyone had to follow. As a young boy I recall going down the list in my black genuine imitation leather King James Bible. (It was a really cool Bible; it had a zipper and everything. Why it had a zipper I have no idea, but at the time it seemed pretty neat!)

I remember going through Deuteronomy 5 and reading the commands, surprised at a number of things. I was first taken aback by the fact that the commandments weren't simply listed and labeled 1 to 10. As a child it wasn't exactly obvious which command was which, but I gradually figured it out. As I did, I performed a mental checklist to see how I measured up. After all, wasn't that what the commands were for? To see how good we were doing? (I know I am not alone in having felt this way. Admit it. At one time or another you have had a similar list. You may even have a pencil in hand right now.)

When I read over the commandments back then I barely spent any time at all on the first commandment. It seemed so simple, so straightforward. You just had to avoid worshipping another God. Easy! How could anyone mess this up? I viewed it in the same way I view the silly warning labels we find on things nowadays, such as the stroller warning label that says "Remove child before folding," or the label on self-defense pepper spray that says "Caution: May irritate eyes." The first commandment was a mere formality, intended only for the ignorant few. I thought, "Only a complete imbecile could violate the first commandment! How hard could it be?" It was unimaginable to me that anyone with even the most minuscule amount of faith would consider worshipping or following another god. Like a map with only one road on it, the direction seemed pretty clear to me.

Since I could not imagine trying to follow any other path, I could not envision any obvious present-day application of the commandment. I thought that perhaps this commandment was written for the primitive and simple Israelites around back when it was written. "That's it!" I decided. That was why it was included, for simple people like the Israelites. No one today would have issues with this, would they?

I know now that I was wrong. The meaning is much deeper and less apparent than I realized. This seemingly simple commandment merits serious consideration. God put it first for a reason. The commandment has application not only for those "primitive" Israelites but for us as well, for the meaning of the command is far greater than my child-like reasoning could comprehend. Not only does its meaning apply today but also its admonition as well. It is much easier to violate the first commandment than we might think. Worshipping other gods is not a rare sin that tempts only an ignorant few; it is a danger to all of us. The first prescription treats a disease that plagues all of humanity.

God in His infinite wisdom was fully aware of human nature and knew how easily people, and especially the children of Israel, could be tempted to worship other gods. Knowing the importance of worshipping only Him, and the ease with which the people could be led astray, God emphasized the commandment's importance by making it first on His list.

God knew there was a tendency for His people to turn to false gods. When we look at the story of the Exodus, the manner in which God delivered His people, we see the origins of the inclination to wander and how God directly attacked the disposition in His people.

God clearly demonstrated to the people of Israel that He alone was God. In spite of God's direct communication the history of the nation of Israel reveals how easily the people forgot this first commandment. Sadly, as we review God's word, we will see that we are not unlike the Israelites. In spite of God's clear communication to us we are easily tempted to turn away, and we readily fall.

At the heart of the first commandment is the uniqueness, or holiness, of God. There is no one and nothing like Him. A survey of the Old Testament reveals that the primary sin of the people of Israel was not that they rejected God's existence altogether and became atheists. Neither did they tear down God's temple and replace it with the temple of another God. The common sins were that they would either turn from God to other gods or would turn to other gods in addition to the One true God.

Why would the people turn away like this? We have already mentioned how easy and natural it can be for people to take on the characteristics of the culture in which they live. If not careful, over time people of faith will find themselves acting like those of the secular world around them. The Israelites who followed Moses out of bondage had lived in the land of Egypt for 400 years. For four centuries they were surrounded by and inundated with the teachings and beliefs of the polytheistic Egyptians. As a result of this exposure there was a chance that some would see God as merely one of many gods instead of as the one and only God He was and is. It was easy for the Israelites to get it wrong with regard to God's uniqueness.

The temptation to misunderstand the nature and uniqueness of God was not left behind them when the people fled Egypt. The new land they were entering had similarly false beliefs in multiple deities. The temptation to worship false gods was, for the children of Israel, inescapable. Although this may seem to us a simple snare to avoid, it was not for the children of Israel. The Egyptian religion had a profound impact on their thinking. Understanding the Egyptian culture and religion is key to understanding the troubles faced by God's people.

Corrupt Egyptian Influences

A review of the religious culture of the Egyptians reveals that they had multiple gods who they believed oversaw and controlled every area of life. Common things such as changes in weather, agricultural successes and failures, fertility, and even birth and death were each under the influence of a specific god. Through the worship of each god the people gained a sense that they could influence these things and the world around them.

If the Egyptians could make their rain god happy, they would get the rain they needed. A proper sacrifice to the fertility god would bring about a desired child. Pleasing the god of the dead would guarantee a loved one's safe passage to the netherworld. There was an Egyptian god for just about every significant natural process or life event. For the Egyptians the key to success in life was to appease the correct god at the right time—this was how all Egyptians thought, and by extension how many of their Hebrew slaves thought. The thinking associated with such polytheism would have to be unlearned if God was to be appropriately worshipped by His people. This was the situation in which the Jews found themselves.

Knowing how difficult it would be for the people to understand and believe that He alone was God, God gave them tangible evidence of His preeminence. He accomplished this through the plagues he sent upon the Egyptians. Each plague was directed at an area of life that was under the "control" of an Egyptian god. God reveals to us that the plagues were designed to demonstrate his supremacy.

> The Israelites set out from Rameses on the fifteenth day of the first month, the day after the Passover. They marched out boldly in full view of all the Egyptians, who were burying all their firstborn, whom the LORD had struck down among them; **for the LORD had brought judgment on their gods**. (Num 33:3–4, emphasis added)

The Ten Plagues

Through each of the ten plagues God demonstrated that the Egyptian gods were false and powerless and that He was true, powerful, and in control of everything. A look at each of the plagues bears this out.

In the first plague, the Nile River was turned to blood. Turning the Nile into blood can be viewed as an attack on a number of Egyptian gods. Hapi was the god of the Nile River and Hatmeyt was the fish goddess. Given that the entire Nile was transformed (at least that which could be seen by those involved), this would obviously be a blow to the reputation of the Nile god! Similarly, what did it say about the power or reality of a fish god who could not protect fish? With this one gesture God demonstrated not only the falseness of these Egyptian gods but also his control over water, that most essential element and giver of life and agricultural blessing.

The second plague involved an epidemic of frogs "covering the land of Egypt." Heqt, a fertility goddess, was symbolized by the frog. This plague made a powerful statement. Stop and picture for a minute what it must have been like. The stench of the frogs decaying would have been overwhelming. Everywhere people looked lay evidence that this Egyptian god was powerless. If she wasn't powerless, why didn't she intervene and stop the plague? For days after the frogs quit coming the smell remained as a reminder of the God of Israel's greatness and supremacy.

The third plague of lice may have been directed against the "earth" god, Geb. When God pronounced this plague it was initiated by Aaron striking the dust of the ground with his staff. The dust (or earth) then turned into gnats (or lice). The superiority of the God of Israel in this act was noted even by the Egyptian magicians who said, "this is the finger of God!" (Exod 8:19). Instead of blessing coming from the ground in the form of produce, curse came in the form of bugs.

The next plague, the fourth, involved a swarm of flies coming upon Pharaoh, his officials, and the Egyptian people. It was the first of the plagues that spared the region in which the Jews lived, the land of Goshen. With this plague God began distinguishing not only Himself as supreme, but His people as distinct as well. God was identifying Himself as uniquely God, and solely as the God of the children of Israel. This was an amazing theological shift for the people. The Egyptians "chose" gods to worship; here the One true God was declaring His choice of His people! The plague can be viewed as an attack either on the Egyptian god Kheper who was symbolized as a flying beetle, or on Amun, the god of the wind. Neither god was able to stop the flies that tormented the beleaguered Egyptians.

With the fifth and subsequent plagues the consequences grew more serious. Fish could be replenished from higher up the Nile, and frogs were not essential to the Egyptian economy. Lice and flies were annoying, but could be brushed off. The fifth plague caused lasting harm to the Egyptian economy. Cattle and other livestock died. Where was Apis the bull god or Hathor the goddess who was symbolized by a cow? Neither of these "powerful" gods was able to save the Egyptians' herds.

The sixth plague was more personal than the previous plagues. For the first time the people were attacked directly as God sent painful boils upon the skin of the Egyptians and their animals. Hiding inside didn't make a difference; no one could escape the pain. It was a lesson impossible to ignore. Even Pharaoh's magicians were unable to stand before Moses when the boils struck. Whether this was due to pain, shame, or embarrassment is unclear. What was clear then and now is that Imhotep, the god of healing, was unable to save the people of Egypt. The God of Israel was supreme.

Prior to the seventh plague God (through Moses) warned Pharaoh that the stakes were increasing: "this time I will send the *full force* of my plagues against you and against your officials and your people, so you may know that there is no one like me in all the earth" (Exod 9:14, emphasis added). We see from the passage that the Egyptians themselves were becoming aware that the God of Israel was different from the gods they worshipped. Many were realizing that their gods were powerless to protect them from this God's wrath. When Moses warned of the impending deadly hailstorm those that trusted in Nut, the sky goddess, or Seth, the god of storms, to save their herds hopelessly watched the animals die as they were struck down with massive hailstones. The wiser ones among the Egyptian people, those who were learning of the true God's power, took their animals to shelter. And what power it was! The very weather was at His command. Each clap of thunder, bolt of lightning, and gust of wind declared the uniqueness of the Lord, the Mighty One of Israel.

The seventh plague, the terrible hail, posed not just a threat to life but to the Egyptians' agricultural economy. The flax and barley crops were destroyed. When the hail subsided the devastation remained. For months afterward the effects lingered.

The eighth plague further damaged the produce of the land, as swarms of locusts devoured what was left of the crops. The Egyptians had to be wondering how this could happen. As with most polytheistic cultures, much of Egyptian religious ritual was centered on the harvest. The powerful god Osiris was believed to come to life with each harvest. Where was he now?

With each plague the God of Israel was declaring His total sufficiency, uniqueness, and supremacy. It was the One and only God who was sending all of these plagues that attacked the core of Egyptian life and worship.

With the ninth plague God further established His dominance over all creation by extending the plague to the very heavens. Ra the sun god was proved to be nothing but a myth as darkness spread across the land for three days. The darkness was so thick that it could be felt. Yet the darkness did not spread everywhere. The people of Israel were spared. How amazing it was, and how powerfully was the message delivered, when the Israelites lived in light for three days. No natural phenomenon could explain this. The only possible explanation was that the great God of Israel had performed this deed.

The tenth and final plague (death of the firstborn son) attacked the very pulse of Egyptian society. It struck the cult of Pharaoh worship, as his own son was among the dead. It established that life itself flowed from the God of Israel. In the final terrible plague God completed a circle that encompassed every aspect of human existence. Food, water, weather, health, light and dark, and now life itself were shown to be unaffected and unprotected by the Egyptian gods. What person living through this could possibly doubt that there was only One true God? And that the One true God was the God of Israel?

God had given both the Egyptians and the Israelites a complete demonstration of His existence, His power, and His grace. In His grace He had taken the time to declare His essence in painstaking fashion. Every human sense experienced His power. The people heard, saw, tasted, smelled, and felt the devastation. This was not mindless destruction; it was clear communication. The plagues were sent for a reason. God spoke to Moses and expressly told him why the plagues had been sent: "that you may tell your children and grandchildren how I dealt harshly with the Egyptians and how I performed my signs among them, and that you may know that I am the LORD" (Exod 10:2).

And this is the essence of the first commandment. God is *the* Lord. He is not *a* god. He is not "one among many." He is not the chief of the gods. He is *the* God. God showed and told the people that they should have no other gods for the simple reason that there *are* no other gods.

It is amazing to see that even after all of the plagues the Egyptians endured this lesson remained unlearned. Over and over we read that Pharaoh and his officials spoke to Moses of "his God" or addressed Moses using the phrase "your God." They did not say "the LORD" or just "God." Implied in each conversation was an acknowledgement of the God of Israel's existence, but a rejection of His supremacy. The Egyptians did not doubt that there was a God of Israel, He just wasn't the only God there was, and He wasn't theirs. Even though Pharaoh eventually referred to God as "the LORD," His ultimate behavior in chasing after the Israelites revealed continued unbelief. So ingrained in polytheism was their Egyptian culture that they clung to it in spite of overwhelming evidence to the contrary.

Israel's Divided Affection

The deep-rooted polytheism impacted the children of Israel. Old Testament history reveals it was difficult for the people of Israel to believe in only one God. The tendency to believe in a pantheon of gods, of which the LORD was merely a powerful member, raised its head repeatedly in Israelite history.

Even after spending a generation isolated from pagan people, Scripture tells us that near the end of their forty years of wandering in the desert the lure of sexual temptation led a number of the Israelites to worship a false god. The people ignored the lessons of the plagues and rejected the commandments they had received and worshipped the Moabite god Baal of Peor (Num 25:1–3). The tendency to stray is described throughout the books of Judges and 1 and 2 Kings. Over and over the worship of other gods marks the major failure of the nation.

In spite of all of Moses' admonitions and God's demonstrations, this apparently simple command to worship only Him was repeatedly broken. The people of Israel could not worship God alone. They continually divided their devotion.

We learn much about human nature, and much about the nature of God, from the history of the nation of Israel with regard to the first commandment. We see that exclusivity of devotion is very important to God. He alone is to be worshipped and He will accept nothing else.

When it comes to exclusive devotion I think of a conversation from a few years ago. A patient and I were making small talk after a visit and, as it was approaching New Year's Day the conversation drifted into talk about college football. In the course of the conversation she mentioned some friends of hers who were diehard fans of the USC Trojans. These friends didn't just root for the Trojans, they bled cardinal and gold, the team colors. They flew a USC flag outside their door, dressed in team colors, and even sent out USC Christmas cards every year.

Each year the friends had a big party around New Year's. The football game in which USC was a part was a focal point of the gathering. The friends decked themselves and their home out in full USC regalia. Cardinal and gold decorations abounded. My patient told me that one year her daughter thought it would be funny to show up to the party wearing a UCLA sweatshirt. (For those who are uninformed UCLA and USC are bitter rivals. If you are from USC you must *hate* UCLA.) When the friends opened the door of their home and saw the UCLA sweatshirt, they failed to see the humor. They didn't even let the girl in the door! She had to drive home and change clothes, because the friends insisted that no one wearing a UCLA shirt was welcome in their house!

These people's devotion to USC was a consuming passion for them. It drove them to root for their team, and for their team alone. There was no room in their lives for any other team. In their home, there was undivided commitment. They would not tolerate any affection for any other school. It was USC and USC alone.

God Commands Exclusive Worship

This silly devotion to a college football team is a good example of what God wants from His people. God requires to be worshipped exclusively. He will not tolerate or accept any devotion to anything else. He demands undivided and complete attention from His people. There is no place in His house for anyone who would worship anything else. He makes this clear over and over in Scripture.

Notice the words God uses to describe Himself and His attitude about other gods to the people of Israel:

> You shall not bow down to them or worship them; **for I, the LORD your God, am a jealous God.** (Exod 20:5, emphasis added)

The word here in the Hebrew that is translated as jealous means—jealous! (Not the petty jealousy humans feel, but rather the appropriate truth that He will not share the affections and worship of His people.) He wants each of us, and He wants ALL of each of us! He will settle for nothing less. He is angered by those who think He will share. Sadly, in spite of how clearly God stated His truth that the people must worship Him alone, the children of Israel repeatedly failed in this regard and worshipped other gods.

It is easy to think that we would not be so foolish, that we would never worship something or someone else, but a close look at our culture and the church of today reveals otherwise. Many churches that were at one time bastions of the faith have slipped into theological liberalism and declared that there is more than one way to God. Many other churches have watered down their teaching by blending in ideas and teachings from other non-Christian faiths. From Oprah Winfrey's new age "Christianity" to a humanistic emphasis on self and positive thinking, people have turned to other "gods."

The "wandering away" aspect is frequently missed because the church today, like the people of Israel so long ago, doesn't completely turn from God and reject all of His truth. It instead allows other gods, those of humanism and secular thought, to gain a portion of its devotion. For a God who shares Himself with no one, this is abominable sin. This is a violation of His first commandment.

While Christians may say that we would never water down or distort our faith in that way, or that we would never divide our devotions, we are no less at risk for failing to obey the first commandment than were the Jews of so long ago. Believers are not to worship or serve *any* other gods. In His Sermon on the Mount of Olives, Jesus stated how easily we could serve the wrong things:

No one can serve two masters. Either he will hate the one and love the other, or he will be devoted to the one and despise the other. You cannot serve both God and Money. (Matt 6:24)

With these words Jesus introduced to the people a false god that they had not previously considered. For people in America today, it is a god with which we are all too familiar. According to Jesus, money (material wealth) is a god that demands our service and devotion. Materialism is a god that longs to be worshipped. The demands of materialism are so strong as to make its pursuit and simultaneous service of God impossible.

It is worth noting the exact words that Jesus used. The word "money" is an ancient Aramaic word, "mamonas." According to biblical scholar W. E. Vine, it has a root meaning of riches.[1] Implied in "riches" is an ability to depend on those riches. The word "amen," which implies that which is sure and can be trusted, is derived from this root word. One way to understand the meaning is that you cannot put your trust in riches and simultaneously put your trust in God. This is why (according to Jesus) it is impossible to serve wealth and God.

This doesn't mean that it is wrong to be wealthy. Jesus specifically stated that it is the service of wealth that is the problem. Jesus uses a slavery analogy in His words. By referring to two masters, He is implying that each master, God and wealth, have responsibilities to be met, rules to be obeyed, and devotion required. He is further telling people that the devotion, responsibilities, and obligations of serving wealth are invariably at odds with the devotions, responsibilities, and obligations of serving God.

It is impossible to faithfully serve two masters who have different demands and goals. A slave that had two masters who gave instructions opposite to one another would find himself forced to make choices. He couldn't serve both. If one master said slaughter a sheep for dinner, and the other said take the sheep to pasture, the slave would have to obey one and only one of the masters. In choosing which master he obeys, he chooses the master he will serve. In obeying one master he is rejecting the other. The disobedience toward the one master would be a rejection of that master's authority. He cannot serve both.

Jesus was saying that the demands of God's kingdom—obedience to His commands and serving Him—requires a rejection of the demands of another master, the master of financial security. According to Jesus this conflict is unavoidable. You cannot wholeheartedly pursue earthly riches and God's glory. The service of wealth requires a rejection of God's law, and the service of God will require one to forego the pursuit and service of wealth.

God, or Money?

I have seen this truth over and over again in my own life. Time after time I have had to let go of financial security as I followed God's law. One particular example comes to mind as I write.

Several years ago my wife Lisa and I were under the care of an infertility specialist. Infertility care is very expensive and, as I had just started medical practice, we did not have a lot of money. After several months of trying we reached the point where the next step would require Lisa to undergo exploratory surgery to look for a cause of the problem. Since our insurance company did not pay for infertility treatment I was very concerned about how much the surgery would cost. I asked the doctor for an estimated cost for the procedure.

He looked puzzled and asked me why I needed to know. I told him our insurance would not pay for the surgery. "They will if it is done for pain," he replied, with a hint of a wink. He was telling me that if the diagnosis given to the insurance for the surgery was pain, the insurance would cover it. All my wife had to do was say "Ow!" and the procedure would be free. We would save thousands of dollars.

We had a choice and a very clear one. We could follow God's law and be truthful and be responsible for the cost of the surgery, or we could lie. We could not afford the procedure. To pay the money would mean going into significant debt. I looked him in the eye and firmly said, "There isn't any pain." He paused for a moment and then seemed to get the message. We could not totally follow God's law and totally pursue wealth. We had to choose a master. Lisa did not have the surgery.

Whether it is in the hours believers work, the money we give to the church, the business contacts we avoid or the networking parties we decline to attend, Christians will repeatedly have choices to make. If we are wholeheartedly devoted to God, if He is our only God, we will find ourselves in the position of saying "No" to the service of wealth.

As worshippers reflect on Jesus' teaching, the meaning of the first commandment comes into sharper focus. God demands that we worship Him and Him alone. He demands undivided devotion. He does this because it is the only way He can be worshipped. If believers try to worship any other god, or follow any other religious teaching, we will have to reject God at some point. If we try to pursue any purpose other than the one He has laid out for us, we will at some point have to reject God. God, who loves us and wants what is best for us, understands that any path that isn't His eventually leads us away from Him.

As Christians think about this we should look at our own lives and ask ourselves, "Is my heart divided?" Is there any place where we are serving another master or worshipping another God? Like the children of Israel have we accepted the beliefs of the world around us and are we drifting away from serving the one true Master?

Jesus pointed out the most alluring master when He addressed materialism and wealth, but there are others. There are gods of humanism and self-esteem, gods of pleasure and lust, and for some, the gods of children and family. Each of us should take the time to look at our lives and ask, "Do I have any gods besides God?" The answer may surprise us.

Swallow the Medicine

The first prescription is to follow the One Road, to worship the one God alone. As with all prescriptions, it must be taken and followed if it is to work. This section will help you determine if you are "taking the medicine" just as God prescribed.

A good place to begin in self-evaluation is to ask, "Is there anything in my life that is taking a place that should rightfully belong to God?

Here are a few possible danger zones:

- God alone deserves our worship. Are we worshipping anything or anyone else? When we think of worship, it helps to think of commitment and devotion, or to think about that which is most important in our minds. Wealth is an easy thing to worship, but we can worship pleasure and even our own accomplishments as well.
- We should put our trust in God alone. Are we trusting in anything or anyone instead of God? Over and over in the Psalms we are reminded of how important it is to trust in God. "But I trust in you, O LORD; I say, 'You are my God'" (Psalm 31:14). If we look to anything besides God for reassurance, hope, or security, we are giving to someone else that which belongs only to God. He alone is the source of our financial, emotional, and physical security. I have seen people trust wealth, spouses, parents, and children when they should have been trusting God.

- God desires our complete love and devotion. Is there anything to which we are more devoted than God? I have heard many people answer this question in the negative, but then skip church or time with God to play golf, take children to soccer, or indulge in a hobby. I know of one man who never attends church during football season because he doesn't want to miss any NFL games! (I always want to ask him, "Haven't you ever heard of TiVO or VCRs?")

Take the time to make your own list of questions. Ask God to help you turn away from anything that would keep you from Him. Ask God to heal you from the diseases of rebellion and pride that can cause you to wander away from Him.

Prescription #2

Understand the Nature of God

You shall not make for yourself an idol in the form of anything in heaven above or on the earth beneath or in the waters
below. Deuteronomy 5:8

*O*ne of the great challenges in medical practice is explaining
complicated physiologic processes to people who have absolutely no idea how the body works. How do you explain pneumonia
to someone who doesn't understand what the lungs do? How do you
explain a heart attack? (Especially since nothing is actually attacking
the heart and the heart isn't attacking anything else either!) How do
you explain high blood pressure to a patient who has no idea what
blood pressure is in the first place?

A story from my residency training illustrates just how challenging communication can be for a doctor. A patient came in to
see one of my fellow resident physicians for warts. The patient was
poorly educated and understood very little about health, illness, and
how the body worked, and she had no idea that the growths on her
body were warts—she only knew that there was something extra
that wasn't there before. When asked why she was in to see the
doctor the patient said she had "extra meat" on her hands.

The doctor tried to determine if there was anyone in the family
from whom she might have contracted the warts, and asked if anyone
in the family had any similar lesions. The doctor was met with a

blank stare. The word "lesion" had no meaning for her at all. The physician realized this and rephrased the question, asking if anyone had similar growths on their body. Again came the blank stare, as the concept of a "growth" was similarly beyond the patient's comprehension. It dawned on the doctor that the patient had an extremely limited vocabulary. The doctor shrugged her shoulders and restated the question: "Does anyone else have any extra meat anywhere?" A look of understanding quickly appeared on the patient's face, and she replied, "Oh, no, no one else!"

The patient could understand the doctor only when she spoke the patient's language. In this case, like so many others, the patient's language did not allow for an accurate description of what was going on. The physician had to settle for a partial understanding or risk there being no comprehension at all.

The danger with using imperfect descriptions is that sometimes they can lead people to completely wrong conclusions. Medical journals frequently describe stories of exactly how far off a patient's understanding can be. One of my favorites concerns a patient who was given a rectal suppository for vomiting. A few days later the doctor received a note with a telephone message: "Mrs. Jones would like new medication. Old one not working, and large waxy pills are too difficult to swallow."

As challenging as it is for untrained lay people to understand medicine, that difficulty is nothing compared to that of finite man trying to comprehend infinite God. This handicap doesn't stop men from trying, for there is an innate longing for humans to understand and explain God. In spite of this desire human beings need to exercise great care in order to avert mistakes in our description. God isn't like us, and is in fact far beyond our understanding. Only with this admission in mind can we begin to grasp the second commandment, the prescription to ascertain the nature of God.

When it comes to keeping the second commandment, most would presume innocence. I seriously doubt that anyone reading this book has ever constructed an idol. The closest I have come to making anything idol-like was a rather poorly constructed animal "thingy" I made out of Play-Doh as a child. Given the lack of religious intent in my handiwork, I am confident that I did not violate the commandment. In fact, those who observed my creation would most certainly attest that it in no way resembled or approached the form of *anything* in heaven above, earth beneath, or waters below. It looked like a yellow lump with lopsided bulges where legs were supposed to be. The only religious use possible would be if there was a cult somewhere that worshipped a deformed sea sponge god. (My Play-Doh sculptures fell into the "decide what it is after someone else tells you what it looks like" category of artwork.)

Modern Idols

Although this may seem facetious, I suspect it is only a slight exaggeration of how most people approach the second commandment. Many people seem to believe that all that the commandment implies is the absence of animal objects that represent God. As a result, they read the commandment, think "I would never do that!" and move on. I know that while growing up I never thought the commandment applied to me at all. I can remember thinking that the only modern-day application was for missionaries who were travelling to primitive third world countries. When confronted with pagan deity symbols such as in Hindu worship, the missionary could point to this commandment to demonstrate the error in the people's thinking.

Later, I thought the commandment more appropriately applied to people such as those on-the-fringe Roman Catholics who venerate purported "appearances" of the Virgin Mary. Although I do believe people violate the commandment when they pray to "images" formed by shadows on fences or burned into the bread of toasted cheese sandwiches, there is more to the commandment than prohibiting such silly displays.

If we hope to fully understand the message of the commandment against idols, we will need to consider the circumstances of the people to whom the commandment was originally given—the recently delivered nation of Israel. We saw with the first commandment that the polytheism which surrounded the Israelites led to a tendency to turn to false gods. Over time the Jewish people adopted the religious beliefs of the cultures in which they lived and ultimately turned away from God.

Just as the thoughts of a plurality of gods led to one type of sin—the worship of other gods—so too could the misunderstanding of the nature of deity in general lead to another sin. The people of Israel in Egypt (and later Canaan) were not only surrounded by the worship of false gods but also by people who had false ides about the very nature of god-ness. Just like my patients who have completely wrong thinking about physiology, the indigenous people demonstrated erroneous thinking about theology.

It is natural for people to tend to think similarly as the people around them and take on the preconceptions and myths of their culture. Cultural beliefs are almost always wrong when it comes to religion, for it is impossible for finite man to fully understand infinite God. It is the correction of such mistaken thinking about God that lies at the heart of the second commandment.

As a doctor I have found myself forced to address people's preconceptions and misinformed thinking on almost a daily basis. I face not only wrong thinking about medicine but also I frequently have to correct faulty impressions about doctors. When people hear the title "Doctor" they think they will encounter a certain type of person. For some the title implies a wise old person. For others it may mean a very dry personality, lack of humor, and elitism. Whatever the preconception is about what "doctors" are like, I never seem to fit it. I have become convinced that very few people think a doctor will in any way resemble a "normal" person.

What's a Doctor Supposed to Look Like?

The fact that there are preconceptions about doctors' personalities was brought home to me years ago by an inmate at a local Southern California prison. While I was in medical school I was a member of a church softball team that regularly played a team of inmates from a prison in Chino, California.

Every other Saturday throughout the spring and summer we arrived at the prison gate by 8 A.M. The other players and I made our way through the metal detectors, baggage inspections, and guardrooms out onto the athletic field in the middle of the prison. There we would match our modest athletic skills against those of a group of the largest and most tattooed men I had ever seen, the inmate softball team. Winning wasn't really our objective. It was our hope that by playing regularly we would develop relationships with the inmates that would allow us to tell them about Jesus Christ. This noble goal was more difficult than we imagined. People like those inmates didn't naturally strike up conversations with church people like us.

When I realized that the inmates were a little leery about us I determined to break the ice in the only way I knew how, with humor. Not knock-knock joke humor, but sarcastic, make-fun-of-your-opponent, friendly guy-competition type humor. In the parlance of the day, I ragged on the other team as much as I could. When we were down by seventeen runs, I yelled continually that we had them right where we wanted them. When a massive player who had shown he could hit a ball over 400 feet came to the plate, I told my teammates to move in closer because the guy couldn't hit a lick. I joked about the inmates' tattoos and their bandanas. Over time, the inmates started joking back. Once they saw me as just another person, barriers began to break down.

The last time I played in the prison was the Saturday after I graduated from medical school. I was moving away to start my residency training and wouldn't be able to make the commitment any longer. I made it a point to say good-bye to all of the inmates that I knew. One of them asked me where I was going. I told him that I had just finished medical school and was starting my family medicine training farther north.

He got a big grin on his face and started laughing. "You a doctor?" he laughed. He laughed louder, pointed at me and shook his head. "You ain't no doctor!" He continued to cackle as he jogged out to his position in the outfield. He looked back over his shoulder and said it again, "You ain't no doctor!" It seems he believed he knew what doctors were like. He had been to doctors and from what he knew about them, I was no doctor!

His preconceptions of what a physician was like came from his personal experience and from what he had learned from others. He was not ignorant about the medical profession. He had seen doctors. He "knew" that they did not joke around, were not smart-alecks and definitely did not spend Saturday mornings playing softball in a prison. For him to accept me as a physician would require him to change his whole thinking about the medical profession.

Changed Thinking Required

The people of Israel were in a similar predicament. A correct understanding of God's nature required a change in their thinking. Because they had lived among the polytheistic Egyptians for so long, it would have been natural for the people of Israel to embrace Egyptian thoughts about deity. They had seen gods, they had worshipped gods, so they thought they knew what gods were like. They thought wrong, and their erroneous notions would have to be rejected if they were going to worship God correctly.

While the commandment expressly forbids idolatry, the formation of a physical image of God, it also concerns the avoidance of the thought processes that lead to such idolatry in the first place. For the Israelites, these mistaken ideas were a natural consequence of interaction with the societies in which they lived. When we look at the gods Egyptians worshipped, it is easy to see how the attributes and characteristics of these gods could lead to wrong thinking about the attributes and characteristics of the one true God.

Egypt's Gods

Although ancient Egypt recognized many different gods, there were a number of common threads in the religious practices associated with each of them. The majority of Egyptian religious practices were geographic in nature, as different cities often had special deities associated with them. Although a specific religious practice might start off in a localized area it would frequently spread, as worship of a particular god would spread from one area to another as a city's god rose in prominence. Political and military successes of a city were often attributed to its god; thus, as a city grew in power it would also grow in religious influence. Egyptian history is filled with stories of brief rises and falls in a specific god's popularity that are directly tied to the rise and fall of its city of worship. Egyptians viewed gods as closely aligned with and attached to the places they were worshipped.[1]

We learn much about how Egyptians viewed deity in general by their specific religious practices. The temple stood as the center of worship for each god or goddess. Temples were constructed specifically in honor of particular deities. Egyptians did not view the temple as merely a venue for worship, but as the specific location for human interaction with the supernatural. Although considered immortal, Egyptians believed a tangible, physical aspect of deity was represented in temple worship. Egyptians believed the temple was the actual physical dwelling place of the god.[2] The priests who lived there carried out rituals and sacrifices that were believed to provide for the physical needs of the god being worshipped. Food, clothing and anything else the god needed was met in this way. When the idol or image of the god was clothed, the god was clothed. When the idol was fed, the god was nourished. Thus to the Egyptians, the physical world directly impacted the well-being of the spiritual world, and gods were thought to respond to the physical blessings and honors given to them in temple worship.[3]

Even though the Egyptians constructed temples devoted uniquely to each god, the majority were not worshipped in isolation. Groupings of deities were very common in Egypt. In the Old Kingdom of Egypt centered in Heliopolis (an area to the north of modern Cairo) a group of nine gods was the principal focus. These gods were considered the primary gods involved in creation, and were the major deities in Egypt for nearly 3000 years. In the city of Hermopolis mythology centered around eight gods, four male and four female. The male gods are thought to have been represented with frog heads, the females with serpent heads. In other smaller cities and regions of Egypt triads of gods were common. One of the most well-known was the triad of Thebes. This trio and its chief god, Amun, serve as a good example[4] of the general attributes and characteristics of Egyptian theology, and allow for a better understanding of the attitudes addressed in the second commandment's prohibition of idolatry.[5]

The city of Thebes, located about 500 miles south of the Mediterranean Sea on the banks of the Nile River, was a major city in ancient Egypt. The triumvirate of gods worshipped there consisted of the god Amun, his Consort Mut, and their son, the moon god Khunsu.

In the earlier years of Amun mythology he was evidently viewed primarily as the supernatural embodiment of air or wind. This view is supported by one of the meanings associated with his name, that of "the hidden one."[6] The invisibility of air naturally leads to a sense of hidden deity; further, since air (or wind) is one of the major "elements" of nature, Amun was considered to be a significant and powerful God.[7]

It is an understandable progression in thought that the mythology of Amun began with his possessing the hidden aspects of air and wind in general, and grew into the belief that Amun was the breath of life itself. Particularly at Thebes, Amun was eventually viewed as the creator and even the father of the gods. With this ascension in veneration came the assignment of a spouse, for the most powerful god would surely have a wife. The wife of Amun, by association the "Divine Mother" of creation from whom life arose, was the goddess Mut. Over time, belief in Amun's nature changed further and, instead of being completely hidden he was thought to have a human form.

About 1500 years prior to the birth of Christ, Thebes reached prominence in Egypt. With the rise of Thebes as the major city in all of Egypt came the wider worship of Amun. Whereas before he was worshipped only as the supreme deity regionally, Amun was gradually worshipped nationally. By that time the essence of Amun had been merged with that of the sun god Ra, and the subsequent "compound" deity Amun-Ra became chief of all the gods.

Around 300 years after the rise of Amun-Ra worship the seat of Egyptian power moved northward to the previous capital. When it did, Thebes declined in prominence. With the decline of Thebes came the downfall of its patron deity. Although Amun worship continued in Thebes for some time, nationally the focus turned to the sibling gods Osiris and Isis. The story of the god Amun (his worship, rise, and fall) tells us a lot about how Egyptians viewed the nature of the gods they worshipped.

Undoubtedly the Israelites' conception of deity and of the essence of the divine was influenced greatly by Egyptian mythology. It would have been natural for them to think that their God was similar to the gods they had known all of their lives. When we learn that the attributes assigned to Egyptian "gods" were understood and accepted by the Israelites, the meaning of the second commandment comes to life.

Egyptian gods were not truly separate from the physical realm. They were born and some even died. Although they lived in a realm inaccessible to mortals, they also interacted directly with the material world. They relied on food and drink for sustenance and were by no means totally self-sufficient and self-reliant. They depended on others to meet their needs and accomplish their purposes.

The gods of Egypt not only engaged the physical world but also were material in their essence. They had physical bodies. The idols were not merely symbolic in their representations but were thought to be actual likenesses. The Egyptian gods came in human and animal forms. Due to their physical limitations they experienced many things mortals did. They could be ill or wounded, and in some cases even die.

In addition to human physical characteristics, the gods possessed human emotions as well. They became angry, jealous, and sad. They held grudges, sought revenge, and fought one another. Further, the gods' emotions were not solely their own. Their moods and actions could be influenced by the deeds of their subjects. The Egyptians believed that offerings could appease anger and change the behavior of their gods.

Simply put, the gods of Egyptian mythology were not transcendent and holy. Nor were they unique and immutable. They were physical, material beings in many ways similar to human beings. In order to understand idolatry we must recognize not only that Egyptian gods *were* represented by idols but also that they *could* be represented by idols. Because they were not distinct from the physical realm, that sphere could be utilized to accurately express their essence and nature.

The transcendent and eternal God of Israel is completely different, and the second commandment repudiates the thinking that he is describable by physical means. When Moses said to the people, "You shall not make for yourself an idol in the form of anything in heaven above or on the earth beneath or in the waters below" (Deut 5:8), he was addressing this Egyptian mindset of physical deity. Such an inclination would eventually lead the Israelites to believe that they could accurately represent the God who had delivered them in a physical way, and ultimately led them to make an idol.

God's Essence Can't Be Idolized

This second commandment then was not just a prohibition against making idols to other gods (this was covered by the first commandment) but was rather aimed at any tendency among the children of Israel to make idols of *the true God*. They were to avoid idols not because idolatry meant they were turning to an Egyptian god, but because *there is nothing in heaven or earth* that could accurately convey the image of the true God.

It is impossible to physically describe God because He is totally apart from creation. Unlike the false gods of Egypt, God is transcendent and holy, immutable and eternal, and completely unaffected by the world He created. He is all-sufficient and totally self-sustaining. There is nothing that God needs and nothing we can give to Him. He just is. Any attempt at physical imagery will (by definition) detract from who He is, since He transcends the physical realm. His divine nature simply cannot be physically expressed.

Correct thinking about the nature of God—His eternal spiritual (nonphysical) nature—comprises the foundation of the second commandment, God's second prescription for healthy lives. God addressed this root essence of His nature when He first revealed himself to Moses and spoke to him in the burning bush. When Moses said to God, "Suppose I go to the Israelites and say to them, 'The God of your fathers has sent me to you,' and they ask me, 'What is his name?' Then what shall I tell them?" God said to Moses, "I AM WHO I AM. This is what you are to say to the Israelites: 'I AM has sent me to you'" (Exod 3:13–14).

God told Moses—"I AM." God's name was a complete and total statement of separation, holiness, and self-sufficiency. He simply is. Regardless of the condition of the world or the actions of individuals, He is. He remains as He is, eternally, unaffected by human behavior. He is the same now as He was to Abraham, Isaac, and Jacob, and He will continue unchanged through all eternity. This complete independence from His creation contrasts directly with the deities of the Egyptians. They were dependent on people; God is totally self-sufficient. They had physical natures; God transcends the physical world.

Acknowledging the nonphysical nature of eternal God does not preclude God interacting with His people on a physical plane; we know He does. But unlike the gods of Egypt, God interacts with people of His own volition and for His own purposes. This truth is borne out in the circumstances of God's Divine intervention as revealed in the Exodus account. The children of Israel were under bondage to the Egyptians and they cried out to God. God responded to their cry. They offered no sacrifices in exchange for deliverance, and there was no temple or idol to which gifts were given. God responded not because of what His people did but because it was His nature to respond, as He had promised. The "I AM," the One who had always been their God, intervened in His own time and in His own way.

Persistent Idolatry Despite God's Faithfulness

In spite of the fact that God acted solely of His own accord, it is clear from the actions of the Israelites that they did not comprehend the uniqueness of their God. Moses made sure Pharaoh and the people knew that there was no one like the LORD (Exod 8:10, 9:14), and the plagues demonstrated this uniqueness. Nevertheless, it was not long before the children of Israel began treating the LORD as if He were similar to the gods they had left behind.

A close look at the Exodus account reveals that it was just a matter of weeks before the people of Israel violated the second commandment and made an idol. In Exodus we see that the first Passover feast began on the fourteenth day of the first month. On the twenty-first day of that month the angel of the LORD struck down the firstborn of Egypt and the people were set free. Shortly thereafter they witnessed Pharaoh's army being swallowed by the Red Sea. A few days later, just twenty-two days after they fled Egypt, they were already grumbling and talking as if they were following a fickle, mind-changing God who had decided to let them die in the desert.

Despite their grumbling and lack of appreciation for who He was, God in His grace satisfied their hunger by miraculously sending bread from heaven. It seems that God's provision had little impact on their thinking, for only a short time later the people were complaining about a lack of water and accusing Moses again of leading them into the desert to die.

On the first day of the third month after they had fled Egypt (the *New Living Translation* says exactly two months to the day), they arrived at Mount Sinai. (Exod 19:1). On the third day of that month God descended in the form of a flame on the mountain and the people heard His voice calling Moses up on the summit.

While on the mountain, God spoke the Ten Commandments and the law to Moses. Moses then came down and delivered the law to the people. The people replied, "Everything the LORD has said we will do!" (Exod 24:3). After about seven days Moses scaled the mountain again and he remained there for forty days. It was during those forty days that the people came to Aaron and begged, "Make us gods who will go before us" (Exod 32:1).

Only sixty-three days after the Passover the people arrived at Sinai. Nobody knows how long Moses was on the mountain the first time, but the text implies it was not long. If we add the seven days he waited before returning to the mountain to the forty days he remained atop the second time, that is forty-seven days. If we add the sixty-three days after the Passover we get a total of 110 days. It seems from the narrative that the time between mountain ascensions was not too great. If we put this all together, it is not unreasonable to believe that the request for an idol occurred about 150 days or less from the Passover, the time of God's great deliverance. What an incredibly short memory! Less than five months after their rescue they asked for a physical representation of the God who had saved them! Less than two months after promising to keep God's commandments they asked for an idol!

As amazing as it is to think that the people would make such a request, it is even more astonishing that Aaron, the brother of Moses and firsthand witness to all God had done, actually listened to them. He took the gold the people brought to him and fashioned a calf. When he had finished it, he placed it before the people. When they saw the idol they said, "These are your gods O Israel, who led you out of Egypt" (Exod 32:4). They were in essence saying that they considered the golden calf to be the exact representation of the gods that had delivered them from Egypt.

After the people professed their belief in the idol, Aaron built an altar before the golden calf and declared a festival "to the LORD," to the God whose name was "I AM." In proclaiming a festival to "The LORD" Aaron said, in effect, that this idol was an accurate representation of the God of Israel. According to Aaron, the God of Israel was a lot like a cow! It was this cow-like god that had delivered them!

Less than five months after being miraculously delivered from Egypt and less than two months after promising to do all the LORD had said, the people created their own gods! Such idolatry provided ample testimony to how ingrained in their thinking the false concept of deity was. They believed it was possible to decide on their own how God should be represented. Aaron and the people decided He was like a cow. When we consider that they had seen God appear to them as fire on a mountain in billowing smoke, lightning, and thunder, and that they had seen His presence as a pillar of fire at night and a pillar of smoke by day, their actions seem unbelievable. In spite of all God had done they decided for themselves that the most appropriate representation of their amazingly powerful god was a baby cow!

Aaron, the high priest and brother of Moses, was complicit in the sin. Although he did not refer to the calf as emblematic of the "gods" that had delivered them, he did consider it a representation of "the LORD." Even he did not understand that the God of Israel was truly supernatural, truly apart from this earthly existence. Apparently Aaron thought it was perfectly reasonable to assign to the God of Israel the physical body of a cow. The error in thinking that God was physical was evidently lost on him. He did not fully appreciate the second commandment.

Just Another God?

Unfortunately for the children of Israel, this false thinking about the true nature of God did not end with the golden calf. In spite of God's discipline and punishment they continued to view God as humanistic and animalistic in both His nature and form. To them He was not any different in this way from the gods of Egypt. When it came to understanding the nature of God, their thought processes were defective. They just did not get it.

We see similar error with regard to the nature of God later on in the response of the people to the report of the spies sent into Canaan (Num 13–14). God had promised the land of Canaan to their forefathers Abraham, Isaac, and Jacob. He had confirmed that promise to Moses and specifically sent the lawgiver to lead them out of their slavery and into the Promised Land. Yet when it came time to enter the land the people doubted God's promise. Although God had demonstrated His protection and provision repeatedly they refused to believe that He would safely guide them into the new territory. The only explanation for their rejection is that they did not grasp the nature of their God. They thought He was like the gods of Egypt and that it was possible He had changed his mind.

They doubted God because they misunderstood deity. They thought all "gods" were alike. Egyptian gods were fickle and varying, just like people. The Hebrew people thought the God of Israel was no different. When confronted with a setback or a challenge their default response was that God had changed His mind, because in their way of thinking that is what gods did.

As we reflect on these attitudes, it seems obvious that the prohibition against idolatry was not just an admonition against building a statue. It was a warning against thinking about God as physical, material, and subject to the whims and fancies of the physical realm. Obedience to the one true God could occur only if the Israelites let go of and unlearned all of their flawed thinking. A reading of the Old Testament shows that this was not easy for the Israelites to do.

Those who seek to live obediently to God today are in a very similar situation. If we wish to think correctly about God, we must understand that He is not like anything here on earth. We must realize that true faith is based on who God *is*, not on a god who is as we think He should be. As created beings it is our place to strive to learn who God is, to discover His attributes, and to acknowledge who He has declared Himself to be. He is not defined by our culture or by our preconceptions. He is unlike anything we can comprehend.

Modern Idolatry

As was true for the Israelites, Christians cannot decide for themselves the form God is to take. It is not our place to determine what God must be like or to lay out in advance the characteristics of deity. Since we live in a world that is continually defining God on its own terms it will take effort for us to think about God correctly.

In the introductory chapters I related the story of the nurse who had declared that she believed in God but she did so "in her own way." Although this is inherently impossible (we can only truly believe in God His way), it demonstrates a dominant line of religious thought in our culture. We repeatedly see and hear of people trying to define God on their own. Some even do this while proclaiming Christian faith!

It is my belief that this "personal faith"—defining God for oneself—is every bit as idolatrous as a golden calf. Whether the idol is formed of clay, wood, gold, or ideology, it is still an idol. Any attempt to define God according to human or worldly terms and imagery is idolatry.

It requires no advanced degree in sociology to see that people today are just as bound by false thinking about God as were the Israelites. The unsound thinking and philosophy of the surrounding culture influences people today just as much as it did the people of Israel thousands of years ago. It is important to recognize this erroneous thinking if we hope to be free from its influence.

Whole books have been written specifically dealing with specious modern philosophy, so I do not think it necessary to devote time to an extensive review of all such thought. But it is important to be able to identify such intellectual idolatry when it appears. We do not have to look far to see it—it is all around us!

In February of 2007 I went with my family to see the movie *The Bridge to Terabithia*. The film tracked a friendship between a young boy and a young girl. The friendship of these two slightly outcast kids was a source of strength for them as they dealt with the struggles of their preadolescent existence. Late in the movie the girl is killed in a tragic accident. The boy was devastated. In one scene he sobs in his father's arms. As his father attempts to console him, he asks his dad if the girl will end up in hell. The father replies, "I don't know much about God, but I do know he is not going to send that little girl to hell."

The message in the father's response was simple. He was stating his understanding of the nature and character of God. He had created for himself a belief system wherein the God he had chosen to believe in would act according to certain rules. In his view, God was obligated to eternally spare those he, the man, deemed worthy. He believed the girl was good, so God would have to spare her. Faith in Christ or alignment with God's plan was unnecessary.

The movie father's words represent a common universalism held by our culture. Most people in America believe that if there is a heaven, all "basically good" people will get to go there. It is assumed that any God worth believing in would allow these "good" people in. We can all know who is heaven-bound, because all "good" people are endowed with the ability to define what is "good." As a result, anyone can confidently say whom God is going to accept. God becomes a servant to the beliefs of people. He is made into the image of man and given the mind and values of humanity. This is idolatry!

Anyone who has attended the funeral of a non-Christian person has almost certainly heard these values expressed. I have attended many funerals where the "goodness" of the deceased was put forth as evidence that the person was now in heaven. People are "sure" that "God" will act in the manner they desire, and that He is moved and motivated by their values, estimations, and actions. If we stop and think about it we must admit that the second commandment is violated in these funeral sermons. In their eulogies, people form God in the image of men! People have changed the materials with which their idols are made, but they are making idols nonetheless. They have exchanged the gold used by Aaron for thoughts, and have similarly crafted a god in an image they desire.

Another common fashion in which God is falsely depicted (a phrase which is perhaps as excellent and concise a definition of idol-atry as I can conjure) is as simply a "big man." I have heard God described as "the big guy," "the man upstairs," and even by former baseball manager Tommy Lasorda as "the Big Dodger in the Sky." Such imagery is common in popular culture. I can recall a "Far Side" cartoon where God is a contestant on *Jeopardy*, drawn as a larger-than-life Old Man with billowing white hair. One of the world's most famous works of art, the *Creation of Adam* by Michelangelo, portrays God as a white-haired man in white garments.

The ceiling of the Sistine Chapel may be great art, but it is lousy theology! Numbers 23:19 begins with the profoundly true statement, "God is not a man." Those five words concisely settle the issue. End of story. God is not like us! Men change, God doesn't. Humans age, God doesn't. All of the faults, limitations, and foibles of humanity belong only to people. God is holy and perfect and any attempt to declare otherwise is idolatrous.

I could give many more examples of idolatrous thought commonly present in our culture, but the point has been made. The world in which we live typically chooses either to deny God's existence altogether or to simply deny the truth of His God-ness by making Him out to be a man. If we want to worship God as He desires and maintain right thinking about Him, it is imperative that we be aware of such thinking and be prepared to confront it.

We must also recognize that such thought is not limited to the unchurched or faithless. Incorrect thinking about God infects the church as well. It clearly had infiltrated the Jewish church in Jesus' day and He addressed it in the Sermon on the Mount:

And when you pray, ***do not keep on babbling like pagans***, for they think they will be heard because of their many words. Do not be like them, for your Father knows what you need before you ask him. (Matt 6:7–8, emphasis added)

In this passage Jesus warned people that they could be influenced by the pagan world around them into thinking wrongly about God. The pagan religions of the day included a practice of prayer through "endless repetition." It seems they believed that such recitation was essential if one wanted to gain a god's favor. They believed that the gods would be influenced and changed by human actions. The Jews of Jesus' day had adopted a similar attitude and practice. Jesus made it clear—God the Father was not like those other "gods." He is eternal and omniscient. He is holy and separate from His creation.

The impetus for such horrendous thinking frequently comes from the world and its beliefs, but sometimes it comes from within the church itself. I have heard many preachers try to adapt a message to fit the sensibilities of unbelievers. It is dangerous to make the gospel message palatable to those who do not believe. It is very easy to leave out parts of the message or to alter its content. As a result God is frequently portrayed as something less than He is. He is made into the form of man.

Demeaning descriptions of God are common in our culture. I have seen T-shirts that declare "Jesus is my Homeboy" and that "Jesus is my Best Friend." When such condescension becomes common, it should not surprise us to see purported believers treat Jesus as they would treat another person. They call Him when they need Him, talk to Him when *they* want, and neglect Him when life gets too busy. Although this is the way people typically treat other people, it is not the way people should respond to a Holy God.

Correcting Idolatrous Thinking

If we are to correct this abysmal thinking in the church, we must do all we can to eliminate all falsehood and worldly teaching about God. We ought to reject any attempt to make Him a part of this world or subject to its ways. We cannot make Him to be like anything in heaven above or earth below, and we need to make sure we train our children to avoid this sin as well. It is not enough to simply say "avoid idolatry," we have to train ourselves and our children to recognize and confront it. This all begins with how we think about God.

Christians should be prepared to confront erroneous conceptions of God. We need to recognize the idolatry of making God out to be like a man, an animal, or an earthly force. Opportunities to identify this wrong thinking present themselves regularly. Movies such as *Bruce Almighty* and *Evan Almighty*, along with TV shows such as *Joan of Arcadia* and *Touched by an Angel* present images of God that are simply false. They portray God as something He isn't. The fact that solid moral messages sometimes emanate from these shows and movies doesn't change the fact that they say horrendous things about God. Believers must reject false thinking and remind each other and our children that God is not like that!

We cannot overestimate the danger of false thinking about God. Many modern-day cults have their origins in erroneous beliefs about the nature of God. One of the most common failings of many cults centers on changing the definition of who God is. Jehovah's Witnesses reduce Jesus to a glorified man. Mormonism claims that the God of this world is a created being from another world who was glorified to become a God. In both cases, by Charles Taze Russell for Jehovah's Witnesses and by Joseph Smith for Mormons, men formulated their own perceptions of God's nature and then built a religion on that false foundation.

The defense against such false religion must be based on a correct understanding of who God is. There can be no doubt or argument that such knowledge must come from Scripture. No other source offers a final, authoritative correction. A perfect example that can easily be taught to children is found in the Lord's Prayer. Look at the words of Jesus.

This, then, is how you should pray: "Our Father in heaven, hallowed be your name." (Matt 6:9)

When Christians talk to God they need to remember whom they are addressing. We are not talking to a man. We are entreating Almighty God. God's children need to understand who He is, where He is, and what He is. When we address God, we ought to approach Him correctly. In this prayer Jesus provides instruction as to how God should be addressed. Proper consideration of who He is supplies a solid foundation for thinking correctly about His nature.

The "who" of God is simply stated in the first two words of the prayer, "Our Father." He is our Father, the source of our origins, the giver of life and identity. He is the One who provides; He is the One who loves and protects. Although this title is a term of endearment, it is *not* a term of equality. In the culture Jesus addressed, the role of father was one that merited respect and honor. No one would presume to address their father casually, flippantly, or disrespectfully.

When I consider this instruction I think of how I would respond to an invitation to meet the president of the United States. No matter how the invitation was addressed to me, my mode of address to the president would be the same. I would refer to him as, "Mr. President." (Or, in the event that a woman serves in that office, "Madam President.") Even if the invitation were addressed to, "My good friend Bart," I would address him as "Mr. President." If he said to me, "We're friends, call me by my first name," I would respond with, "Thank you, Mr. President." Why? Because the position merits respect, and there is no way I could address him otherwise.

This attitude should dominate our hearts as we approach the throne of God. Believers have been justified, made righteous, and granted access to boldly approach the throne of grace to obtain help, but we must still remember who is on the throne. We are beseeching our heavenly Father. When we pray with our children, we should take care to address God with respect and deference. As we do, we reinforce the truth about his nature in teaching our children.

The second part of the introduction to the Lord's Prayer reads "who is in heaven." Christians need to remember not only whom it is we are speaking to but also where He resides. He is in heaven. God is not of this earth. He is otherworldly, supernatural, distinct. Not only is He separate from this world and its limitations but also beyond it. God transcends time and space. When we dwell on this preeminence we shake off any tendencies to view Him as small and confined to our realm, or as incapable of meeting our needs. When believers pray in this way, we are reminded of a vital component of God's nature: He is not a part of this physical world.

The Lord's Prayer doesn't just remind us that God is our Father and that He dwells in heaven. The prayer tells us *what* God is. He is holy. We are told to pray, "Holy is your name." Holy, (that is) separate, distinct, and unlike any other. Believers cannot approach God like anyone else, because He isn't. Jesus tells us that an understanding of God's nature and of His name is a crucial part of prayer. We cannot commune with God and yet entertain faulty thinking about His character. When Christians say, "Holy is your name" we confess, "There is none like you." This notion strikes at the heart of idolatrous thought, for when we think that He is like anything else we take the first steps on the road to idol worship.

As the Levites proclaimed in Nehemiah 9:5–7: "Stand up and praise the LORD your God, who is from everlasting to everlasting. Blessed be your glorious name, and may it be exalted above all blessing and praise. You alone are the LORD. You made the heavens, even the highest heavens, and all their starry host, the earth and all that is on it, the seas and all that is in them. You give life to everything, and the multitudes of heaven worship you. You are the LORD God…"

Swallow the Medicine

Here is the second prescription. God expects us to correctly understand His nature. Before moving on to the next commandment, stop and take time to check your own thinking about God. Look closely and investigate whether or not your attitudes about God have been infected and damaged by the world around you. If they have, ask God to heal and change your thoughts, allowing you to experience the transformation that comes when the Great Physician endows you with His truth.

For Further Reflection

- When you think of God, what do you think of? Do you envision a man? Do you view Him as limited? Take some time to reflect on the amazingness of God. If you need help, read through the Psalms, or look up the words to such great hymns as "How Great Thou Art." Intentionally work to correct wrong thinking.
- How do you talk to God? Is there a sense of awe and wonder or is He just another person? Take a moment daily to talk to God about who He is.
- How do you respond when you are confronted with erroneous ideas about God? Do you allow wrong thinking to just slide by? Stop and review what you have seen and heard about God in the media. Is He accurately portrayed? If not did you catch it, and did you respond to it?

Don't Ask God to Do It Your Way

Thou shalt not take the name of the LORD thy God in vain: for the LORD will not hold him guiltless that taketh his name in vain. Deuteronomy 5:11 (KJV)

You shall not misuse the name of the LORD your God, for the LORD will not hold anyone guiltless who misuses his name. Deuteronomy 5:11

*W*hen it comes to Godly prescriptions, the benefits of this third one are initially elusive. It is difficult to comprehend why the way we say God's name is so important and why saying it wrongly is so harmful to our spiritual health. Most people are familiar with the commandment and as commonly understood it seems pretty simple in its application. For as long as I can remember, I believed I understood this third commandment perfectly.

For me as a child "taking the Lord's name in vain" (as stated in the King James Version) was a reference to the manner in which the actual word "God" was used. There were good ways and bad ways you could say "God." Good ways included such phrases as "God bless you" or "thank God." Bad ways included anything casual such as "Oh my God" or "swear to God." Most importantly I was taught never to use God's name as a swear word. Saying "God damn" was the worst possible violation of the commandment, a grievous sin.

This admonition against using God's name in vain was drilled into my head as the definitive guide to appropriate verbal behavior. It is one of the more curious aspects of my childhood that in a home best described as remarkably ungodly, this commandment was frequently quoted. I grew up with the constant fear that if I ever were to slip up and say "God" inappropriately the consequences would be dire. Although the third commandment was often referenced in my home, I do not believe it was understood at all. There was little reverence for God in my family's daily life. For us the commandment was simply a matter of avoiding a few swear words or casual phrases and nothing more. There was no deeper meaning.

When it comes to language, my family reminds me of the boy Ralphie's in the holiday movie *A Christmas Story*. In the film, in addition to the main story line of Ralphie's pursuit of an official Red Ryder, carbine-action, two-hundred-shot-range model air rifle, there is a sub-story involving his father's use of foul language. Throughout the movie Ralphie's dad endlessly mutters unintelligible profanity. In one scene the narrator (adult Ralphie) states that his father "worked in profanity the way other artists might work in oils or clay. It was his true medium; a master." As a result there is considerable humor when Ralphie gets in trouble for using the "Queen-mother" of all swear words while helping his dad change a tire. From the story we learn that his father commonly used the expletive, but the family acted as if the word had never before been spoken.

This was my childhood. My mother and stepfather cursed like drunken sailors. I was exposed to vulgarity of a sort that even today would be reserved for R- and NC-17-rated movies. In spite of my parents' fluency in all things profane if I used even a hint of foul language I was harshly beaten. I vividly remember getting spanked at the age of seven for singing in the shower a ditty I had learned at school; "Yankee Doodle went to town riding on a rocket, turned the corner just in time to pee on Davey Crockett." To this day I can see my mother's angry, contorted face as she delivered the blows. How dare I talk in such a way! Another beating came as a result of my angrily calling one of my brothers a "fart with a cherry on top." (How profane of me!)

While all "foul language" led to punishment, nothing resulted in greater retribution than "taking the name of the Lord in vain." In my family "not taking in vain" meant that you could not use the word "God" in any speech not intentionally religious. Phrases such as "Oh my God" were strictly taboo. In fact, just to be safe, we weren't even allowed to say "Oh my gosh," for doing so came too close to violating the command. Just like Ralphie, I grew up hearing a steady stream of "God D—s" and "Jesus Christs" (many times with Jesus being given vulgar middle names as well), but I was taught, and taught well, that for me this was forbidden. I was NEVER to use the name of the Lord "in vain" like that.

I spent the next thirty or more years of my life with the unchallenged belief in this interpretation of the third commandment. It was all about how you used the word "God" or the name of Jesus. As a result of this belief I confidently thought that I had never violated the commandment. I might get angry and occasionally slip into a profanity, but I would NEVER stoop that low. Over my entire life I have never used the name of God or Jesus in anger. Like so many other people from my generation a subconscious unspoken fear lurked that to do so would result in some unnamed, terrible punishment. I just knew that God would respond with a vengeance if I dared to offend Him by misusing His name. I had visions of lightning bolts, falling boulders, and giant hammers just waiting to crush my head if I said the wrong words.

Meaning of the Command

Over the last few years, particularly in the time spent contemplating this book, I have come to realize that my old interpretation and application of the third commandment needed a reevaluation. There is much more to the commandment than swearing. It does not make much sense for an Almighty, Eternal, and Holy God to devote the third spot on His commandment list to a simple warning against speaking His name in anger. Many human offenses seem more harmful than that, and more worthy of Divine admonition, than quibbling about a name. The commandment cannot be solely about words. The God who cares deeply about our spiritual health had another purpose and deeper meaning in mind when He gave this command.

The meaning of the commandment was apparently obvious to the Israelites. We know this because the command was not accompanied by any specific qualification or detailed explanation. The third commandment is very brief and to the point—don't misuse the name of God. The meaning was clear to those hearing it at that time, as unmistakable as a doctor's recommendation to "take two aspirin and call me in the morning" is to people today. When Moses told the Israelites they were not to misuse the name of the Lord, they knew exactly what he meant.

What, then, does it mean to misuse the name of the Lord?

Whatever it means, we can be sure that misusing God's name was not an uncommon problem. In the Ten Commandments the Great Physician was not addressing incredibly rare and exotic diseases; He was after common and preventable conditions of the soul. As with all of God's admonitions, we can be certain that God would not have bothered to declare a prohibition against misusing His name unless there was an inherent and frequent tendency for people to do so. Not only must the tendency be frequent but also strong. The fact that God specifically told the people to avoid the behavior implies that conscious thought and effort would be required to avert it. Something innate in human nature causes people to disobey the commandment.

As we have seen before, the errant behaviors and attitudes of Israel frequently stemmed from immersion in the cultures that surrounded them. The tendency to misuse the name of God is no different in this regard. The Israelites almost certainly learned erroneous speaking about God from the pagan world around them. It is reasonable to believe that the Egyptians and the Canaanites habitually used the names of their gods in ways that would not be acceptable if similarly applied to the name of the one true God. Looking at how these cultures invoked the names of their gods is one way to learn what it means to misuse God's name. Scripture helps us understand the proscribed behavior.

Few instances in Scripture refer specifically to the names of other gods, but the handful of passages where such references are made provide insight. Two familiar passages reveal valuable information about how the names of pagan gods were used.

How NOT to Invoke God's Name

The first passage describes David's stand against Goliath from 1 Samuel. The shepherd boy David had volunteered to fight against the Philistine giant Goliath. David was offered King Saul's personal armor for the battle, but he turned it down. After refusing to wear the king's armor David left his presence, went to a brook, and selected five smooth stones for his sling. Unprotected by armor and with only the five stones as weapons, David went out to meet the Philistine giant. As David came near, we learn Goliath's response:

> Meanwhile, the Philistine, with his shield bearer in front of him, kept coming closer to David. He looked David over and saw that he was only a boy, ruddy and handsome, and he despised him. He said to David, "Am I a dog, that you come at me with sticks?" *And the Philistine cursed David by his gods.* (1 Sam 17:41–43, emphasis added)

Goliath invoked the names of his pagan gods and called upon them to impart harm upon David. Although the exact words are not given, we can guess at how it might have gone. We can envision something along the lines of "May the all-powerful Dagon, mighty god of the Philistines destroy you!" Undoubtedly Goliath believed that his gods would respond to his words, which were almost certainly a prayer of destruction on David.

We know from history and tradition that such a curse wasn't just name-calling, but rather a prayer of negative consequences. Nelson's Bible dictionary states it well: "In Bible times, a curse such as would have been spoken by Goliath was considered to be more than a mere wish that evil would befall one's enemies. It was believed to possess the power to bring about the evil the cursor spoke."[1]

Goliath believed that when he invoked the names of his gods he was ensuring that they would act in the fashion he desired—a point that should not pass by modern readers too quickly. It was a type of human control over the divine to invoke the name of a god. Gods were moved when their names were spoken. It is very similar to the genie-in-the-bottle mentality with which we are all familiar. Although a genie is incredibly powerful, his powers are subject to the one who holds the lamp. It seems that the pagan culture of which Goliath was a part, and by which the people of Israel were surrounded, believed that when the name of one of their "gods" was used the god was compelled to act. People controlled a god by invoking his (or her) name.

Similar attitudes about controlling gods appear to have been held by the prophets and followers of the pagan god Baal. In their fateful encounter with Elijah on Mount Carmel, the prophets of Baal demonstrated their belief in human ability to influence a god's behavior.

> Elijah went before the people and said, "How long will you waver between two opinions? If the LORD is God, follow him; but if Baal is God, follow him." But the people said nothing. Then Elijah said to them, "I am the only one of the LORD's prophets left, but Baal has four hundred and fifty prophets. Get two bulls for us. Let them choose one for themselves, and let them cut it into pieces and put it on the wood but not set fire to it. I will prepare the other bull and put it on the wood but not set fire to it. Then you call on the name of your god, and I will call on the name of the LORD. The god who answers by fire—he is God." Then all the people said, "What you say is good." Elijah said to the prophets of Baal, "Choose one of the bulls and prepare it first, since there are so many of you. Call on the name of your god, but do not light the fire." So they took the bull given them and prepared it. Then they called on the name of Baal from morning till noon. "O Baal, answer us!" they shouted. But there was no response; no one answered. And they danced around the altar they had made. (1 Kings 18:21–26)

It was the belief of these false prophets that their behavior, their invoking of Baal's name, would cause Baal to act in the manner they desired. As the passage continues, they went so far as to engage in self-mutilation as a means of influencing Baal's behavior.

> So they shouted louder and slashed themselves with swords and spears, as was their custom, until their blood flowed. Midday passed, and they continued their frantic prophesying until the time for the evening sacrifice. But there was no response, no one answered, no one paid attention. (1 Kings 18:28–29)

Why would the prophets of Baal do this? What possible advantage could be gained by self-mutilation? Undoubtedly they felt they could influence Baal's behavior through their actions. Notice the terminology used in the NIV to describe their behavior: "frantic prophesying." When we recall that the root of the word "prophesy" is to speak in the name of God, the events become clearer. They were declaring what they wanted Baal to do. The prophets of Baal screamed, yelled, called on the name of Baal, and cut themselves, *as was their custom*. They acted like this all of the time. It was their firmly held belief that such behavior would influence Baal to do *what they wanted*.

Although these stories are brief, they demonstrate a common thread. In each case, the pagan individuals involved believed that they could control the actions of their god by invoking his name. The religious constructs under which they operated taught that gods were subject to human will. This view of deity, that gods are limited and malleable, is totally contrary to the sovereign nature of the one true God. God is under no man's control. If this attitude of limited deity were true, God would not be the almighty, holy, and self-sufficient God that He is.

I believe the third commandment addresses this limited power, man-influencing-God mindset. God is reminding His people that He cannot be controlled by men. The people of Israel were forbidden from invoking the name of their God to bring about divine action. God did not work that way. They were not to view Him as a genie or a puppet or in any way under their control. To consider Him as controllable and limited was wrong thinking about God, so wrong that such thought invited grievous consequences. God made it clear that He does things His way, not man's, and humans should not expect Him to give in to their wishes and demands.

In spite of the clarity of the command and the implied warning within it, it was, like all of the commandments, frequently violated. A look at a specific time when a child of Israel failed to follow the command proves enlightening.

Failure to Follow

1 Samuel 15 describes the story of an Israelite victory over the Philistines. The narrative begins with King Saul—apparently immobilized by fear—too afraid to fight against the superior Philistine force. Saul and his small army of 600 men are hiding out in a place called Gibeah. Seemingly frustrated by his father's inaction, Saul's son Jonathan takes matters into his own hands. He and his armor bearer attack a Philistine outpost alone, just the two of them against more than twenty armed fighting men. It was an amazing act of courage and faith. The text gives the impression that Jonathan attacked with his armor bearer behind him. We get the idea that as Jonathan plowed forward through his foes he would wound, kill, or knock down a Philistine soldier, and his armor bearer would follow behind and finish them off! In a very short time the two of them had killed twenty of their foes!

God moved mightily after Jonathan's fearless display of faith. The book of Samuel describes it:

> Then panic struck the whole (Philistine) army—those in the camp and field, and those in the outposts and raiding parties—and the ground shook. It was a panic sent by God. Saul's lookouts at Gibeah in Benjamin saw the army melting away in all directions. (1 Sam 14:15–16)

When Saul saw what was happening, that the Philistines were in a panic, he mustered his forces and joined the battle. It is significant to note the differences in attitude between Jonathan and Saul. Jonathan went out in faith before there was any tangible or visible evidence of God's deliverance. Saul did not respond until he could see that something was happening and he was certain that he could win.

The writer makes it evident that this is what was happening.

Then Saul and all his men assembled and went to the battle. They found the Philistines in total confusion, striking each other with their swords. Those Hebrews who had previously been with the Philistines and had gone up with them to their camp went over to the Israelites who were with Saul and Jonathan. When all the Israelites who had hidden in the hill country of Ephraim heard that the Philistines were on the run, they joined the battle in hot pursuit. So the LORD rescued Israel that day, and the battle moved on beyond Beth Aven. (1 Sam 14:20–23)

When Saul arrived at the battle the Philistines were already in confusion. The battle was nearly won. The people of Israel had united in battle, traitors had returned to the cause, and victory was imminent. Given the circumstances and the odds against the people of Israel there could be no doubt that victory was at hand, and that it was all the LORD's doing.

But Saul, the man who had recently been cowering in fear, tried to make God's victory his. Here's the account:

Now the men of Israel were in distress that day, because Saul had bound the people under an oath, saying, "Cursed be any man who eats food before evening comes, **before I have avenged myself** on my enemies!" So none of the troops tasted food. (1 Sam 14:24, emphasis added)

The victory was God's doing, but Saul exploited it for personal revenge. That Saul was trying to take for himself that which rightly belonged to God became more obvious as events unfolded. Unaware of his father's foolish curse against any who would eat, Jonathan snacked on some wild honey during the battle. Out of fear all of the other Israelite soldiers ate nothing. The victory was limited in its scope because the remaining Israelite warriors were fatigued due to the imposed fast. When the battle was finally over, the soldiers' hunger and post-battle adrenaline rush caused them to violate God's dietary laws by eating bloody meat. What should have been a great and glorious victory ended in shame.

Perhaps because he realized that he had done something wrong, when Saul saw what his men were doing he "got religion":

> Then Saul built an altar to the LORD; it was the first time he had done this. Saul said, "Let us go down after the Philistines by night and plunder them till dawn, and let us not leave one of them alive." "Do whatever seems best to you," they replied. But the priest said, "Let us inquire of God here." So Saul asked God, "Shall I go down after the Philistines? Will you give them into Israel's hand?" But God did not answer him that day. (1 Sam 14:35–37)

After building the altar Saul decided to demand something from God. Saul wanted God's blessing and action to help him go out and finish the victory, one that would already have been completed were it not for his foolish action in forbidding his troops food!

When God didn't answer his prayer, Saul declared that someone must have sinned.

> Saul therefore said, "Come here, all you who are leaders of the army, and let us find out what sin has been committed today. As surely as the LORD who rescues Israel lives, even if it lies with my son Jonathan, he must die." But not one of the men said a word. (1 Sam 14:38–39)

I believe the silence was due to the fact that they all understood that any man who spoke what was on his mind risked getting killed. I don't think that saying, "Um, King Saul, if we are talking about sin today, I wonder if maybe the sin was when you decided to take credit for God's victory?" would have gone over too well. Instead of acknowledging his own failure, Saul declared that someone else must have sinned, and he was going to find out who it was!

And how did Saul declare his self-righteous intent to discover the sinner's identity and stomp out evil? He invoked the name of God! God had not responded as Saul had wanted, so now Saul declared in the name of God that *he* was going to cleanse sin from Israel. "As surely as the LORD lives!" Saul dramatically proclaimed. He tied God's very existence to Saul's behavior. He acted as if God was subservient to him. He invoked the name of God in a useless, selfish manner. Saul took the name of the Lord in vain.

When lots were taken and it came down to assigning guilt to either Jonathan or Saul, so confident was Saul in his self-righteousness that he commanded that the lot be cast between he and his son. When his son was chosen, Saul asked Jonathan to admit sin. Jonathan admitted to eating, but not to sinning. Saul then pronounced sentence on Jonathan, again referring to God by saying, "May God deal with me, be it ever so severely, if you do not die!" (1 Sam 14:44)

Finally the men of Israel had had enough and called Saul on his sin. They loved Jonathan and they were not going to see him killed. It is interesting to see the words they used when they responded to Saul's arrogance:

But the men said to Saul, "Should Jonathan die—he who has brought about this great deliverance in Israel? Never! *As surely as the LORD lives*, not a hair of his head will fall to the ground, for he did this today with God's help." So the men rescued Jonathan, and he was not put to death. (1 Sam 14:45, emphasis added)

"As surely as the LORD lives." They invoked the name of God on behalf of Jonathan!

The men stood up to Saul and he was shown to be the self-centered unrighteous man that he was. Shamed, he gave up the pursuit of the Philistines. By refusing to respond to Saul's demands God showed that He did not accede to Saul's wishes. Unfortunately for Saul, he did not learn the lesson. He continued to believe that God was obligated to serve him instead of realizing he was obligated to serve God. His failure to learn became his undoing. It wasn't just the fact that he misused the name of God that led to his downfall, but the misuse of God's name revealed his abysmal thinking about God, his incorrect understanding of who God was. It was flawed thinking that ultimately led to Saul's failure. Saul's diseased thinking was revealed in the words he spoke. He misused God's name because he did not recognize God's sovereignty, nor His transcendence and holiness. If Saul had thought correctly about God he never would have spoken so foolishly in the first place, and he never would have fallen. Spoken behavior followed unspoken attitude. As Jesus said, "For out of the overflow of the heart the mouth speaks" (Matt 12:34).

The meaning and application of the third commandment now comes into focus. It is not simply avoiding the utterance of God's name in a frivolous manner (although this is a reasonable inclusion). It is an admonition against invoking the name of God as we attempt to accomplish *our* own selfish goals, as we go about *our* business. The commandment precludes the *misuse*, not the correct use, of God's name. We are not to speak God's name and expect Him to respond to our every whim.

Correct Use of God's Name

What then constitutes the correct use of God's name? If the misuse involves applying God's name to achieve our personal goals, it follows that the correct use of God's name accomplishes His plans and purposes. The truth of this application is borne out in Scripture. Another look at the story of David and Goliath reveals appropriate use of the name of God by David. We previously noted Goliath's invocation of the names of his pagan gods as he cursed David. David responded to Goliath's taunts by using the name of His God, the God of Israel.

David said to the Philistine, "You come against me with sword and spear and javelin, **but I come against you in the name of the LORD Almighty, the God of the armies of**

Israel, whom you have defied. **This day the LORD will hand you over to me**, and I'll strike you down and cut off your head. Today I will give the carcasses of the Philistine army to the birds of the air and the beasts of the earth, and the whole world will know that there is a God in Israel. All those gathered here will know that it is not by sword or spear that the LORD saves; **for the battle is the LORD's**, and he will give all of you into our hands. (1 Sam 17:45–47, emphasis added)

What a contrast from King Saul! When God initiated a great victory against the Philistines, Saul stepped in to claim it for himself. Saul then tried to make God follow his plan by wrongly using God's name. David, on the other hand, gave God glory and credit for the victory, before the battle even began! David came against Goliath and challenged him for his affront not to the armies of Saul, or even of Israel, but for the fact that he dared defy the LORD Almighty! David understood the battle was about glorifying God, and about David following God's plan, not God following David's.

David's initial response to Goliath's challenge supports the conclusion that David was fighting in the name of the Lord:

David asked the men standing near him, "What will be done for the man who kills this Philistine and removes this disgrace from Israel? Who is this uncircumcised Philistine that he should defy the armies of the living God?" (1 Sam 17:26)

David went forth in God's name to accomplish God's purposes, and a great victory resulted. When David used God's name it was with a proper understanding of the God he was proclaiming, an acknowledgment of God's plan, and an eye toward God's greater glory. He used, but clearly did not *misuse*, God's name. David did not violate the commandment, he followed it!

A correct understanding of the name of God and how it can be wrongly applied is not limited to Old Testament examples. Knowing the true meaning of the commandment brings new insight to the teachings of Jesus about the use of His name as well. The fact that the commandment was intended not only for the ancient Israelites is seen when Jesus commented on the tendency to misuse God's name. Note his admonition against using God's name when making vows.

> "But I tell you, do not swear at all: either by heaven, for it is God's throne; or by the earth, for it is his footstool; or by Jerusalem, for it is the city of the Great King. And do not swear by your head, for you cannot make even one hair white or black. Simply let your 'Yes' be 'Yes,' and your 'No,' 'No'; anything beyond this comes from the evil one." (Matt 5:34–37)

Since we do not have total control even over our own lives, we cannot be sure that we will keep all promises we make. The passage forbids invoking God's name, His heaven, His city, or anything under His dominion as assurance that we will do what we say. Saying "may God strike me dead," "I swear to God," or "as God is my witness" diminishes the name of God. We are implying by our words that God is either validating or vouching for our actions. When Jesus said that anything beyond our simple word "comes from the evil one," He meant that such vows are an affront to God. The notion that humans can impact God by our words is a lie, which, like all lies, has its origins in the devil himself.

Just as the third commandment in the Old Testament did not mean that people should *never* use the name of God, Jesus' teaching in the New Testament does not prohibit the use of His name in any fashion either. Jesus made reference to the proper use of His name in one of His final teachings to his disciples in John 14.

> "I tell you the truth, anyone who has faith in me will do what I have been doing. He will do even greater things than these, because I am going to the Father. And I will do whatever you ask in my name, so that the Son may bring glory to the Father. You may ask me for anything in my name, and I will do it. If you love me, you will obey what I command." (John 14:12–15)

Study of this and other passages like it reveals that people are not instructed to avoid using Jesus' name, in fact we are specifically taught to use it. Invoking the name of Jesus becomes crucial when we make requests of the Father, and the use of His name is connected to a positive response to our petitions.

There are only two possible ways that this could come about. Either the use of Jesus' name legitimizes the request being made, or there is something in the request that legitimizes the use of His name. Simple logic and an understanding of what it means to invoke someone's name make it obvious that the latter is correct. Appropriate use is determined by the appropriateness of the request.

Many circumstances in modern life dictate when the concept of using someone's name applies. Phrases such as "Stop in the name of the law" are a common part of our vernacular. When yelled by a police officer on TV or in person, we instantly understand the command. The police officer is not creating law on the spot, nor is the officer declaring himself to be the final authority on the law by saying that the law is whatever he says it is. He or she is declaring that the law is clearly known, and that as a *representative of that understood law,* he is proclaiming its application. The officer in essence is saying, "We all know what the law says, and as a designated representative of that law, I am telling you to stop!"

Ambassadors for Christ

Similar representation can be seen in diplomacy. When an ambassador to the United Nations addresses the assembly in the name of the United States, he or she is not declaring a personal opinion and expecting the United States government to back it up. The ambassador cannot say whatever he wants and later go back to the president and say, "You have to do what I said, I used your name!" The ambassador must represent what he or she already understands to be the position of the nation represented. The invocation of the name is merely a means to communicate that he or she is acting not according to personal wishes but according to the dictates of the United States government.

This is exactly how believers are to use the name of Christ. We are not to consider our needs or conclude that we know how things should be and then tell God that He must do what we ask "in Jesus' name." To do so would be tantamount to God the Father subjecting Himself to our will. The idea that God is subject to our will stands in direct violation of the third commandment. God is not our genie!

Logically speaking, if we could force God to act by using the name of Jesus, He would not be truly God. The constancy, immutability (not susceptible to change), and sovereignty of God dictate that He does what He does in the way He wants and for the purposes that He sets forth. He is never subject to the whims of man.

Considering the two options on why and how Jesus' name is to be used, it becomes evident that it is not the use of Jesus' name that validates our requests. Rather, it is the godly nature of a request that validates the use of Jesus' name. When we pray and ask for things in Jesus' name, we are saying—in essence—that we are acting as His representatives on earth. In effect, we are ambassadors representing His interests. When we invoke the name of Jesus, we say to God the Father that we know that our requests align perfectly with the declared purposes of God the Son. We are saying, "I know that this is what Jesus would want, and I am asking for it in His name!"

When we comprehend what it means to correctly use the name of Jesus, we can then understand what Jesus meant when He made the promise about asking things of God the Father in His name. The positive response of the Father to the use of Jesus' name is neither an indication of our authority nor a declaration of our ability to get things from God. It is rather a declaration of the unity in purpose and essence of the Father and the Son. When we ask things in Jesus' name and according to His purpose, we can be assured of God the Father's response, *because Jesus' purposes are the Father's purposes as well.*

There is a natural progression in thought here: (1) We are instructed to use the name of Jesus when we pray, (2) When we pray in Jesus' name we are to pray according to His and God the Father's plan, (3) Jesus is the name of God incarnate, the physical expression of the divine, and (4) When we misuse Jesus' name, we misuse the name of God.

When we invoke the name of Jesus, the name of God Incarnate, for our own selfish reasons in an effort to get what we desire, we violate the third commandment! We demonstrate a false perception of God and His sovereignty and we diminish His power and authority.

Misuse of Jesus' Name

This truth should change our attitude about the commandment and about the people of Israel. Like many of the commandments it is easy to think that we are better than those foolish Israelites and that we would never violate God's law as they did. However, when we understand the true meaning of "You shall not misuse the name of the LORD your God" and consider that it applies to the name of Jesus, we see that the opposite is true. Modern-day Christians violate this command on a regular basis, perhaps even more so than the people of Israel!

Whenever we attach Jesus' name onto the end of our prayers with the thought that we have improved our chances of being heard, we violate the commandment. Whenever we flippantly pray for something we want for ourselves "in Jesus' name" we sin. This is far more common than we would like to admit. I committed this sin regularly as a child, most frequently between the months of April and September, when I consistently prayed for the Los Angeles Dodgers in Jesus' name! A review of baseball history provides proof that invoking Jesus' name did nothing to help the Dodgers win a World Series during those years!

Not only do individual churchgoers regularly violate the commandment by casually invoking Jesus' name but also their pastors frequently teach in direct opposition to the commandment! I have heard preachers proclaim that believers could and should use the name of Christ to pray for success, wealth, and health. Prosperity teachers guarantee success in life if people would only speak their desires in Jesus' name. Some go so far as to say that we can demand that God accede to our requests, announcing that because we are heirs of God in Christ we can therefore demand our inheritance here on earth! As if *that* were God's eternal plan and purpose! Prosperity preachers such as these essentially teach that God is a genie-type god. They instruct people to take God's name in vain, to use His name frivolously.

Sadly, Christian parents often teach children to ask God for things in the same erroneous way. For most of us it is unintentional, but the fact remains that we frequently teach our children that they can get what they want if they pray "in Jesus' name." It was only when I started writing this chapter that I became aware of how consistently I had instructed my children to pray in this way. In our nighttime prayers over the years we repeatedly asked God for things such as good test scores, success in sports, and other trivial blessings. Each and every prayer was concluded with the words, "in Jesus' Name." Looking back, I ask myself, "What was I thinking?" Did I honestly believe that because we asked for all of these things in Jesus' name that somehow we were more likely to receive them? If I didn't believe that, why did I pray in that way?

Reflection on such such-serving prayers brings to mind the time I took my medical school admission test. It was the biggest exam of my life. A poor score would essentially doom any chances at a medical career. As I had learned in church over the years, I asked people to pray that I would do well, that I would relax, have a clear mind, and that all of my studying would pay off. I specifically asked God to give me a good score. When I received the results and learned I had achieved a high score, I attributed my success to all of the prayers that had been offered on my behalf. Although it was a pleasant and noble thought, I think it shows that I misunderstood prayer. Godly prayer is prayed in accordance with God's will. How did I know that God wanted me to do well on the test? How did I know that there wasn't some other plan for my life besides medical school?

Proper Prayers

With a new understanding of what it means to pray in Jesus' name, wouldn't a more correct prayer have been:

"God, you have led me to this place. I have followed your leading as I have pursued this career. You have allowed me to reach this point, and I have felt a sense of your guidance as I have followed this path. I go in faith to take this test. I have faithfully prepared by doing my best, and I trust you to fulfill your purpose in me today. Allow me to perform as you have ordained, and I will give you all the glory. In Jesus' name"?

What a difference! Instead of asking God to act on my behalf, I would have been acknowledging God's sovereignty and accepting His plan! Lest anyone think that this is not the normal pattern in which we should pray, Christians need look no further than the Lord's Prayer for confirmation of this truth.

"This, then, is how you should pray: 'Our Father in heaven, hallowed be your name, your kingdom come, **your will be done** on earth as it is in heaven. **Give us today our daily bread**. Forgive us our debts, as we also have forgiven our debtors. And lead us not into temptation, but deliver us from the evil one.'" (Matt 6:9–13, emphasis added)

The Lord's Prayer is a prayer of submission to God's will—"Your will be done." The only things requested from God are those which He has already promised; namely provision for the day and forgiveness of sins. Jesus nowhere suggests that we are to ask God for anything we want for our own purposes.

So how then do we pray? How do we use the name of Christ? If we are only supposed to petition the name of Jesus in accordance with the will of God, how do we know what His will is? The easy answer is by praying in accordance with Scripture. A prayer consistent with God's Word is a prayer that can be made in Jesus' name. But what about those instances where Scripture is either silent or not clear?

An answer can be found in Romans 12:1–2:

Therefore, I urge you, brothers, in view of God's mercy, to offer your bodies as living sacrifices, holy and pleasing to God—this is your spiritual act of worship. Do not conform

115

any longer to the pattern of this world, but be transformed by the renewing of your mind. Then you will be able to test and approve what God's will is—his good, pleasing and perfect will.

When we lay ourselves on the altar of God, focus on His mercy, and allow our hearts and minds to be transformed by the Spirit of God, we will be able to test and know what God's will is and pray accordingly. Prayers offered in this manner demonstrate that we have followed God's prescription, and that we don't even want Him to do things our way!

Swallow the Medicine

Following God's prescription means being very careful with our words, prayers, and how we speak about, for, and to God. The following questions can help you determine if you are taking God's Word as prescribed, or if you need to call in for a refill.

- How do you pray? Are your prayers a litany of requests, or are they about "His will being done"? Focus on His plans and not your wants.
- Do you casually invoke God's name when making a promise or a vow? When we see or hear others in the media or in person do so, do you point out to your children the truth that God is not bound by our words? What do your promises and vows say about your attitude toward God?
- Do you teach your children how to know God's will? By teaching our children God's plans as revealed in Scripture and by modeling for them lives that are sacrificially given to God, we teach them how to live and think about God.
- How do you use the name of Jesus in prayer? Christians should remind one another and our children continually what it means to pray in Jesus' name, and make sure we understand that its use does not guarantee God's blessing.
- Do you ever think, talk, or read about God's name in Scripture? The stories of David, Saul, and other people in the

Bible can teach us about the name of God. Christian parents need to learn these stories and teach them to our children. As we do we show them what it means to use, and misuse, God's name.

Prescription #4

Remember What God Has Done

O bserve the Sabbath day by keeping it holy, as the LORD your God has commanded you. Six days you shall labor and do all your work, but the seventh day is a Sabbath to the LORD your God. On it you shall not do any work, neither you, nor your son or daughter, nor your manservant or maidservant, nor your ox, your donkey or any of your animals, nor the alien within your gates, so that your manservant and maidservant may rest, as you do. Remember that you were slaves in Egypt and that the LORD your God brought you out of there with a mighty hand and an outstretched arm. Therefore the LORD your God has commanded you to observe the Sabbath day. Deuteronomy 5:12–15

I love holidays. I love the food, I love the sports, and I love being with my family. I look forward to church on Easter morning, fireworks and barbecues on the Fourth of July, turkey and football on Thanksgiving, and the looks on my children's faces every Christmas morning. Holidays are so much more fun when shared with those we love.

In addition to the celebrations and the activity of each holiday, I enjoy taking time and reflecting on the meaning behind each holiday as well. I love talking about the birth of Christ on Christmas and thinking about what that night in Bethlehem was like. I love talking about His resurrection on Easter and what it means that Jesus defeated death. I love patriotic stories on the Fourth of July and gratefully looking back each Thanksgiving on all of the things God has done. Holidays are special, each in their own way.

My love of holidays was not inherited from my parents. Holidays were anything but happy for me as a child. As an unwanted child in a broken family, holidays were more a time of loneliness and sadness than they were a time of laughter and celebration. Holidays were observed dutifully and out of a sense of obligation rather than with a sense of meaning or excitement. I cannot remember a single Christmas or Easter where Jesus was the focus of the family gathering. The spiritual meanings of these holy days were either overlooked or forgotten.

Grateful for My First Thanksgiving

One of the first meaningful holidays of my life came on Thanksgiving when I was eighteen years old. I had moved out of the house in October of that year, just six weeks after my eighteenth birthday. I moved in with four friends in a two-and-a-half bedroom house in Whittier, California. The "half-bedroom" was a small five-foot by ten-foot enclosed back porch that served as my sleeping quarters. It was so small that there was no room for the closet door to open once a bed was placed there!

I had lived there for about six weeks when Thanksgiving arrived. I did not own a car, and I was not able to get to any of my family's Thanksgiving dinners, so instead of spending the day with my family I volunteered to join some people from my church who were making a trip to Skid Row in Los Angeles. Together we helped serve Thanksgiving dinners to the poor and homeless people who lived in that wretched area. I can remember the looks of gratitude on some faces, and the looks of shame and embarrassment on others, as we handed out the food. I remember watching as some men ravenously devoured their meals, almost inhaling the food in their hunger. I watched as many—their stomachs primarily accustomed to alcohol and occasional scraps—found they were unable to tolerate so much food. They became sick on the spot and could not keep their meals down. Some of them ate only a few bites of their meal before giving up and walking away.

When the food service was over early in the afternoon we all left Skid Row and went back to our homes. My roommates had gone to be with their families, so I found myself alone in the house. I sat at the table and ate my Thanksgiving dinner. The meal was meager, only a tuna fish sandwich and a few slices of bacon, yet I was thankful. I was thankful that I had a place to live. I was thankful that I had a tuna fish sandwich to eat. I was thankful that I had friends, and I was thankful that God loved me. In many ways, that day marked my first real Thanksgiving, for it was the first Thanksgiving where *being thankful* was a focus of my meal. On that day the meaning of the holiday became very real to me.

As I think back on that day I realize that a holiday without its meaning is not a holiday at all. If the meaning is overlooked or ignored it is nothing more than another day off.

In considering what it means to observe the Sabbath day it is important to remember that when God set aside one day a week for His Sabbath, He intended it to be much more than just another day off. He desired it to be filled with meaning. He expected it to be a "holy day," a holiday. Like all holidays, observing the Sabbath properly requires that we understand the meaning of the Sabbath. God's prescription to remember the day is meaningless without comprehending what the day is about.

AUniversally Ignored Command

For believers today, perhaps no commandment is more overlooked and less understood than this fourth one. In my family this command was given no attention at all. Even in a nonreligious home such as mine some of the other commandments were occasionally quoted. I was told not to lie and to not misuse God's name. I was even told not to have a picture of Jesus because it might be a form of idolatry. Yet at no time was I ever instructed to keep the Sabbath. Looking back I cannot remember the word Sabbath ever being spoken!

Ignorance of the Sabbath commandment continued into my teen years. Even when I began to attend church regularly the commandment continued to be overlooked. I cannot think of a single time when I was encouraged by a pastor to keep a Sabbath, or a single time when the commandment was mentioned. It was implied that this was a command for the Jews, the people of Israel, and that as a result it no longer mattered. It was applicable only for Old Testament times.

The only people of faith for whom Sabbath-keeping seemed to hold any significance were the Seventh-day Adventists. Their beliefs concerning the Sabbath had no impact on me, for in the Baptist church I attended I was told that they were weird and on the theological fringe. As a result their Sabbath views were easily ignored. A conversation I had with a member of the Adventist faith as a teenager supported this biased view. I was told that I was destined for eternal hellfire because I went to church on Sunday instead of Saturday, and that no Sabbath-breaker such as I would inherit eternal life. I was not particularly literate in Scripture at that time, but I was pretty sure this man was wrong in his interpretation of the fourth commandment. Whatever it meant to keep the Sabbath, I was pretty sure my eternal salvation didn't depend on it.

For years, in fact for my entire life before beginning work on this book, I continued with the belief that I did not need to concern myself with Sabbath-keeping. My attitude changed dramatically as I began to write this chapter. I have come to believe the commandment holds a significance that has been missed and ignored. Although a failure to keep the Sabbath does not impact my eternal standing before God, He would not have included it on His top ten list if it wasn't crucial.

Significance of the Sabbath

What is so important about the Sabbath day? Why is it essential to remember or observe one day over others? Isn't Sabbath-keeping just about going to church? Or, for the Israelites, wasn't it just about going to the temple? In exploring the history of the Sabbath and of God's commandment regarding it we will see much more to the command than mere church or temple attendance.

The command must entail more than just going to the temple because the Israelites of Moses' and Jesus' day did not, and in fact could not, go to the temple on a weekly basis. For many of the people throughout the history of Israel there was no nearby temple. In all of Israel there was only one tabernacle and later, once it was built by Solomon, only one temple. There was no way for all of the people to travel to the place of worship on a weekly basis, so temple attendance could not be what God was requiring of His people.

Far more than attending a worship ceremony, as we look closely at Scripture we will see that the Sabbath commandment was specifically designed to help people think correctly about God. The rest associated with the Sabbath was not the objective of the commandment but rather the means to accomplish the commandment's intent, right thinking about God. As with many of the Ten Commandments proper thinking is at the heart of the command to remember the Sabbath day.

The first three commandments also addressed people's conception of God. They reminded the people of God's unique and holy nature, His transcendence, and His separateness from the will and whimsy of man. Following closely on the heels of those commands came the instruction to keep God's Sabbath. It is logical to conclude that there was and is something embodied in Sabbath-keeping that is essential to understanding God and His nature.

If we hope to understand what the essential truths of the Sabbath are, we need to go back to the very beginning, to the book of Genesis. The concept of Sabbath began at the dawn of creation and was described by Moses in the creation account.

> By the seventh day God had finished the work he had been doing; so on the seventh day he rested from all his work. And God blessed the seventh day and made it holy, because on it he rested from all the work of creating that he had done. (Gen 2:2–3)

In the Hebrew the word translated as "rest" is shabat. This word, when best translated, appears to mean "to cease" or stop.[1] It does not mean to rest as we do when we are tired from exertion. It does not describe a recovery period during which strength is regained. God would not need to rest from any exertion, so we can know with certainty that the initial Sabbath did not refer to a rest in this type of restorative sense. God did not rest because He was tired. The reason God rested, or ceased, from His work is because He was *done*. Note what Moses said in the first part of verse 2—by the seventh day God had *finished* the work. The NASB says God had *completed* His work.

Simply put, on the first Sabbath, on the seventh day of creation, God stopped working because there was *nothing* left to be done. The work of creation had been completed. There was nothing more to create, nothing more to establish, and nothing more to do regarding creation. This completed work of God, a completeness of His being and of His doing, was the focus of the first Sabbath rest. God's completed work forms the basis for the fourth commandment.

It's Not Merely About Resting

Thus, Sabbath-keeping is not about us resting from our labors. It is not about us not working. It is a time for us to remember the completeness of God's creative work. It is a time to focus on who God is and what He has done, on what He has finished.

The completeness of God's work reflects the unique completeness of God's character. Only He is complete, only He has nothing left to do, only He has nothing further to accomplish, and only He has no improvements to make to His character. He can rest, or stop, because there is nothing else He needs to do. This completeness of God became the focus for the Israelites on each Sabbath. The Sabbath day was a day set aside to reflect on the completeness of God as revealed in the finished work of His creation.

A look at other times in Scripture when the importance of Sabbath-keeping was communicated to the people reveals the completeness of God as a common thread in each instruction. The commandment was restated to the people of Israel in Exodus 31, where this theme is repeated.

> "Say to the Israelites, 'You must observe my Sabbaths. This will be a sign between me and you for the generations to

come, **so you may know that I am the LORD**, who makes you holy.'" (Exod 31:13, emphasis added)

"It **will be a sign between me and the Israelites forever**, for in six days the LORD made the heavens and the earth, and on the seventh day he abstained from work and rested." (Exod 31:17, emphasis added)

These words indicate that the Sabbath represented something. It was a sign meant to last throughout all generations. It served to remind the people about who God was and what He had done.

With this biblical perspective of the Sabbath as a time to reflect on God's work and His character, we can understand its importance. When we remember its meaning, the seriousness with which Sabbath transgressions were punished makes sense. If it was just about taking a day off each week or only about abstaining from work, severe punishments for Sabbath-breakers would make little sense. Serious punishments were reserved for serious offenses, and the punishment for violating the Sabbath was death! Scripture describes what happened to a man who gathered wood on a Sabbath day:

While the Israelites were in the desert, a man was found gathering wood on the Sabbath day. Those who found him gathering wood brought him to Moses and Aaron and the whole assembly, and they kept him in custody, because it was not clear what should be done to him. Then the LORD said to Moses, "The man must die. The whole assembly must stone him outside the camp." So the assembly took him outside the camp and stoned him to death, as the LORD commanded Moses. (Num 15:32–36)

The man died not merely because he picked up wood. There was nothing inherent in wood-gathering that merited such a harsh response. The man was killed because he violated the Sabbath. It is significant to note that he did not incur the death penalty simply because he violated one of God's commandments. There are other commandments for which the penalty of disobedience was not death.

People did not suffer death if they were ever caught in a lie, or for stealing, or for being jealous. So it was not just that the wood-gatherer broke one of the commands that brought the death sentence. He was killed for violating the Sabbath. There was something significant in Sabbath-keeping and Sabbath-breaking that justified such a severe sentence. That something significant involved an appropriate understanding of the nature of God. Something in the man's actions reflected a poor understanding of God himself. Said differently, violating the Sabbath was a type of blasphemy—a way of saying something horrendous about God.

It's About Remembering God's Work

God cares about His name and His reputation, and He had set aside a day in which He was to be remembered and celebrated. In particular His completed work was to be extolled as an example of His divine completeness. The Creator's completed work was to be acknowledged through the resting of His people.

This is not to say that the completeness of God in creation was the only aspect of God's nature to be reflected upon each Sabbath. There are other aspects of God's work and character upon which the people were instructed to meditate each Sabbath day. In those passages in which other instructions about Sabbath-keeping were given, the Israelites were reminded that the Sabbath day was a day set aside to reflect on the character of God.

> Remember that you were slaves in Egypt and that the LORD your God brought you out of there with a mighty hand and an outstretched arm. Therefore the LORD your God has commanded you to observe the Sabbath day. (Deut 5:15)

This passage shows that the people were to reflect on the deliverance of God as well. As they remembered how God had liberated them and how he had shown Himself to be the only God, they would further comprehend His nature. He was God over all creation and all aspects of creation. He was God over everything. The gods of Egypt were not like Him. Their work was not complete and neither were they. The sun god Ra rode his sun chariot across the sky every day, over and over. The God of Israel set the sun and moon in their places once for all time. Egyptian gods continued to do battle, evolve, and change. The God of Israel was complete and unchanging.

It makes sense that God's deliverance from Egyptian bondage was a focus of the Sabbath day. It provided an opportunity to contrast the truth of the Creator who was their God from the false gods they left behind. In many of the Egyptian creation myths, one god (frequently Ra) created other gods who then went on to complete the work of creation. None of the Egyptian gods were complete, nor were they self-sustaining and originative in their creation works. In fact, all of the gods of Egypt were believed to have either arisen at creation or to have been created themselves. The God of Israel was self-sufficient and the originator of all things. He was, is, and forever will be different. As they rested on each Sabbath, the people would remember these truths about God as they reflected on their deliverance from Egypt.

It is easy to understand the importance of reflecting on God as creator, and of the uniqueness of God in His creative work. But why were the Israelites commanded to stop all work themselves? Why was it such an egregious sin to violate the Sabbath day?

One way to answer the question of why work needed to stop is by asking what the result of *not* working was. What did the people lose by not working? The answer seems silly, but it is important. When the people did not work they left something undone. Consider that as they sat on the Sabbath, weeds were not being pulled from the fields, fields were not being mowed, and animals were not being fed. For those who had a trade, tables weren't being built, pots were not being turned on the wheel, and clothes were not being sewn. The contrast is clear. As they thought about all of their work that was *not* done, they were to remember that God's work was complete. As they took a break from working to meet their daily needs they had time to reflect on the One who promised to meet every need they had.

A former pastor of mine used to remind people "God is God, and you are not." On the Sabbath day the people were to acknowledge that "God was complete, and they were not." They were to

126

remember "God's work is done, and yours is not." The contrast between the self-sufficiency and perfection of God and the imperfection and ongoing struggles of man is too important to be missed or ignored. The Sabbath was a day set aside to make sure that the contrast wasn't missed.

Remembering God's Provision

Another meaning underlying Sabbath-keeping was trusting God to provide. By leaving work undone or incomplete the people were forever losing a revenue-generating opportunity. They were giving up time they could never get back. They had to trust God that the time lost would not hurt them later. This trust would come as they reflected on God's past provision, which was ample evidence that He would provide again. Recall the admonition from Deuteronomy 5:15: "***Remember*** that you were slaves in Egypt and that the LORD your God brought you out of there with a mighty hand and an outstretched arm. Therefore the LORD your God has commanded you to observe the Sabbath day" (emphasis added). The people were supposed to reflect and recall how God had provided.

As the Israelites rested from their labor they would have the time and opportunity to think about their God and what He had done for them. That this is the intent of the Sabbath is further evidenced by the instructions contained in the commandment. God's people were told that they were supposed to "observe" the Sabbath day and "keep it holy."

The word translated as "observe" is the Hebrew word "shamar." "Shamar" means more in the Hebrew than simple recognition and acknowledgment of something. It refers to guarding or watching over something. There is a sense of protection and caution implied in the term. The people were to make sure that they not only personally obeyed the command but also that other Israelites did as well.

God charged His people to guard the day and to keep it holy. The day was to be treated differently from all other days. It was a holy day, or as we would call it today, a holiday. Like all holidays there were things done on the Sabbath that weren't done on other days. Just as Valentine's Day is especially romantic, the Fourth of July is especially patriotic, and St. Patrick's Day is especially Irish, the Sabbath had meaning all its own. Like the holidays we celebrate, it was to be a national holiday, observed throughout the nation.

Unfortunately for the children of Israel, this was a commandment they constantly violated. Time and again the children of Israel ignored God's law in this regard. Frequently, failure to keep the Sabbath comprised a major part of their overall disobedience and turning from God. The end of the book of Nehemiah portrays a particularly sad occasion when this was true. Early in the Nehemiah story the people had celebrated the rebuilding of the temple upon their return from captivity in Babylon. When the temple was finished the people of Israel gathered together in celebration and made a written promise to follow all of God's law. They specifically promised to keep the Sabbath.

But the people quickly forgot their promises. After the work was finished, Nehemiah was summoned to Babylon for a number of years. When he returned to Jerusalem he discovered the people's disobedience. Nehemiah records the experience in the final chapter of his account.

> In those days I saw men in Judah treading winepresses on the Sabbath and bringing in grain and loading it on donkeys, together with wine, grapes, figs and all other kinds of loads. And they were bringing all this into Jerusalem on the Sabbath. Therefore I warned them against selling food on that day. Men from Tyre who lived in Jerusalem were bringing in fish and all kinds of merchandise and selling them in Jerusalem on the Sabbath to the people of Judah. I rebuked the nobles of Judah and said to them, "What is this wicked thing you are doing—desecrating the Sabbath day? Didn't your forefathers do the same things, so that our God brought all this calamity upon us and upon this city? Now you are stirring up more wrath against Israel by desecrating the Sabbath." (Neh 13:15–18)

How soon the people displayed ignorance of the God to whom they had made their promises. It is remarkable to see how completely they had ignored both God's law and their vow to obey it. If they had truly understood God's character, they would have honored Him on the Sabbath day and kept the Sabbath. Conversely, if they had appropriately observed the Sabbath and used the time to focus on God's deeds and work, they would have understood His character!

The people of Israel had gotten so caught up in the business of everyday life that they had forgotten to focus on God. This tendency toward busy-ness is not limited to ancient Israelites; it is present in all of us. Human nature insists that we think of ourselves and our immediate needs instead of God. If we are going to think rightly about God, we must take time to intentionally focus on Him. This type of thinking requires that we stop doing everything else. There must be times when God has our undivided attention!

Still a Sabbath Today?

Is Sabbath-keeping still important today? Careful reading of the New Testament reveals that the early church did not keep the Sabbath in the way it was commanded in the Old Testament, because the people gathered together on a completely different day of the week. In Acts 15, when the elders in Jerusalem gave specific instructions to the Gentile churches, Sabbath-keeping was not on the list. The question then arises—if the Sabbath is no longer kept as it was in the Old Testament, is it still vital? Is there a New Testament or modern-day equivalent?

If we keep in mind the Old Testament purpose of Sabbath; namely a time purposely set aside to focus on the work and person of God, in the New Testament we see a similar observance intended for today. God has given us, the church, a specific time during which we are to stop normal activity and focus on Him. The early church, in its regular meetings practiced an observance specifically intended to remind them of what God had done for them. In this observance believers followed precise instructions from Jesus on how they were to focus on what He had done for them. He gave these instructions in the upper room on the night He was betrayed:

And he took bread, gave thanks and broke it, and gave it
to them, saying, "This is my body given for you; do this in
remembrance of me." In the same way, after the supper he
took the cup, saying, "This cup is the new covenant in my
blood, which is poured out for you." (Luke 22:19–20)

The Lord's Supper as Sabbath

The observance of Communion, or the Lord's Table or Supper,
is the specific time and practice set aside by Jesus for His disciples
to reflect on His work. It was the designated moment when they
were to remember all that Jesus had done for them. In the same way
that the children of Israel were commanded to intentionally stop on
the Sabbath and reflect on the completeness of God in creation, so
also the redeemed children of God were instructed to reflect on the
completed work of Christ in redemption as they observed the Lord's
Table. The Apostle Paul told the church at Corinth that they were to
specifically remember Jesus every time they partook the bread and
wine. Communion was and is a time set aside to remember what
Jesus did.

Some might say that equating the observance of communion
with the Old Testament observance of the Sabbath is a bit of a
stretch. Nowhere in the Bible is communion (by itself) described
as a modern-day Sabbath. Although it is not definitively called a
substitute for the Sabbath observance, it has many similarities that
cannot be ignored.

Consider the importance given to the proper observance of communion. In addition to being a reflection of the completed work
of Christ, communion is given a degree of significance that sur-
passes any other New Testament action. Although communion does
not impart salvation or change a person's eternal standing before
God, the failure to appropriately observe the Supper was associated
with adverse consequences. Just as in the Old Testament Sabbath-
breaking constituted a capital crime, improper observance of communion brought punishment as well. The Apostle Paul speaks
candidly in his letter to the Church at Corinth:

For I received from the Lord what I also passed on to you: The Lord Jesus, on the night he was betrayed, took bread, and when he had given thanks, he broke it and said, "This is my body, which is for you; do this in remembrance of me." In the same way, after supper he took the cup, saying, "This cup is the new covenant in my blood; do this, whenever you drink it, in remembrance of me." For whenever you eat this bread and drink this cup, you proclaim the Lord's death until he comes. Therefore, whoever eats the bread or drinks the cup of the Lord in an unworthy manner will be guilty of sinning against the body and blood of the Lord. A man ought to examine himself before he eats of the bread and drinks of the cup. For anyone who eats and drinks without recognizing the body of the Lord eats and drinks judgment on himself. *That is why many among you are weak and sick, and a number of you have fallen asleep.* (1 Cor 11:23–30, emphasis added)

Paul said that many were weak, sick, or had even died as a result of failing to remember the work of Christ as they took communion. Is this not similar to the Sabbath?

Paul elucidates in verse 26 that communion was set aside as a time to reflect on the completed work of Christ. Its purpose and meaning went far beyond eating bread and drinking wine. Communion was (and is) a physical, tangible way of proclaiming the Lord's death until He comes. It is a declaration of the finished work of Christ. It cannot be thought of as merely declaring that Jesus died. It must also be a way of announcing what that death accomplished.

What did Christ's death accomplish? Here are some things Christians can focus on when we come to the Lord's Table:

- Jesus' death brought us to God
- For Christ died for sins once for all, the righteous for the unrighteous, to bring you to God. He was put to death in the body but made alive by the Spirit. (1 Pet 3:18)
- Jesus' death brought about our righteousness and justification
  Consequently, just as the result of one trespass was condemnation for all men, so also the result of one act of righteous-

ness was justification that brings life for all men. For just as through the disobedience of the one man the many were made sinners, so also through the obedience of the one man the many will be made righteous. (Rom 5:18–19)

- Jesus' death brought reconciliation with God
  But now he has reconciled you by Christ's physical body through death to present you holy in his sight, without blemish and free from accusation. (Col 1:22)

Reconciliation, justification, and righteousness represent the completed work of Christ. When Jesus said, "It is finished" on the cross, it was these works that were completed on our behalf. Our reconciliation, restoration, and justification were accomplished completely and without limit by His perfect sacrifice. Having finalized that work, Jesus sat down (after His ascension) at the right hand of God. Just as God rested on the seventh day because His creative work was finished, so also Jesus sat down on His heavenly throne at the consummation of His redemptive work (Heb 12:3).

Thus, in proclaiming the death of Christ in communion, believers celebrate and remember His completed work. Jesus' broken body and shed blood fully satisfied God's wrath and once and for all purchased our redemption. This similarity to Sabbath-keeping, this reflection on finished work, does not end with simple remembrance and proclamation. In these admonitions about the sobriety with which communion was to be observed and in the consequences associated with its improper observance, communion does appear to be equivalent to the Sabbath day. Note again the words of the Apostle Paul:

Therefore, whoever eats the bread or drinks the cup of the Lord in an unworthy manner will be guilty of sinning against the body and blood of the Lord. A man ought to examine himself before he eats of the bread and drinks of the cup. For anyone who eats and drinks without recognizing the body of the Lord eats and drinks judgment on himself. That is why many among you are weak and sick, and a number of you have fallen asleep. (1 Cor 11:27–30)

Eating the bread and drinking the cup in an unworthy manner was described as sinning against the actual person and work of Christ. It was not just bad manners or rudeness. By disrespecting this sacrament the person was showing disdain for Jesus Himself. Is this not similar to the failure to respect God in the Sabbath?

The deeper significance of communion—that it is more than a simple feast—is clear in 1 Cor 11:28. When the Lord's Table is celebrated, it is a specific recognition of the person and work of Christ. Just as the simple act of avoiding work on the Sabbath does not equate with Sabbath-keeping (it must also include a specific meditation on God's work), so too simply drinking the cup and eating the bread does not equate with keeping communion. The act of eating and drinking is significant only because of what it proclaims and represents. Without the proper focus on God in Christ, the observance is empty of meaning and insulting to God. It is so dishonoring that it brings judgment upon the individual who demeans God in this way.

How serious is the failure to appropriately keep communion? How dangerous is it to not dwell on the completed work of Christ and on His perfect sacrifice? Just as the failure to keep the Sabbath was a capital crime, so too Paul tells us that the failure to remember in communion the perfect and final sacrifice of the Savior brings harmful physical consequences. For some people it can even result in death. Communion is a big deal! Honoring God by intentionally commemorating the completed work of Christ is a foundational part of the Christian life.

This is a sobering thought, isn't it? When I stop and consider some of the thoughts that have passed through my mind as communion trays were passed in church, I feel ashamed. In truth, for many years I spent as much time focusing on trying to grab the cup of juice in the middle of the tray or on trying to snag the biggest piece of cracker as I did on what Jesus did for me. Undoubtedly, it is only by God's grace that I am not already dead!

As essential as keeping communion is supposed to be, it clearly wasn't important to everyone in the church at Corinth. There were enough people taking the cup and the bread improperly to cause

Paul to pen a harsh admonition. It seems there were some who gave no thought at all to what they were doing.

If we are honest, we must admit that many Christians approach communion as the Corinthians did. I have sat through enough communion services in the thirty-plus years I have attended church to know that for many, communion is anything but a time of reflection on the person and work of Christ. In fact I can remember only very few occasions when I was encouraged to reflect on the completed work of Christ at all. The passage in 1 Corinthians 11 is frequently read, and I am often encouraged to examine myself, but it is only rarely that the leader of the service has encouraged the congregation to reflect on what Jesus did on the cross or what He accomplished with His death.

Focusing on the Cross Leads to Gratitude

Yet this is the very thing Jesus was encouraging us to remember! The bread is a reminder of His body broken for us. The cup is a reminder of His blood, shed for us. What was the result of His broken body and shed blood? Our salvation! Our atonement! Our redemption! Our reconciliation! When we meditate on what Jesus did for us, on His complete and final payment for our sins, we are naturally driven to examine ourselves. We are compelled to search our hearts to see if we are living the lives of gratitude and service that true remembrance of Jesus requires.

Self-examination is possible only when done by the light of God that shines forth in the person of His Son. It is in comparing ourselves to Him, to His perfection, that we realize our unworthiness. It is then that the appropriate spirit of humility and gratitude arises in our souls. It is then that we truly remember what was done for us!

Oh, that we would understand how crucial remembrance is to our lives! Forgetfulness is too often a major characteristic of those who profess to know God. Forgetfulness was a problem for the people of Israel, and it is for us today. In the Spirit of the fourth commandment it is my prayer that we will take the time to remember all of Who He is and what He has done.

Swallow the Medicine

Believers today are not compelled to observe the Sabbath exactly as the Jews did, but we are commanded to remember God and what He has done for us. The prescription to remember what God has done is essential for all who want to live healthy and productive lives. I encourage each reader to pause and reflect on Christ's work and sacrifice on your behalf. It may even help to take a piece of bread and a cup of juice or wine and have a private communion service. As you do, ask yourself these questions:

- What has God done for me? Think about all of the gifts that you have been given.
- How have I acted ungratefully toward God? Think of all the times when you have failed to remember God's work in saving you, in loving you. Tell Him you are sorry. Thank Him for His forgiveness.
- Think about all that Jesus did on the cross. Pause and remember the thorns, the nails, and the pain. Ask yourself why, and reflect on the answer, given in Romans 5:8—"But God demonstrates his own love for us in this: While we were still sinners, Christ died for us."

Prescription #5

Honor the Parents God Gave You

Honor your father and your mother, as the LORD your God has commanded you, so that you may live long and that it may go well with you in the land the LORD your God is giving you. Deuteronomy 5:16

*I*t is a shared reality for all of us that—just as with following a doctor's advice—listening to God isn't always easy. When it comes to following God's treatment plans for our lives, we can be inconsistent and noncompliant. We all have good days and bad days, good months and bad months, good years and bad years. When it comes to honoring my parents, especially with regard to my attitude toward my parents, year sixteen of my life was definitely not a good year. My father and mother both let me down that year in ways I will never forget.

Painful Upbringing

My father's diminishment in my sight came when he took my brothers and me on a trip to the central valley of California the summer after I turned sixteen. We had gone to visit relatives for a family reunion. We stayed with some cousins that I had never seen before and have never seen again. During the visit, my twin brother and I were especially bored with the adult conversation one evening and asked about going to a movie. My father suggested we see the movie *Oh, God!*, a comedy he thought was very funny. We had heard about the film, which starred the octogenarian George Burns as "god." We didn't want to see the movie, primarily because we didn't like the idea of God being portrayed as an old man with a cigar. My father couldn't understand our objections, and attacked us for being self-righteous. As the discussion went on he completely lost his temper.

It is amazing to think that not wanting to see a movie could generate such a visceral response, but it did. My dad was furious. In my mind I can still see the rage in his red face and still hear the venom in his voice as it quivered in shouted fury. I can also vividly remember the fear I felt. Pinned against a wall in the cousins' garage with nowhere to go, I endured the torrent of words and waited to see what he would do to me. He had a history of violent outbursts, and had physically abused my stepmother and stepbrothers on many occasions. I was certain I was going to be hurt and hurt badly.

My fear of pain was soon justified. When his yelling and threats failed to get me to change my mind, he slapped me across the face. He just stood and stared at me after the blow, pausing for a moment to see what I would do. It was as if he was waiting for me to retaliate so he could strike again. Instead of striking back in anger, I found that I was suddenly possessed by a strange sense of calm. With tears rolling down my face I felt fear leave me. I looked my father in the eye and calmly said, "You can beat me all you want, but I will not change what I believe. I am not going." There was another tense moment of silence as my father internally debated what to do next. In that instant he seemed to realize he had lost. He was a man who controlled people through fear, and since I was no longer afraid, he did not know how to respond. He shook his head, muttered a final insult, and walked away.

On that night, in a relative's garage, I lost a great deal of respect for my father. It was then that I began to understand that my father did not love me, and in fact couldn't love me. He did not understand me, my beliefs, or my feelings at all. If he didn't understand who I was, how could he love me?

The explosion did not occur only because I had refused to go to a movie that night. Tensions had been building between my father and me for over a year. I was growing and changing in ways that my father could not accept. The more I grew in my faith, the more my agnostic and angry father hated who I was.

I had not always been vocal about my faith. Although I had believed in Jesus since the age of five, I had not regularly attended church. As a result of my lack of spiritual training I had not lived out my faith. I didn't talk about what I believed in, mostly because I didn't know exactly what I believed, and didn't recognize my dad's lack of faith. Like many young children I just assumed that everybody in my family believed in God and that my father was no exception, so there was no reason to talk to him about religion. For the first fifteen years of my life we never discussed God at all.

Things changed by the time I reached the age of sixteen. I had started attending church on my own when I was fifteen years old and soon was deeply involved. The small church I attended had a vibrant youth group led by a young pastor who consistently challenged us to boldly live out our faith. I began to speak out to others about what I believed in, and to be concerned about my father's lack of faith. I loved my dad and when I recognized his unbelief I desperately wanted him to come to faith in Christ.

Unfortunately for our relationship he construed my awkward attempts to talk to him as attacks on his character and authority. Instead of being able to clearly explain to him what I believed, I found myself frequently having to listen to my father's attacks on my faith. He did not have any solid arguments against faith, but that did not keep him from trying to prove my beliefs foolish whenever he had the chance. Our relationship had been very tense and on the verge of a blowup for quite some time. It all came to a head on the night he struck me.

Although completely different in many ways from the relationship I had with my father, my relationship with my mother, who divorced my father, the first of her four husbands, was strained as well. My mother never spoke out against my faith and in fact liked the fact that my brothers and I were regularly attending church. She even seemed excited about our newfound commitment to Christ. She was pretty well-versed in the basics of Christianity and had attended a Bible study group several years earlier. However, in spite of her acknowledgment of biblical truth she did not make any noticeable attempt to live according to what the Bible taught. While for years she was able to maintain her semireligious façade, her lack of seriousness about God became undeniably obvious when I was sixteen years old.

Four years earlier my mother had divorced her second husband. For the ensuing four years she lived the life of a single mom, barely scraping by financially and far too busy to have any hope of a social life. Things changed the year I turned sixteen. A man who worked at the same car dealership as she began to show an interest in her. He pursued her aggressively, and she was swept away by the attention. The man wanted to be with her but had no desire to be with her teenage children. My mother found herself forced to make a choice. It was him or us. She chose him.

She asked my former stepfather, the second husband whom she had divorced four years earlier, to move back into our home to look after us. She then moved in with her boyfriend. Because my mother and stepfather had divorced, I was no longer legally related to the man entrusted with our care. What made matters worse was the fact that he had physically abused me when I was a child, viciously beating me on many occasions. I had thought that I was freed from ever having to deal with him again, yet there I was living with him! There was no way to justify what my mother had done. She had completely abandoned my brothers and me. Just as my father had as a result of his temper, in my mother's immorality she lost my respect that year.

These stories mark just two examples of how dysfunctional my relationship with my parents was. My father was a violent, intimidating, and possibly mentally ill man. My mother was an insecure alcoholic who neither wanted nor loved me as a child. Neither of them provided me with any of the love and encouragement I so desperately craved. By almost any measure they were failures as parents.

Honoring Dishonorable Parents

As a child of such a broken and dysfunctional family, honoring my parents is a concept with which I have struggled mightily over the years. I have frequently wondered how I could possibly give honor to people who were, for so much of my life, anything but honorable in their actions. Yet God commands that we *all* honor our parents.

The feelings and emotions I had for my parents over the years led me to wonder how I could ever follow the fifth commandment. For years I was filled with a sense of inadequacy and failure every time I heard the words "Honor your father and mother." I wanted to obey God, yet I had no idea how it was possible to obey Him in this way. My parents were anything but honorable people.

Even as I write these words the feelings of sadness, loss, and guilt about my parents come flooding back. Although I was a well-behaved, pretty good kid overall, the lack of respect I have had for both of my parents often causes me to feel that I have failed miserably in respect to this commandment. There have even been a few occasions over the years when, upon hearing this commandment, the thought "Seriously God, have you seen my parents?" went through my mind. How can a person honor his parents when he doesn't even like them?

In trying to answer that question, others arise. What exactly does it mean to honor one's parents? What does it mean to dishonor parents? Why is it so important? Why does God include this command on His list of ten? Knowing that the previous commandments gave insight into the person of God, what does this commandment tell us about God's character or plan?

What Is Honor?

The best place to start in answering these questions is with an appropriate understanding of what it means to honor someone. I believe that a large part of the difficulty in comprehending and applying this commandment comes from a poor understanding of honor.

When I think of the word honor, I think of medals, statues, banquets, and celebrations of achievement. I think of a recent family trip to Washington DC, where we visited the monuments to Abraham Lincoln, George Washington, Franklin Roosevelt, and Thomas Jefferson. While there we also went to Arlington National Cemetery, where honor is given to many of our country's war heroes and great men and women. In all of those places great people are given tribute through elaborate statues or engraved stones placed in solemn settings and embellished with eloquent engravings. The monuments inspire awe and respect and leave no room for doubting that the Americans being remembered were truly honorable and worthy of acclaim. These are the things most of us think of when we consider what it means to honor someone.

The type of honor on display in Washington DC, although impressive, is not the only possible meaning of the word. Honor isn't always showy and isn't reserved only for the most revered citizens. The type of honor the children of Israel were asked to give to their parents was different from what my family saw in our nation's capital. Unquestionably, God commands that parents are to be treated differently from other people, but I do not think the Israelites were being asked to erect statues and monuments to their moms and dads! Whatever God intended when He commanded that parents be honored, it must have been something that applies to all parents in all circumstances, for there were no qualifications or limitations added to the commandment.

Therefore parents are to be honored, yet honor doesn't necessarily mean statues. It must mean something else, and if we are to appropriately obey the command we will need to know what that something else is. The meaning of the word "honor" is a good place to start. The word for honor in Hebrew is not an easy word to translate. Like many Hebrew words, it has multiple meanings depending on the context. The Hebrew word is "kabed" (*Vine's Dictionary of Old Testament Words*).[1] It implies weightiness, heaviness, a quantity, or a positive reputation. It is used in various other places to suggest such things as rank, wealth, glory, or splendor. While it can be used in a "Washington Monument" sense, it doesn't usually have that meaning. It doesn't necessarily suggest something elaborate, yet there is a sense in the word of giving greater substance, weight, or respect to parents than we give to others. Parents are not to be treated just like everyone else.

This leads to other questions. What does biblical honoring look like? How exactly should we treat our parents differently? What kind of action in the lives of the Israelites did this command spur? Fortunately, God inspired very wise men to describe for us ways in which parents can be honored. Specific instructions regarding honoring parents were written in the book of Proverbs. The writers gave tangible advice as to how parents were to be treated. Consider these examples:

> Listen, my son, to your father's instruction and do not forsake your mother's teaching. They will be a garland to grace your head and a chain to adorn your neck. My son, if sinners entice you, do not give in to them. (Prov 1:8–10)

> My son, do not forget my teaching, but keep my commands in your heart, for they will prolong your life many years and bring you prosperity. (Prov 3:1–2)

> Listen, my sons, to a father's instruction; pay attention and gain understanding. I give you sound learning, so do not forsake my teaching. (Prov 4:1–2)

> My son, keep your father's commands and do not forsake your mother's teaching. Bind them upon your heart forever; fasten them around your neck. When you walk, they will guide you; when you sleep, they will watch over you; when you awake, they will speak to you. (Prov 6:20–22)

Over and over we see the admonition to listen to and follow the advice, instruction, and teachings of one's parents. It is clear from the Proverbs that giving weight, authority, and respect to parental advice comprises one aspect of giving honor. Further implied in these Proverbs is that conscious effort is required if one wishes to follow parental counsel. The writers advise the reader to "not forget," "not forsake," and "bind on your heart." The strength of these admonitions implies a natural tendency to disregard the godly advice spoken through parents. Our sin natures and pride result in a tendency to rebel and go our own way and thereby disgrace our parents. Conversely, when children listen to and obey parental advice they give honor to their parents. By obeying God in this way, the God who gave us parents and their advice is honored as well.

Biblical Clues About Honor

In Moses' instructions regarding the law we find another hint of what it means to honor parents. Immediately after Moses read the law to the people he challenged parents to teach it to their children. It was the job of parents, their holy obligation, to guide children in walking with God. As we saw in the opening chapter, parents were to teach God's law as an integral part of everyday life. It is logical to conclude that listening to that parental instruction and obeying it was what God wanted all Israelite children to do. When children do what God wants, they are blessed, and the family receives honor. It can be summed up this way—when a child listens to parental instruction and becomes a godly person, he brings honor to his parents.

This honor that results from applying the lessons parents teach can be given to any parent, even ones who would be considered less than honorable. My father was anything but encouraging in regard to my faith, and in many ways he was a negative influence in my life. Nevertheless, there were some positive values he passed on to me. My father believed in providing for one's family, and he stressed the importance of getting a decent job. He encouraged me to use the gifts that I had been given and to not discount my abilities. He believed in working for what you had in life, and taught the importance of effort. This was good counsel, in fact godly counsel, even though it did not come from a godly man. When I provide for my family and use the skills God has given me to succeed in life, I honor my father's teaching, and I honor my father.

In similar fashion my mother, who did not attend church regularly and who battled alcoholism for much of her life, was used by God to pass on His truth. For reasons that I cannot recall, when I was in second grade my mother decided to read through a book of Bible stories with my brother and me. Although our home did not follow biblical values for most of my life, and to my recollection was filled more with cigarette smoke than the Holy Spirit, the lessons I learned from those stories provided a foundation for my faith. The impact of the stories I was taught so long ago continues to this day. My current commitment to Christ, and the writing of this book, honors the work of God in her.

Now some would say that there has to be more to honoring one's parents than this. It can not only be about following God and learning from our parents, we must *do* something. Although there is more to honoring one's parents than following God's instructions, there is no denying that God put parents into our lives to make us and shape us into the people He wants us to be. If we do not honor God's work through our parents, any other form of praise and honor we give them will be empty and meaningless. If we ignore parental advice and become dishonorable people, any other praise or tribute we give them is worthless. If my son grew up to be an unrepentant axe murderer, it would provide me no comfort to know that he regularly praised me to the other inmates in prison! If my daughter accumulated great riches through dishonest means, I would not be honored if she used those riches to build a beautiful monument for me. Parents cannot be truly honored by children who reject God's ways.

My wife and I have made it a point to teach our children that they honor us not by achieving worldly success but by becoming godly people. Worldly success has no meaning apart from godliness. As crucial as this value is it seems to be ignored by many Christians today. In a culture that has pursued success at any cost acting honorably is a lost virtue.

The world's inability to understand this value was made clear to me in a parent-teacher conference we had when our son was in third grade. The teacher was primarily focused on telling us of our son's academic achievements. He is a bright child and he had done well academically. She spent the majority of the allotted time reviewing how well he had done in his studies. Almost as an afterthought, at the end of the conference she told us that he had had some "issues" with another student, and had been reprimanded for his behavior. She gave no details, but assured us that it was "taken care of" and that we need not worry. She then acted as if she wanted to move on to another subject. She was surprised when we stopped her and wanted to know more. Our concern caught her off guard. We wanted to know exactly what our son had done and how it had been handled. I stressed that I was much more concerned about behavioral issues than academics. She had a look of disbelief when I told her I would rather have my son grow up to be a garbage collector with character than to be an immoral US president.

My wife and I focused on our son's behavior at school because we embraced the fundamental truth that it is simply not possible to be truly honored by a dishonorable child. Academic success was meaningless if he was not acting honorably. After much prodding, the teacher told us that he had been mocking and teasing a special needs child on the playground. When we learned of what our son had done, we took additional action to address the character issue that caused his behavior. The punishment seemed severe to the teacher because she did not place the same significance on loving the less-fortunate as we did. We made sure that our son learned that loving others was one of the most important things in life, of far greater import than scholastic achievement. To this day our son remembers the lessons he learned from that episode. Academic success is of no value if one does not have godly character.

King Rehoboam's Dishonor

Scripture provides an excellent example of how a child can be successful, yet dishonorable, in the story of Rehoboam, the eldest son of King Solomon. His story is found in 1 Kings 12.

When Solomon died and Rehoboam became king, it was a challenging time in the land of Israel. It is apparent from the passage that the wisdom that had characterized the early years of Solomon's reign was not a part of its end. The people felt they had been abused and mistreated by Solomon. In their frustration with their mistreatment they turned to Jeroboam, a man exiled by Solomon, to be their spokesperson. On the day that Rehoboam was introduced as

Solomon's successor the people had Jeroboam approach the new king and ask if he was going to continue in the abusive fashion of his father:

> So they sent for Jeroboam, and he and the whole assembly of Israel went to Rehoboam and said to him: "Your father put a heavy yoke on us, but now lighten the harsh labor and the heavy yoke he put on us, and we will serve you." (1 Kings 12:3–4)

The people of Israel (through Jeroboam) gave Rehoboam a choice. He could continue in the oppressive pattern of his father or he could respond with a conciliatory tone. There was risk in either response. Harshness could result in rebellion and conflict. A kinder response could be deemed soft and might weaken his ability to rule. While the choice appears obvious to readers who look back on it, it clearly was not obvious to Rehoboam. He did not immediately know how to respond.

Initially Rehoboam followed the counsel of his father Solomon who wrote, "He who guards his lips guards his life, but he who speaks rashly will come to ruin" (Prov 13:3). Rehoboam wisely asked for three days to consider his response. This deliberation was also in keeping with his father's advice. Three different proverbs declare that many advisers assure victory and success (Prov 11:14, 15:22, and 24:6). Rehoboam went to others for counsel, first asking advice from the elders who had given counsel to his father Solomon.

That interaction with the elders was where his adherence to his dad's advice ended. He didn't listen to the counsel he received. He rejected it, and instead sought out the advice of his young friends. In arrogance the friends advised Rehoboam to "man up" and tell the people that he was, in so many words, bigger and badder than his dad had ever been. Although his father had told him, "A gentle answer turns away wrath, but a harsh word stirs up anger" (Prov 15:1), Rehoboam responded harshly to Jeroboam's request. Ignoring his father's instruction to answer gently resulted in the anger that the proverb promised. The people rebelled, the kingdom was divided, and Rehoboam barely escaped with his life.

When we focus on the fact that Rehoboam was King Solomon's son the story takes on profound significance. When Solomon wrote the proverbs urging sons to listen to instruction, keep God's commands, heed the warnings of their mother, and remember all they had been taught, he was writing those words specifically for his children. These words of wisdom were written to Rehoboam. Through these proverbs, Solomon taught Rehoboam all he needed to live wisely. If Rehoboam wanted to honor his parents the proverbs showed what he needed to do. The story of Jeroboam's request and Rehoboam's response demonstrates that Rehoboam didn't follow his father's counsel.

In reading the passage it is impossible to disagree with the truth that Rehoboam failed to honor his father and mother. Although he was the king of Israel and extremely wealthy, his refusal to follow his father's godly counsel and the resultant disaster brought dishonor to his family. We can say this with confidence even though we have no record of what the actual relationship was between Rehoboam and Solomon. Rehoboam could have been loving, kind, courteous, polite, and respectful to his parents. Even if he was, by his actions he ultimately did not honor his father.

It is also clear that Rehoboam's ability to honor his father was not dependent on his father's godliness. Rehoboam could have honored his father Solomon even though Solomon had turned away from God at the end of his life. (Scripture tells us that Solomon was led astray by his pagan wives and concubines.) Solomon's later sin did not cancel out the truths of the proverbs that he had written earlier. Solomon was not worthy of honor at the end of his life, but Rehoboam could still have honored him with godly behavior. The example of Rehoboam reminds us that we do not honor our parents because they are honorable, but because *we* are.

Honor Parents by Taking Care of Them

With the knowledge and understanding that we honor our parents by being honorable people comes a potential danger. It is possible to get so caught up in doing "honorable things" that we forget our parents altogether! There are things we owe our parents beyond our good behavior and moral conduct. Scripture teaches that we are to be mindful of the physical needs of our parents as well. Jesus addressed this duty in one of his dialogues with the Pharisees.

> "For God said, 'Honor your father and mother' and 'Anyone who curses his father or mother must be put to death.' But you say that if a man says to his father or mother, 'Whatever help you might otherwise have received from me is a gift devoted to God,' he is not to 'honor his father' with it. Thus you nullify the word of God for the sake of your tradition. You hypocrites! Isaiah was right when he prophesied about you: 'These people honor me with their lips, but their hearts are far from me. They worship me in vain; their teachings are but rules taught by men.'" (Matt 15:4–9)

There is an obligation implied in Jesus' teaching to meet the physical needs of parents. It appears that the Pharisees of Jesus' day had developed "godly" practices that resulted in ignoring their parents' basic needs! Instead of giving material goods to their mothers and fathers, they made promises to give those goods to God. We know that promises and making vows were very important to the Pharisees and that vows could only be broken in the most extreme circumstances. By making a vow that material gifts were set apart for God's use they made it a "sin" to use those gifts to help their parents—if they helped their parents they would break their vows to God. (Amazingly, the fact that a vow was made contrary to the expressed law of God was not one of those extreme circumstances in which a vow could be broken!)

Jesus' rebuke of the Pharisees attests that providing for material needs is an important aspect of honoring parents. The fact that Jesus referred to the gifts as "help" the parents might have received implies that the parents had a true need. The parents were in a tough spot and the Pharisee son in question had the ability to do something about it. It was in the descendant's power to alter the difficult circumstances in which the parents had found themselves, but the descendant chose not to and justified his behavior by making a vow.

Jesus' admonition was not that the Israelites were obligated to give to parents who did not have needs; He was not compelling anyone to give to someone who was self-sufficient. Jesus' use of this example implies that the behavior of the Pharisees represents a violation of the command to honor one's parents. It could not be disputed. By neglecting their physical needs the Pharisees were not honoring their parents.

The use of needy parents as an example shows another implication of the commandment. Jesus was talking about adult children. There is no way that a young child would have the means to help his parents, so Jesus had to be talking about an adult responsibility. It is evident from the example Jesus gave that the obligation to help parents never ends. It extends into the "grown-up" years.

The issue of adult children striving to honor their parents is something I encounter on a regular basis. As a family physician I frequently counsel children of aging parents. A common question is how to provide for senior citizens who are no longer able to care for themselves. I have seen devout people struggle with the question of whether or not adult children are obligated to have their parents live with them. They wonder if it is wrong to place parents into assisted living or nursing homes. On many occasions the children are contemplating how to care for parents who were abusive and neglectful. These adult children wonder what their obligations are and often come to me for advice.

Jesus' challenge to the Pharisees provides insight in caring for incapacitated and dependent parents as well. We have seen that the duty to care for our parents is not limited by age. The obligation continues into our adult years, and it never ceases. Nevertheless, as long-lasting as the obligation is, it is not without some limits. Implied in Jesus' words is an ability to meet the needs in the first place. The Pharisees were not being asked to take vows of poverty in order to help their parents. The Pharisees had the means to provide their parents with assistance; they just didn't want to give it. Instead of helping their families, by the vow they made, they chose to make the money inaccessible. (And actually in a way that would give the Pharisees access to it for their personal use!)

The Pharisees were rebuked not solely because they denied their parents help, but because they used an inappropriate tradition as justification for not helping. They were trying to weasel out of an obligation they clearly had the ability to meet. This interpretation of Jesus' words, that it was the refusal to help when able that was at issue, is consistent with other teachings of Scripture such as Proverbs 3:27: "Do not withhold good from those who deserve it, when it is in your power to act." The Pharisees were withholding good from their parents when they had the power to do otherwise.

As someone who grew up in an unhappy and abusive home, and whose parents have chosen not to have a relationship with me as an adult, I have thought a lot about what this means for me. I have absolutely no desire in my human nature to give anything to my parents. Nevertheless, I have come to the conclusion that if my parents were ever bereft of the essentials of life, I would be obligated to respond. It seems to me that this is part of the commandment. Given the opportunity, I would do what I could to make sure my parents had food, shelter, and clothing. This doesn't mean I would have to take them into my home. The help I offer might be given so they could live in a rented room or in a shelter, but I would make sure they did not starve or go homeless. To do less would be to dishonor them. My duty in this fashion is independent of the quality of their parenting. They deserve help simply because they are my parents. They are the parents that God gave me. Even if no other reason exists, that is all the reason I need in order to help.

Helping parents in this way fulfills the commandment. We can honor our parents by meeting their needs, and we can do this regardless of their obedience to God.

We have spent time considering how we are to act toward our parents. It is also important to consider how we *talk* about our parents. If we are to honor them, we need to be careful not to speak ill of them. This isn't always easy, especially for those who were not blessed with godly mothers and fathers. Fortunately, honoring parents does not mean that it is a child's obligation to praise parents who are not praiseworthy. (As a child of a dysfunctional home, there is not a lot to praise about my upbringing. To heap praise upon my parents would be to lie, and clearly that is not God's desire.)

Honoring by Avoiding Negative Comments

Even for those of us who can find little good to say about our parents, if we are to honor them we cannot berate them. We must resist the temptation to speak ill of what our parents have done. Recounting our parents' failures to others is pointless and wrong. When we avoid negative remarks, we honor our dishonorable parents.

An example of this type of honoring is described in the book of Genesis. In Genesis 9 we read an account of a time when Noah acted in a dishonorable fashion and yet was honored by two of his three sons. Noah had planted a vineyard and made wine. It seems from the passage that Noah had celebrated a little too hard one night and had passed out. One of his sons, Ham, found Noah passed out and naked, lying on his bed in his tent. It may have been a truly comical sight and Ham may not have intended to see his father in that way, yet at the moment when Ham saw his father Noah's embarrassment he had a choice. He could keep his father's shame a secret, or he could dishonor his father by telling others.

Unfortunately for Ham, he did not act honorably. He told his brothers what he had seen. It may be reading between the lines, but it seems there was some malice and disrespect in Ham's actions. It is as if Ham took pleasure in his father's embarrassment. When Ham shared what had happened with his brothers they refused to join in his disrespect. Instead of making fun of Noah, they refused to even look at their father in his drunken condition. They took a garment and held it between them, and then walked backwards into Noah's tent and draped it over their father to hide his nakedness. When word got back to Noah about how Ham had blabbed to others about his drunkenness, Noah was livid. Noah deemed Ham's actions as dishonorable and cursed him. Ham was destined to be subservient to his brothers for the rest of his life.

There is much to learn from Ham and his brothers. Even when parents are clearly in the wrong, there is no warrant for making light of their failures. No amount of pain or suffering we feel justifies taking vengeance by attacking their character. When our parents make mistakes, even grave ones, we honor them by not telling others details of their failures, and especially by not putting them down or making fun of their struggles. Our parents deserve better, if only because they are our parents. This is not easy. In writing this chapter it was, at times, difficult to seriously talk about my childhood without attacking my parents, and I have tried to choose my words very carefully.

As we have reflected on what Scripture teaches about honoring parents we see that God has shown what is required of all of us. We are to honor our parents by being honorable ourselves. When we follow God, we make our parents look good. Even in the case of a negative example, all of us have learned some lesson from our parents that has been used of God. We honor our parents by making sure that their basic needs are provided for, and by not maligning them to others. Finally, the obligation to honor our parents endures throughout our lives.

Honor Below Leads to Honor Above

Having reached this understanding about what it means to honor our parents, a natural question arises: Why is this so important? Why did God include this one on His list of the Ten Commandments? We have said before that the commands are more than rules to obey, that greater and deeper spiritual meaning can be found in each one. This is true of the fifth commandment as well. The attitude God demands we have for our parents is representative of the attitude we are to have for Him. The honor we give our earthly parents helps us understand how we are to honor our Heavenly Father.

Throughout Scripture God uses family imagery to describe His relationship with His people. The people of Israel are referred to as His children (Deut 32:5; Isa 45:11; Ps 103:13). Christians are called children of God (Luke 20:36; John 1:12–13; Rom 8:16). Jesus told his disciples that God is our Heavenly Father (Matt 6:6). Jesus called His followers His brothers (Matt 12:48). Time and space do not allow for an exhaustive list, but it is obvious that earthly familial relationships are representative of a person's relationship with God.

This symbolism of family relationships is made particularly clear in Paul's letter to the Ephesians. In Ephesians 6 Paul writes:

Children, obey your parents in the Lord, for this is right. (Eph 6:1)

Children obey God when they obey their parents. When we submit to the real and physical authority of our parents, we submit to God. When we submit to the parents we see, we are submitting to the God we cannot see. Obedience, which can be defined as relinquishing control and independence, is a fundamental part of what it means to be a Christian. We cannot follow our own will and desires and also follow Christ. We must subject ourselves, *all* of ourselves, to His control. We learn to do this by subjecting ourselves to our parents. Obedience to God and obedience to parents are inseparable.

As Paul concluded his letter to the Ephesians he took the time to remind the children in this young church of the importance of obeying parents. Paul said of obeying parents—"This is right." Any sense or thought children might have had to the contrary, any belief they had that they were free from parental constraints, was wiped out with these three words. Paul made it clear that obeying parents, honoring one's father and mother, is a commandment that endures. It was the right way to behave thousands of years ago, and it is the right way to behave now.

It is no coincidence that this instruction of Paul's regarding obedience came right after his instructions to husbands and wives. After describing the manner in which the husband's role as head of the family was similar to Christ's as head of the church, Paul directed his words to the role of children. The husband, as the father, represents Christ on Earth. Paul emphasizes the point that—at the risk of redundancy—when we obey our parents, we obey God.

Implied in Paul's exhortation to obey is the understanding that there will be times that the children either do not understand or even agree with their parents. (If they agreed with their parents' instruction, obedience would not be an issue, they would do it naturally. Obedience is only a necessary instruction for the times when there is incomplete understanding or agreement.) Is this not true about our relationship with God as well? Are we not obligated to obey even when we do not fully understand or agree?

We do not always understand God's laws. Yet we are required to obey Him. When it comes to tithing, forgiving those who have unjustly wronged us, or denying ourselves things we truly desire, we do not always comprehend why we should obey. This lack of knowledge in no way diminishes our imperative to obey. We must do as God commands, whether it makes sense to us or not. We learn this by obeying our earthly parents.

Obedience is key to a godly life. As Samuel famously told the disobedient Israelite King Saul so long ago, "To obey is better than sacrifice!" Every time moms respond to a child's challenge with the words, "Because I said so!" they are teaching their kids how to obey God. When a parent says to do something, no additional explanation should be required. (An obvious exception would be something contrary to God's expressed will.) We obey our parents because they are our parents. The same is true for our Heavenly Father. We are to obey God without questioning reasons or outcomes. We obey God because He is God. And as we do, we honor Him.

Parents serve their children well when they grasp these principles and apply them. When children are allowed to challenge parental authority, they are developing habits that are destructive to the walk of faith. Parents need to teach children to obey, regardless of incomplete knowledge and understanding because, as Paul said, it is right!

Swallow the Medicine

The prescription to honor the parents God has given us is as hard to swallow as a horse pill, yet it embodies so much of what it means to follow God. God gave every one of us parents through whom He teaches us about Himself. When we honor them, we honor Him. All Christians would do well to reflect on how we measure up to God's standards of honor and obedience, to make sure that the medicine has truly "gone down." The following questions can serve as a "heart test" of sorts with regard to our attitudes about our parents, and about God. Use them to see if the medicine is working as it should.

- How important is honor to you? Do you strive to do the right thing? Are there areas in your life where you are acting dishonorably?
- What lessons about life and God did God teach you through your parents? Take some time and make a list. Thank God for each lesson you learned. If your parents are still alive, consider sharing the list of positive things you learned from them. Even if you had dysfunctional parents, you should be able to find something God taught you through them.
- Are you prepared to help your parents if they have a need? If you are at that place in life where this may become a reality, take the time to discuss it with your spouse and family. Their needs are your needs.
- If you are a parent, are you easy to honor? Do you make it difficult for your children to respect and obey you? Just as children learn to obey God by obeying parents, parents have the opportunity to model God's love to their children.
- What are you teaching your children about obedience? Do you allow them to challenge and question your authority? Are you modeling for them the type of obedience God requires? Discuss these things with your children. Be on the lookout for the symptoms of disrespect, symptoms that reveal a dangerous heart disease! Share with them ways in which God has healed your attitude toward your parents, reminding them that the prescription for honor comes from God Himself!

Prescription #6

Value Human Life

You shall not murder.
Deuteronomy 5:17

*A*s a physician I am amazed at the frequency with which I must state the obvious. Things that I think should be immediately apparent to anyone and everyone simply aren't. I see it over and over again. I have seen a person with an amputated leg—due to poorly controlled diabetes—seem genuinely surprised when he developed a similar infection in his other leg that caused him to lose that one as well. He apparently didn't learn anything from the first amputation! I have counseled unfaithful husbands who seemed surprised by their wives' anger upon learning of their infidelity, expecting immediate forgiveness as if it were their right.

But the most common example I see of the overlooked obvious is in the bewildered looks on the faces of severely obese patients whom I counsel to lose weight. Many times these obese patients have even come in for checkups—visits specifically designed to detect any threats to their long-term health. They are often worried about elevated blood pressure, high cholesterol, and sometimes even funny-looking moles, but seldom ask about weight loss. I have seen such patients more than 100 pounds overweight act as if the need to diet had never entered their mind. Things I would think are obvious, aren't! Over the years I have come to learn that reminding people of the obvious is just a part of my job.

It reminds me of a joke told by Jerry Seinfeld. In the stand-up routine I observed, after making a joke about fat people the audience groaned at its political incorrectness. Jerry reacted to the response of the audience by telling them, "You don't understand fat people. There is a guy right now hearing this who weighs a thousand pounds, and he's thinking, 'Jerry's not talking about me, he's talking about someone with a *serious* weight problem!'" Apparently Jerry knows many of my obese patients, for he clearly gets the fact that not everybody sees the obvious!

When it comes to stating the obvious, I wonder if anything could top the sixth commandment, "You shall not murder!" What could possibly be more obviously wrong than murder? Shouldn't this be a no-brainer? It is rather remarkable to think that God had to remind people of the fact that they shouldn't kill each other. There are certain things in life that people shouldn't need to be told, things that people just know. I think of the words to the old song, "You Don't Mess Around with Jim," by Jim Croce. "You don't tug on Superman's cape, you don't spit into the wind, you don't pull the mask off the old Lone Ranger, and you don't mess around with Jim!" In the song, these were things that everybody knew. They were a given. Not murdering someone is something we would think was similarly unmistakable.

Though the prohibition against murdering anyone should have been clear, it seems not all of the people of Israel "got it." God wouldn't have told the people of Israel not to murder unless there was actually a possibility that they might think there were occasions when unjustly killing somebody was okay. There must have been people among them who thought there were circumstances when either human life didn't matter at all, or in which murder was justified.

How could this be? How could the people of Israel be unclear on such a straightforward concept? Where in the world would they ever get the idea that there were circumstances when unjustly killing someone was okay? A review of the Old Testament reveals that this type of thinking was more common than most would believe. There is more than one example of an incident when someone committed what they considered justifiable murder. When we look at these examples in Scripture we see that the prohibition against murder wasn't as generally understood as one might think, for Moses himself wasn't immune to the problem.

Moses the Murderer

Moses, the man to whom the law was given, the man who saw God face to face and stood before the Israelites, was himself a murderer. He had wrongly taken the life of another man. More than forty years before the first reading of the law and eighty years before the second reading, Moses had violated this unequivocally obvious commandment. The story is recounted in Exodus 2.

> One day, after Moses had grown up, he went out to where his own people were and watched them at their hard labor. He saw an Egyptian beating a Hebrew, one of his own people. Glancing this way and that and seeing no one, he killed the Egyptian and hid him in the sand. The next day he went out and saw two Hebrews fighting. He asked the one in the wrong, "Why are you hitting your fellow Hebrew?" The man said, "Who made you ruler and judge over us? Are you thinking of killing me as you killed the Egyptian?" Then Moses was afraid and thought, "What I did must have become known." When Pharaoh heard of this, he tried to kill Moses, but Moses fled from Pharaoh and went to live in Midian, where he sat down by a well. (Exod 2:11–15)

In this brief and fascinating account we learn much about who the man Moses was at that time. There was Moses, Hebrew-born prince of Egypt, going out to *watch* his people at labor. It doesn't say he went out to help, rescue, or defend his brethren. Moses was not sharing in their struggles. He remained at a distance, watching. He was a prince, not a laborer, and he acted accordingly. From a distance he saw an Egyptian beating a Hebrew, an act that was unquestionably wrong and undeniably brutal. Nevertheless, though it was clearly wrong, it was not a capital crime. The Egyptian was guilty of abuse and deserved to be punished, but he did not deserve to die. We do not get any indication from the passage that the Egyptian was going to kill the Israelite. In fact, we actually get the sense that such beatings were common.

The passage shows that there was at least one person on the scene (Moses) who disagreed with the assessment that the Egyptian did not deserve the death penalty for his actions. So angered was he at the Egyptian's actions, Moses decided that the man should die. Without consulting anyone, or telling anyone in authority, Moses sentenced the Egyptian to death. We cannot know from the text exactly what Moses' motives were, but we can make some educated guesses. It is possible that Moses saw this as an opportunity to advance his standing with the people of Israel. Killing a brutal Egyptian in defense of a fellow Jew would surely gain Moses respect. Alternatively, the nature of the beating may have been particularly offensive, so brutal that it infuriated Moses. Or, perhaps Moses was just having a bad day and was really ticked off.

Whatever the justification or rationalization, one thing is clear. In Moses' mind he gained or achieved something by killing the Egyptian, which to Moses was more important and valuable than the life he took. Perhaps in part because of his princely position, Moses felt he had the right to pass judgment and deliver the sentence. The man's life was simply not that important to him.

The text strongly suggests that even as Moses was carrying out his crime he was aware that his actions would not stand up to scrutiny. Moses was described as "glancing this way and that." Moses checked to see if anyone was watching him. There was no reason for Moses to check to see if anyone else was watching unless he was afraid of being caught. If the killing had been justified, it would not have been necessary for Moses to keep it hidden.

Moses' actions indicated an awareness that he was perpetrating evil. It reminds me of the discipline advice I give to parents. When parents ask me how they can know when their child is ready for discipline, I give them a behavioral answer. Instead of giving them an absolute age I tell parents, "When your child starts to do something, stops to see if you are watching, and then goes ahead and does it anyway, he (or she) is ready for discipline!" By looking to see if their parents are watching, children demonstrate an understanding that they are about to do wrong. What is true for a typical one-year-old today was true for forty-year-old Moses then. When he stopped to look around, he demonstrated his awareness that he was about to do something wrong. And just like a one-year-old, Moses did it anyway!

The fact that Moses' killing of the Egyptian was clearly unjust is further supported by the response of his fellow Hebrews. The events of the following day make that evident. When he tried to stop the two fighting Hebrews they challenged him by saying, "Who made you ruler and judge over us?" They recognized that Moses had wrongly placed himself in a position of deciding who would live or die. The fact that Moses fled when he realized his secret had been discovered provides further evidence of his guilt. Moses had indeed illegitimately placed himself in the position of ruler and judge. He had elevated himself—in his thinking—to such a level of arrogance that he could decide on his own when human life could be taken.

It is this thinking, the elevation of oneself to a position of ruler and judge over others that lies beneath all murderous acts. It isn't the belief that there are certain circumstances under which the taking of life may be necessary that is the problem, but the belief that someone can decide on their own when such circumstances exist. That is the issue. Only God has the right to decide what constitutes a capital offense. Once a person usurps that right he is traveling down a dangerous road. History has proven time and again that people in power can rationalize and justify murder. The wickedness of human nature makes such actions inevitable when people declare themselves rulers and judges.

It is likely that Moses perceived himself as a ruler and judge at least in part due to his Egyptian upbringing. It is not unreasonable to assume that in Egyptian culture it was widely accepted that there were some lives that weren't worth saving; some lives that deserved to be taken. To Moses, the life of a brutal soldier fell into the "deserved to be taken" category.

This type of reasoning wasn't unique to Moses. A reading of the Old Testament shows that this type of thinking wasn't limited solely to those with an Egyptian heritage. Abimelech, the illegitimate son of Gideon, is another person who was similarly guilty.

Murder Fit for a King

In the ninth chapter of Judges we read of the merciless and evil deeds of Abimelech.

> Abimelech son of Jerub-Baal went to his mother's brothers in Shechem and said to them and to all his mother's clan, "Ask all the citizens of Shechem, 'Which is better for you: to have all seventy of Jerub-Baal's sons rule over you, or just one man?' Remember, I am your flesh and blood." When the brothers repeated all this to the citizens of Shechem, they were inclined to follow Abimelech, for they said, "He is our brother." They gave him seventy shekels of silver from the temple of Baal-Berith, and Abimelech used it to hire reckless adventurers, who became his followers. He went to his father's home in Ophrah and on one stone murdered his seventy brothers, the sons of Jerub-Baal. (Judges 9:1–5)

Abimelech decided he wanted to rule over the people of Israel. His claim was based on his standing as a child of the judge Gideon, the previous ruler of the nation. Unfortunately, there were seventy other men who had the same standing as Abimelech and could make similar claims. Abimelech ignored any claims the others might have made and determined that his status as a true child of Shechem gave him the right to decide who was to rule. With his actions Abimelech demonstrated that he considered an unchallenged reign as more important than the lives of his brothers. Once he had reached the conclusion that this "thing" was more important than their lives, it was a short journey to the justification of mass murder. Seventy men, his brothers, were executed at his command. To Abimelech this was a reasonable solution to his political problems.

It seems from the passage in Judges that this line of reasoning was understood and accepted by the people of that day. That Abimelech's actions were believed reasonable by the people of Shechem can be deduced from a number of clues in the text. There was no way that Abimelech could have killed all seventy of his brothers on his own. He needed the cooperation and assistance of others, collaboration he would have to pay for. He was able to hire the men he needed with money given to him by the people of Shechem, the city in which he had been born. The people of Shechem were not wealthy and would not have given Abimelech money without explanation. They had to know what he was going to do with the money.

The response of the people of Shechem after Abimelech's murders gives additional credence to the idea that they were supportive of the killings. The passage describes their actions:

> Then all the citizens of Shechem and Beth Millo gathered beside the great tree at the pillar in Shechem to crown Abimelech king. (Judges 9:6)

The response of the Shechemites to Abimelech's abominable act was acceptance, not rejection. Crowning a man king is not exactly a sign of outrage! Rather than condemning his actions, they considered his actions to be worthy of honor and praise. They rewarded him! It is apparent that in that culture murdering others to consolidate power was considered a sign of able leadership. Abimelech thought and acted the way a king was expected to act, and the people rewarded his kingly behavior.

Sadly for the people of Shechem, they were unaware of the monster they had helped create. The pattern of thought that led Abimelech to kill seventy people later led him to take over a thousand innocent Shechemite lives. Three years after being crowned king by the people of Shechem, they began to question and grumble against his rule. Abimelech defeated their city in battle, and then came against a tower where a thousand unarmed Shechemite men and women had taken refuge. With no apparent remorse, he and his men burned alive the people in the tower.

As horrendous as Abimelech's deeds were, they are understandable in that they were the natural outgrowth of his thought processes and powerful position. He believed it was his right to decide who lived and who died, so he determined for himself which lives were valuable and which lives were not. To Abimelech some things were more important than people. Human life was of little intrinsic value to Abimelech. Such devaluation of life allowed him to act as he did.

Lessons from a Serial Killer

The truth that the devaluation of human life lies at the root of murder was confirmed by the infamous serial killer Jeffrey Dahmer. He shared his beliefs in a television interview recorded shortly before his death. Dahmer, who had killed seventeen people, stated that at the time of the killings he believed that people evolved "out of the slime" and that there was no God and no life after this one. These beliefs diminished his valuation of human life to the point where satisfying his dark urges was more important to him than people. He saw no reason to *not* satisfy his desires. Dahmer's story teaches us that when ambitions become more important than people, terrible things can happen.

I believe that the devaluation of human life as illustrated by Abimelech and Jeffrey Dahmer is at the core of what God intended to address in the sixth commandment. I am convinced that, as with the other commandments we have discussed, God wasn't just addressing the actual act of murder but the revolting thinking that leads to it.

Jesus' Teaching on Murder

Jesus, in the Sermon on the Mount, emphasized the truth that vile thinking leads to murder. His teaching made it clear that devaluing human life is the root cause of all murder.

> "You have heard that it was said to the people long ago, 'Do not murder, and anyone who murders will be subject to judgment.' But I tell you that anyone who is angry with his brother will be subject to judgment. Again, anyone who says to his brother, 'Raca,' is answerable to the Sanhedrin. But anyone who says, 'You fool!' will be in danger of the fire of hell." (Matt 5:21–22)

Jesus' words extend the meaning of the commandment, moving it beyond the limits of action to include attitudes and thought. Just as the blisters of chickenpox are the outward sign of the virus inside, murder is the outward visible display of an unseen diseased heart. With this understanding Jesus, as He did on many other occasions, attacked the evil thinking and attitudes that lead to sin. Jesus' teaching made it difficult, if not impossible, for His listeners to say that they had never violated God's law against murder.

Although there was little likelihood that many in Jesus' audience had ever taken the life of another person, everyone present had verbally attacked or insulted someone or at least thought that way. All who read this book have done the same. All of us have wrongly been angry with someone else. All of us have devalued someone. According to Jesus, this means we will all be judged. We are all guilty of violating the commandment "You shall not murder."

One can get a better understanding of what Jesus meant by looking at the context in which He spoke. Prior to His remarks about murder, Jesus told his listeners that unless their righteousness exceeded that of the Scribes and Pharisees they could not enter the kingdom of heaven. The Scribes and Pharisees taught that the avoidance of murder was tantamount to fulfillment of the law. Jesus said that if they wanted to truly fulfill the law, they would have to exceed this standard. They could not view their brothers with contempt. For all who would follow Jesus, following the law just got a lot more difficult!

The hearts of the Scribes and Pharisees were in the wrong place, and these contemptible attitudes served as motivation for Jesus' words. When we understand the meaning and the use of the word "Raca" the teaching comes more clearly into focus. "Raca" was a term that showed utter contempt and disregard for what someone said or thought. It was a way of saying that someone's opinions were completely worthless. That such an insult was generally thought to be wrong is evident from the passage. Jesus implied that according to the Sanhedrin, the religious leaders of that time, calling someone "Raca" would subject one to being summoned before a religious court. It was a very demeaning term.

Even though "Raca" was a grave insult, use of the term was not forbidden to all Jews. According to New Testament scholar Alfred Edersheim,[1] it was a term used by Rabbis to denigrate those they deemed ignorant and uneducated. Such use by Rabbis was considered acceptable. It was not the use of the term "Raca" that was wrong, but rather the assumption of a layman that he or she was capable of pronouncing such a judgment that was condemned by the Pharisees. According to the religious leaders a commoner could be called Raca by an enlightened leader, but could not, as a lower-class person, place the label on another. It was acting presumptuously that got someone called on the carpet, not verbally attacking someone!

The Sanhedrin (and by extension the Scribes and Pharisees over whom they ruled) passed judgment on anyone who presumed to call another man's ideas worthless, or who devalued someone by viewing them with disgust and disdain. Every one of Jesus' listeners knew it was wrong to address a fellow Jew in this way. It is clear from Jesus' words that these facts were commonly understood. Jesus began with the generally known truth and then took the teaching even further. Jesus taught that devaluing someone wasn't just insulting; it was the root cause of murder. To Jesus, degrading words and attitudes revealed a devaluing heart.

While calling someone "Raca" resulted in earthly judgment, Jesus warned of an even greater crime. In the culture of that day the term for fool, "moros" in the Greek, was a far greater insult. While "Raca" attacked a person's ideas or opinions, "moros" attacked the person himself. "Moros" was an attack on a person's nature. Calling someone a fool was a way of saying that the person had no value whatsoever. It was the greatest possible verbal devaluation of a human being. It seems from Jesus' words that it was widely understood that calling someone a "fool" was so terrible that the perpetrator would be subject to eternal condemnation. Jesus' position was in total agreement with the commonly accepted interpretation of the law; such an attitude was worthy of severe punishment. How people viewed and treated others mattered.

Even though there was an element of truth in what the people had been taught by their religious leaders, their teaching had not gone far enough. Throughout His Sermon on the Mount, Jesus contrasted His teaching with the incomplete teaching of the Jewish religious leaders. The phrases "You have heard that it was said" and "But I tell you that" were combined and repeated several times. The entire Sermon on the Mount was characterized by Jesus' expansion and clarification of the people's understanding of God's law. In His teaching Jesus applied the law not only to outward actions but also to thought. Jesus explained that the law applied to a person's attitudes and motivations.

In His teaching on murder in Matthew 6 Jesus provides such an application. He equated murder with needless anger! Jesus told people they would be judged by how they viewed and treated others. We could paraphrase Jesus' warning by saying, "You'll have to give account of your reasons for being angry, so be careful!" This should be a frightening thought for most of us. If we are truthful we will have to admit that in the majority of cases our anger with others won't stand up well to scrutiny. Our motives are seldom pure. In almost every angry circumstance a close look will reveal that we value some*thing* more than some*one*. Such anger violates the principles laid out by Jesus. When it comes to anger, there is no denying the fact that we are all guilty.

Recognizing the Murderer Within

I came to grips with my own tendency toward unfounded and unrighteous anger a few years ago. A particular circumstance revealed to me how badly I needed to change my attitude. My wife Lisa and I had been given two orchestra seats to a Broadway musical. We didn't get opportunities like this very often and were looking forward to a nice night out. As is common for parents, getting everything in order with the children took longer than expected and we did not get out of the house as early as we would have liked. Nervous that we might miss the first part of the show, I left the house more than a little grumpy. (Lisa will say I was a LOT grumpy.)

My grumpiness remained when we drove up to the theater. We parked in a lot a block away from the theater and quickly headed toward the entrance. In typical guy fashion I decided to jaywalk to save time. I saw that the gap in the traffic wouldn't last very long so I quickly took off across the parking lot, expecting my wife to follow. Lisa did not want to try and dodge traffic in high heels, so she stayed on her side of the street and waited to cross at the light. When I looked back and saw that she had not followed me, all I could think about was being late, and I got angry. My response to her was anything but kind. I didn't say much, but I said enough to make it clear I was angry and that it was going to be her fault if we were late.

The combination of the hurt look on her face and the conviction of the Holy Spirit took effect within seconds. I realized what my words and actions were really saying—that the first few minutes of a Broadway musical were more important to me than my wife's feelings (and safety). How else could my actions be explained? There was no other reasonable or justifiable explanation for my anger. If called upon to answer to God for my actions in that moment I certainly would have been liable for harsh judgment. I was wrong! (Worse than wrong, I was an idiot!)

All of us could fill volumes of books with similar stories of inappropriate anger. There have been innumerable silly things that I have valued more than people. The list is embarrassingly long. Over the years people have been less important to me than money (even small amounts), hurt feelings, highway traffic flow, and even the correctness of a fast food order. If honest, I have to admit that it is hard to remember very many times when my anger toward another person was even remotely appropriate or justifiable. On the vast majority of occasions I was just being a jerk! In every circumstance my heart was in the wrong place.

Poor attitudes about people are common in our culture. We live in a world in which people routinely attack other people as worthless. Talking "smack" makes for good entertainment. We frequently berate and demean people with whom we disagree. Anyone who doubts this need only spend a few seconds reading comments attached to political blog postings. It is not hyperbole to say that there are a number of bloggers and commentators who think people who disagree with them do not deserve to live. (This was particularly true a few years ago when the object of scorn was George W. Bush!)

Although we might say we don't vociferously attack people with whom we disagree, almost all of us are guilty of demeaning others. According to Jesus, this is wrong and a violation of God's commandment. If we are to obey God's commandment we must make conscious efforts to avoid insulting people. As we strive to change in this way we must remember that our good behavior cannot merely be limited to avoiding public outbursts. If we are to truly obey God we must watch our motives and words even in the privacy of our homes.

This is more of a challenge than we may think. When I consider the way in which I have talked about people who have done mean and hurtful things to me, I must confess that too many times the attitudes I have expressed at home have been terribly wrong. Instead of modeling obedience to God's law as Moses commanded, I have frequently violated this commandment in front of my children. (This is particularly true when I drive. I have repeatedly proven that the back seat of the car is not a good place for children to observe and learn how they are to value others!)

Television programs and movies regularly portray this devaluation of humanity. If we are not careful it is easy to get caught up in the disrespect for others that characterizes our society. Christians need to be cautious about the media's influence on our children. There is scarcely any sitcom that does not have as a major foundation for its humor, making fun of people who are less intelligent, less popular, or less attractive than others. Over and over the not-so-subtle message comes through that there are certain people for whom it is okay to make fun of and to demean. The truth that we are ALL created in the image of God and ALL have intrinsic value stands in stark contrast to the demeaning messages with which we are surrounded.

When we consider the worth of human beings, it is important to remember that it is because we are created in God's image that we all possess value. God sent His Son to die for us, demonstrating that worth. Because we know He desires a right relationship with His people, we cannot discard anyone. It is when we understand these truths and take them to heart that we can truly obey His command. This truth medicates our hearts and transforms our lives. When we see mankind as God does, as infinitely valuable, we will find it inconceivable to demean and devalue people, and as a result find it unthinkable to murder.

Swallow the Medicine

Although you may not be a murderer, you have certainly demeaned and devalued someone, sometime. And though the disease of devaluing others may now only be in its incubation period, it can rapidly spread into an outward anger that can infect and harm others. Review these questions as you search your heart, asking God to cure you of the selfishness and pride that could cause you to view others wrongly.

- Is there any person or type of person you don't value as you should? Think about people with whom you frequently disagree. How do you treat them? Consider people who are different from you, such as immigrants, people of other faiths, and people of other races. Is your heart attitude pure?
- Think of the last few times you were angry at or with someone. How did you respond? Did your actions reflect a person who valued people? Or did you value things?
- What kind of jokes do you tell? Do you laugh at the expense of others? Do you find humor in the sufferings of others? What messages are common in the television shows you watch? Are people valued?
- What lessons about valuing people are you teaching your children? Does your life and language lift people up or tear them down?
- In your workplace, do people come first? Would people say you are more concerned about things or about them?

Prescription #7

Be Faithful to Your Spouse

You shall not commit adultery.
Deuteronomy 5:18

*I*n nearly two decades of practice as a family physician I have seen multiple cases of adultery and immorality. As with cancer, heart disease, and asthma, it is a condition constantly on the increase. It is a sad truth that when pondering the introduction to this chapter the challenge wasn't coming up with an example, it was deciding which story to use. I have seen adultery rear its head in many different families, in many different circumstances. I have seen infidelity in people married a short while and I have seen it in people married for over twenty years. I have seen it in religious people and in atheists. I have seen husbands who were unfaithful within a few weeks of the birth of a first child. I have even had a couple who simultaneously discovered their mutual infidelity. They came to me to treat the anxiety they felt when they had caught each other cheating!

Of all the cases I have seen, the most troubling occurred when I had been in private practice for only a few years. The husband was a pastor of a new church in the same town as my office. It was a young and "hip" church, and he was a young and "hip" pastor, complete with flip-flops and surfer lingo. His wife was the perfect wife. She was pretty, friendly, outgoing, and devout. She headed the women's ministry for the church and was widely respected and loved by the congregation.

I first met the couple when she was pregnant with their third child. She had come to me for medical care in the pregnancy. Her seemingly devoted husband was with her at every visit. We talked regularly about issues of faith, and he spoke frequently about what was happening in the church. He never missed an opportunity to demonstrate his faith. When their daughter was born he prayed a dramatic prayer of thanksgiving in the delivery room.

Before long I found myself providing care for many more families in the same church. Once word got out that I was a Christian doctor a veritable stream of church members came my way. I was particularly thrilled that other women came to me for their obstetrical care as I had always loved delivering babies and caring for entire families. Caring for young Christian families was a special added bonus.

Two of the women from the church who came to me for pregnancy care were particularly involved in the church. One was a church administrative assistant who worked in the church office, the other a woman who was actively involved in children's ministry. They were both young, pretty, and outwardly committed Christians. I had no reason to doubt their faith.

Shortly after the two women gave birth to their children, I learned my confidence in them was misplaced. An epidemic of stress struck their church and several members came to see me, distraught and struggling to deal with terrible news they had recently heard. I was told that the pastor of the church had been forced to resign, accused of having affairs with these two women whose babies I had recently delivered. I heard that one of the women had confessed to her sin, while the other adamantly denied it. The confessor, partly out of shame and partly out of a desire to start over, soon moved out of the area. The woman who maintained her innocence left the church and left my practice, angry at all of those who doubted her integrity. I never saw either one of them as a patient again.

I saw the disgraced pastor soon after the scandal broke and he was remarkably unrepentant. He remained a patient for a while, and continued to talk about future ministry and what he believed God had in store. It was awkward for me, as I desperately wanted to challenge him about what he had done but could not find a way to appropriately work my thoughts and feelings into the context of the medical visit. The opportunity never did present itself. He left my practice a few years later.

The pastor's wife divorced him, and eventually found a man who loved and cherished her and her children. I have seen her off and on over the years and she seems to have rebuilt her life. The children seem to be doing well but must struggle with the daily reality of divorce and with the residual anger between their mom and dad.

The church body recovered much more slowly. Disillusioned, a number of families left the church. Many who stayed struggled with trust and wondered how something so awful could have happened. It took several years for the new pastor to overcome the damage that had been done and for healing to occur.

As the doctor for the pastor, the pastor's family, the women involved, many church members, and eventually the new pastor and his family, I saw firsthand the magnitude of the damage and harm that occurred. It is one of the greatest tragedies I have seen in all of my years of practice. This case and the others I have witnessed have convinced me that few sins are as damaging as adultery. The impact of the sin reaches far beyond the immoral person or couple. It extends to children, extended family, friends, and colleagues. It is truly a grievous sin.

As painfully obvious as the consequences of adultery are, there are still many people who do not think they need to do anything special to prevent it. I can only surmise that they do not truly understand the damage done by adultery. God considered adultery significant enough to include its prohibition in His Ten Commandments; important enough to write a prescription against it on tablets of stone.

Even though adultery is clearly a terrible sin, a full understanding of the sin and the commandment against it cannot be gained without a full understanding of God's plans for marriage and sexuality. Like an ink stain on a white blouse (or a blood stain on a white lab coat!), when we grasp the beauty, holiness, and intimacy God intended for marriage and all that marriage represents and symbolizes, the sin of adultery can be seen as the tragedy it is.

God's Original Plan

When we read the story of Adam and Eve it is clear that God had beautiful intentions for marriage from the beginning. The language that God used to describe the bond between this first man and his wife gives us insight into God's design for the marriage relationship.

> For this reason a man will leave his father and mother and be united to his wife, and they will become one flesh. The man and his wife were both naked, and they felt no shame. (Gen 2:24–25)

In this brief passage we see that the initiation of the marital bond is characterized by two processes. First, the individual separates from his or her parents, permanently altering the structure of that previous relationship. The parents are no longer to be the primary source of intimacy, affection, and encouragement. The connection with the parent is replaced by a new and more powerful bond, the bond with the spouse. The passage explains that this leaving of parents and uniting to one's spouse is at the heart of God's plan for marriage. The terminology used to describe this new family, "They will become one flesh," is incredibly powerful.

The second process in the formation of the marital bond is the cleaving, or uniting together, of the man and his wife. God proclaimed that the two individuals would become "one flesh." The bond between husband and wife is so strong, the couple so united, that there is a blurring of individual boundaries. God intended there to be oneness of purpose, heart, thought, and of physical intimacy, even while individual personalities remained.

The oneness of the marital relationship between man and woman is unlike any other. The depths of commitment and love that should characterize this union are far beyond that seen in any other relationship. Implicit in this oneness is that there are aspects of marriage that are unique. There are things shared between a husband and wife that are not, and in truth should not, be shared with anyone else. I know this to be true in my own marriage. My wife knows many things about me that nobody else does. She knows things about me physically and emotionally that I have never shared with anyone else. This is the very definition of intimacy.

The incredible intimacy of the marital bond finds its ultimate expression in the act of sexual intercourse. The bond of sexual intimacy is the tangible, physical expression of the oneness of flesh that God designed. I believe the primary intent of the sexual act, the primary reason God created sexual intimacy, is to form a physical bond that holds a relationship together. Although sexual intimacy happens to be both pleasurable and the means of procreation, neither of these ends represents the ultimate purpose of the sexual union. The ultimate purpose is stated in Genesis 2. Two individuals join and become one flesh. Sexual intimacy unites a man and a woman in a powerful way. So powerful is the bond that significant emotional harm results when a sexual relationship dissolves.

The Impact of Immorality

I have seen in my medical practice the emotional pain that results from broken sexual relationships. The damage I have observed supports the idea that the sexual bond is exclusively designed for marriage. The oneness of flesh created by a sexual union is meant to endure. When couples break the bond much harm is done. I have seen many young people troubled with the intense emotional pain brought on by the loss of a girlfriend or boyfriend who had been their first sexual partner. When they are mature enough to be able to express themselves they have told me of the profound sense of loss. Deep sadness came when they realized that they had given away something they had hoped to share with their life's one true love. Many times they had given themselves away in the belief that they had found their soul mate, only to discover they had lost something they could never get back.

One particular young lady comes to mind. I can recall the visit when she shared her grief. Then twenty-one, she had just been dumped by her boyfriend of the previous five years. He had been her first and only sexual relationship. To her, that was something special. She had thought that he was her life mate, her future husband; yet now that was clearly not to be. She felt used, shamed, and less womanly. She thought she was damaged and less attractive to other men. She had fallen into a major depression that was worsened by an associated anxiety disorder. She required significant doses of medication just to function each day. The medication helped her get through each day, but it did not deaden the emotional pain she was suffering.

Her emotional pain left her with two choices. She could acknowledge the truth that she had sinned and had made a serious error in giving herself to her boyfriend, or she could tell herself that sexual relationships were normal when dating and therefore no cause for shame. She knew the truth and was struggling with its ramifications. She had made a grave mistake, one that could be forgiven yet never undone.

This young woman's loss illustrates the seriousness of sexual immorality prior to marriage. When people give themselves away before marriage, their future marriage loses a degree of intimacy. A secret told to many people isn't really a secret, and when the most intimate act known to mankind is shared with many people, it loses some of its power. I have seen many promiscuous individuals who were later unable to sustain intimate relationships. The powerful bond intended by God was so weakened by casual sex that it appeared lost forever.

As harmful to the soul and psyche as premarital relations are, they pale in comparison to the damage of adultery. Adultery takes emotional havoc to an entirely different level. When someone has sex outside of a marriage, it is a betrayal of trust and intimacy unlike any other. When the marital bond of oneness comes undone, the consequences to families, children, and individuals are incredibly severe. When we understand the terrible damage done it is easy to understand why God included the prohibition against adultery in His Ten Commandments. It is exceptionally important.

Understanding the Blessing of Purity

Adultery's damage can only be understood in the context of the beauty that God intended for marital intimacy. The more beautiful the object that is damaged the more tragic the loss. Graffiti on a bridge overpass is ugly; graffiti on the ceiling of the Sistine Chapel is a catastrophe. All immorality is wrong and sinful, but when the masterpiece that is God's plan for marital purity is ruined by the stain of adultery it isn't just wrong, it's a tragedy.

The greatness of the tragedy of adultery, the violation of the marriage covenant, is profound evidence of the beauty God intended for marriage. Conversations with people who have known no other partner apart from their spouse confirm the beauty intended by God. This exquisite quality is evident in the attitude towards sex I have seen in faithful men. The sexual desires in men who have only been with their wives are not merely desires for sexual release or for a physical act. There is much more to it than the mere pursuit of pleasure; faithful men desire their wives. They don't want to be with just any woman; they want to be with the woman God gave them. This directed desire creates a powerful bond of attachment. When these men think about sex, they think about their wives, as they have no other frame of reference. This passion for their wives is intensely personal and private. By default their wives become their sexual ideal. This is truly a wonderful thing.

The strong attachment that results from undiluted intimacy has additional benefits beyond physical union. When a man's wife is truly his and a woman's husband is truly hers it gives rise to strong nurturing and protective emotions. As years of faithfulness accumulate, the emotion grows. I have seen this in my own marriage. I can honestly say that after twenty-six years of marriage my love for and connection to my wife has grown with every passing day. Love truly blooms with faithfulness over time. As clichéd as it may be, our relationship is the most beautiful thing I have ever experienced.

Country singer John Berry echoes my feelings in his song, "Your Love Amazes Me":[1]

I've seen the seven wonders of the world
I've seen the beauty of diamonds and pearls
But they mean nothing baby
Your love amazes me
I've seen a sunset that would make you cry
And colors of the rainbow, reaching across the sky
The moon in all its phases
Your love amazes me

It was, is, and always will be God's desire that one man and one woman share such a bond. This physical and emotional bond of unity is the foundation of marriage and, by extension, the foundation of the family.

More Than an Earthly Bond

This secondary aspect of marriage—as a godly institution that symbolizes eternal things—is another reason God hates adultery and prohibited it in the Ten Commandments. It is clear from Scripture that the family is an institution ordained by God. It is the primary vehicle for religious instruction and training and it is designed to be representative of man's relationship with God (Eph 5–6). As a result, God has a vested interest in healthy, intact families. Robust, godly families are the objective of the commandment. Adultery destroys families and is (understandably) hated by the God who created them.

To see the horrible consequences of adultery one need look no further than the story of the Israelite King David and the woman Bathsheba (2 Sam 11–12). David's lust for another man's wife led to adultery, murder, and ultimately the death of a child. As the years passed, David's family was plagued by idolatry, immorality, incestuous rape, and sibling murder. David's unfaithfulness in adultery weakened the foundations of his family—with devastating long-term effects.

From David's story we learn about the roots of adultery as well. David's sin was not a spontaneous act arising out of a chance encounter. Although he pursued Bathsheba only after he had unintentionally observed her bathing, the seeds of immorality had taken root many years earlier. A close look at the life of David reveals that his sin with Bathsheba was not the first time he had made a wrong decision about a woman. As with all sin, David's adultery began with a wrong attitude of the heart. Just like David, if we do not avoid the attitudes and desires that can lead us astray, we will fail in our quest to live sexually pure lives.

The story of David's relationships with women began many years prior to Bathsheba. When David killed the Philistine giant Goliath (1 Sam 17), he was promised the daughter of King Saul as his wife. Although the promised daughter was eventually given to another man, Saul ultimately gave his other daughter Michal to be David's wife. David's response to Saul's offer of his daughter's hand tells us much about David as a man. We see from the story that David was a humble man who did not consider himself worthy to be the king's son-in-law. This initial attitude of believing himself unworthy of such a wife suggests David began with a healthy appreciation of the blessing that a wife is.

David's attitude is well described in the text:

Then Saul ordered his attendants: "Speak to David privately and say, 'Look, the king is pleased with you, and his attendants all like you; now become his son-in-law.' They repeated these words to David. But David said, "Do you think it is a small matter to become the king's son-in-law? I'm only a poor man and little known." (1 Sam 18:22–23)

At this point in David's life he was a humble shepherd boy. Although he was adored by the people of Israel, who danced and sang "Saul has slain his thousands, and David his tens of thousands" when David returned from killing Goliath (1 Sam 18:5–7), David refused to view himself as better than anyone else.

Unfortunately for David, this attitude did not last. Not long after David took Saul's daughter Michal as his wife, Saul turned against David and tried to kill him. David and a small band of soldiers found themselves on the run from Saul and his men. They moved from place to place to avoid being captured and killed by King Saul. Eventually they arrived at a desert in a place called Maon. Near where they were staying lived a wealthy but unpleasant man by the name of Nabal. Nabal was married to Abigail, a beautiful and intelligent woman (1 Sam 25:3).

David sent men to Nabal and asked if he might give some blessing and aid to David and his men. Nabal responded to David in a rude and demeaning way:

> Nabal answered David's servants, "Who is this David? Who is this son of Jesse? Many servants are breaking away from their masters these days. Why should I take my bread and water, and the meat I have slaughtered for my shearers, and give it to men coming from who knows where?" (1 Sam 25:10–11)

Nabal said of David something very similar to what David had said of himself a short while earlier. Nabal asked, "Who is this David?" Although David had once questioned his own worthiness when it came to marrying the king's daughter, the events that followed show that the humble *Who am I?* David was gone. In his place was a man filled with a sense of importance and entitlement. *Who am I?* David had been replaced by *How dare he talk to me that way!* David. Nabal's response was an insult to this new David, so David and his men took up arms and set off to avenge their impugned honor.

With vengeance in their hearts they approached the place where Nabal lived. It was their intent to kill not only Nabal, but also every man who worked for him. Only the wise intervention of Abigail prevented a terrible slaughter. She met David and his men while they were coming to attack, bringing food and gifts to appease David's anger. Her thoughtful actions saved the life of her foolish husband and the lives of their servants as well.

Ten days after Abigail's shrewd actions, Nabal died. The beautiful, intelligent, and wealthy Abigail was suddenly single and available—all of which certainly did not go unnoticed. Travelling with David were some 600 men. I have no doubt there was at least one single man among those serving David who would have loved to be blessed with such an amazing woman as a wife. As ecstatic as one of David's men would have been to marry Abigail, none of them were given the chance. Even though he was already married, David decided that he deserved Abigail more than anyone else did. He took her as his second wife.

David had changed. He had gone from someone who felt he did not deserve a wife at all to someone who felt entitled to more than one. He had gone from someone who served others to someone who believed that others existed for him. Here, in his decision to take Abigail, we see the beginning of the attitude that led to his moral failure with Bathsheba. The act with Bathsheba revealed the culmination of the mindset that he was entitled to any woman he wanted. Instead of being a physical expression of the union of one man and one woman, for David sexual intimacy became about his own personal pleasure. He exchanged God's beautiful plan of intimacy for irrational lust, a compulsion that led to his adultery with Bathsheba and the resultant devastating consequences.

As with all sin, David's sin of adultery began with wrong thinking. We have seen in our study of God's commandments that each commandment addresses not just wrong actions, but the wrong thinking that underlies each sin. Adultery is no different. When it comes to sexual sin it is corrupt thinking, believing that sex is only about pleasure, that leads people astray. Although God intended the sexual act to be intensely pleasurable it is not pleasure but intimacy and oneness that God desires for His people. When people focus on pleasure instead of intimacy there is a tendency to devalue the beauty of the oneness that God intended.

Jesus Makes It Clear

Jesus' New Testament teaching about adultery confirms that evil-mindedness is at the heart of the seventh commandment. Jesus specifically addresses wrong attitudes about sexuality in His teaching on adultery in Matthew 5.

"You have heard that it was said, 'Do not commit adultery.' But I tell you that anyone who looks at a woman lustfully has already committed adultery with her in his heart." (Matt 5:27–28)

The key to understanding Jesus' teaching lies in what it means to "look on a woman lustfully." It is not just looking at a woman that is the issue. Jesus is not asking men to go through life with blinders on. Jesus' words indicate that it is not just the look but something in the way that the woman is being looked at that is the source of the sin. It is a lustful look, not just a glance, against which Jesus is speaking. It is that type of look that Jesus equates with adultery.

What is a "lustful" look? The word in the Greek translated as "lustful" means "to long for" or "to desire." The term implies that the person is not desiring relationship, intimacy, and marriage. The desire and longing that characterizes the look is purely physical. It is a desire for pleasure. The "luster" desires the other person in a physical sense only. There is no thought of the person's life, feelings, or standing with God. (Such thinking would by its very nature prevent illegitimate sexual desire!) The lustful person is thinking only of himself, of the pleasure to be gained. This is the type of look of which Jesus is speaking. It is a leer that ignores the heart and soul of the woman. It objectifies her and makes her nothing more than a physical source of pleasure. It is dehumanizing.

The story of David and Bathsheba provides an excellent example of such sinful gazing. We read in the story that David first saw Bathsheba bathing. Stumbling across a beautiful woman who happens to be bathing is not in and of itself sinful. But it is clear that as David looked at Bathsheba, the look became something more than a brief unintentional glance. The look evolved into wanton lust. Although David may have initially been innocent, at some point the sinful attitude toward women that he had previously allowed to possess his heart took over. Just as he had with Abigail years earlier, David viewed Bathsheba as someone who could please him. He wanted Bathsheba for himself, and he felt entitled to her.

David's lust was evident in the actions that followed. He inquired as to who Bathsheba was, not because he was concerned about her life, but because he wanted her. The report that she was married did nothing to squelch his desire. The urge for pleasure controlled his thoughts and drove his actions. David's adultery was the physical expression of what was already in his heart.

This account of David's sin and the teaching of Jesus show that selfishness is at the core of adulterous thoughts and actions. Selfishness causes one to view another person as a source of pleasure instead of as the child of God they are. Selfishness separates the beauty and intimacy of proper sexual relations from the pleasure associated with it. Such selfishness turns sex into a purely physical act devoid of any deeper meaning.

Thinking wrongly about sex undermines the bond of intimacy that is the foundation of marital unity. This is why Jesus warned of violating this union. When the beauty of sexual intimacy is lost, the marital bond is weakened. When a man looks at a woman (or the other way around) as solely a physical object, he is intentionally thinking inappropriately about sex, marriage, and God's plan for men and women.

It is easy to condemn David for his sin, but the tendency to view sex as a purely physical act meant for personal pleasure is present in all of us. Billions of dollars would not be spent on pornography if there were not a large number of people who pursue sexual pleasure apart from true intimacy. Surveys of Christian men's use of pornography have shown time and again that men of faith are not immune to such sexual sin.[2] The tendency to violate God's commandment against adultery seems to be innate. If so, then only through intentional effort can it be avoided.

As seen with the previous commandments there's a natural tendency to violate each of the commands that God gave. For the first receivers of the law this failure was often a result of the influences from the Egyptian culture they had lived in for so long. For the next generation who heard the law from Moses prior to entering the Promised Land, it was often because of the pagan cultures that surrounded them. Although adultery and immorality were characteristic of these outside cultures, it is likely that this particular sin would have been a problem for the people even had they lived in isolation. The tendency to commit adultery and to think immorally about sex is a characteristic of all humanity. It is a natural expression of mankind's sinful nature.

No One Is Immune!

God gave Moses the commandment against adultery knowing full well of man's tendency to commit sexual immorality. An infinitely wise and all-knowing God would not have given a prohibition against adultery if only a few people were apt to fall into the sin. God knew then, and knows now, that sexual immorality is common. In my many years of practice I have seen this truth proven over and over again. The natural sex drive that God designed to be fulfilled in marriage is easily perverted into something else. Research provides further confirmation. I have seen surveys in which 5–25 percent[3] of married individuals admit to infidelity. The sin is remarkably common.

The fact that 75–95 percent of individuals claim to be faithful does not mean that these people are guilt-free. When we consider Jesus' teaching that men who wrongly *view* women are guilty as well, there are very few innocent people. It appears that the majority of people struggle with adultery. "You shall not commit adultery" is clearly on God's top ten list for good reason. Just as murder resulted from devaluing human life, so too, adultery is a result of devaluing sexual intimacy.

Intimacy More Than Physical

As plain as it is that God intended sexual intimacy to be a foundation for the marital bond, I believe that there is much more to the union than a physical connection. Faithfulness in marriage means more than simply avoiding sexual sin. Physical intimacy is the most tangible expression of the intimacy of marriage, but the bond goes far beyond mere sexuality. The oneness God described in the Genesis account includes intimate emotions, thoughts, and words, nonphysical things that are not to be shared outside of marriage. Jesus' words on adultery illustrate the truth that such thoughts and feelings are important.

When Jesus warned against looking at a woman with lust in the heart, He was referring to a woman who was not a man's wife. (It is rather difficult to commit adultery with one's spouse!) I believe it is appropriate to look at one's wife with desire. The longing to be with one's spouse is part of a healthy marriage, desiring someone else is not. Implied in Jesus' teaching is the truth that the desire for sex, and the look that accompanies that desire, are the sole property of one's spouse. If a husband gives such a look to another woman, he is giving away something that only his wife deserves. The marital bond is weakened not only because a lustful look separates sex from marital intimacy but also because the look itself belongs only to one's spouse.

When a marital partner shares with another that which rightly should only be shared with a spouse, he/she violates intimacy and trust. This breach makes adultery especially harmful. There are things in a marriage that are meant to be unique to a marriage. The marriage bed is the most sacred of these trusts, but there are others as well. Just as looking at another person as a source of pleasure is a type of adultery, so also is giving to another person anything that rightfully belongs only to one's spouse.

As I reflect on my own marriage I can think of a number of things that belong only to my wife. In addition to my physical self, only she deserves my sexual desires. To her alone belong my admiring stares and flirtatious smiles. To her alone belongs my heart. No other woman deserves to know my deepest thoughts and fears, my greatest hopes and dreams. The deeper things of my heart are hers and hers alone.

There are words that belong solely to my wife as well. There are compliments that carry with them an admiration and appreciation that rightfully belong only to my wife. While I may tell another woman that her new haircut looks nice or compliment the color of a new outfit, I should not give any praise that communicates any sexual desire. Compliments such as "You look beautiful," "You have the prettiest eyes," or at times even something as seemingly innocuous as "You look really nice today," may be wrongfully giving away admiration that belongs to my wife. Wisdom demands that I be careful in what I say.

Out of love and respect for my wife I have chosen to avoid giving other women any compliments that might make a woman think she was an object of my desire. I will never compliment another woman in a way that might make my wife uncomfortable or jealous. Years ago I was discussing these things with a neighbor of mine. He thought I was being foolish and legalistic. To him words were harmless. As a salesman, he regularly would compliment other women, telling them they were beautiful or that they looked great. I shared with him that I thought that was "verbal adultery," that certain types of praise, particularly praise of someone's physical appearance, could easily be interpreted as expressions of desire or as a type of flirtation. For that reason I felt it best that no woman except for a man's wife should be addressed in this way. Although he could not understand it at the time, as he grew in his faith he realized the wisdom in what I was sharing and changed his behavior.

I have taken steps to intentionally put these attitudes into practice. As a man who has female employees I have learned what to say and not say. I carefully choose words that cannot be misinterpreted as flirtatious. I am very careful in how I compliment female patients. I make a conscious effort to compliment *actions* (such as losing weight) rather than appearance.

It is not just words of praise that should only be given to my wife. There are specific types of attention and time that should not be shared with other women either. Included on the list of things that belong to my wife is intimate time alone. It is very dangerous for a man to spend time alone with another woman. Great caution should be used when it comes to lunches, dinners, or meetings in private. There are very few men who spend so much time with their wives that they have any extra time to share with another woman! I believe that intimate friendships with members of the opposite sex should be avoided, as it is inevitable that things will be shared with such a "friend" that rightfully should have been shared with a spouse.

If we truly desire to follow the spirit of God's instructions regarding sexuality and marriage, we will do whatever we can to preserve all of the types of intimacy marriage includes. Practically speaking, asking ourselves the question "Do these words, actions, or thoughts rightfully belong to my spouse?" will keep us out of a lot of trouble!

Just as wrong thinking leads to sin, right thinking leads to godly behavior. When I began to consider all of what belongs to my wife, my behavior changed. Movies with nudity and sexually provocative content became even more inappropriate. I did not want to give desirous looks to any woman, including one on a movie screen. I began to carefully watch my words. I starting turning down some invitations. As I did, I grew in love and appreciation of the wife God gave me.

Not Just a Man's Problem

While there are many things that men can inadvertently give away to other women, there are things women can give away as well. Just as I should not look at any other woman with desire, women should not set themselves up as the object of any other man's desire. In many ways, provocative dress is the female counterpart to a man's lustful look. There is no one who hasn't walked down a street and seen a woman displaying aspects of her person that should only have been shown to her husband! I am not advocating that women be fully covered as they are in expressions of Islam, but I am encouraging women to reflect on their appearance. Some aspects of a woman's physical beauty do not need to be shown to other men.

As we look at our own thoughts and attitudes about marital intimacy and how they impact the way we see the world we realize just how important our thoughts are. All of the commandments thus far emphasize the importance of how we think. God cares about how we think about sexuality and marriage. God knows that evil actions always begin with evil thoughts and wrong attitudes. The beauty and oneness of marriage can be easily damaged if we do not consciously work to protect it. We live in a world filled with easily accessed pornography, and where casual sex is the order of the day. With the foundation of intimacy under such attack it is not surprising that infidelity, divorce, and single-parent families are so common.

Given the prevalence of sexual immorality in our culture, intentional effort is required if we are to protect our families. Christians need to be vigilant in what we allow into our homes and into our minds. We need to be especially careful in our consumption of media. So much of what's on television and on the internet threatens our families.

Teaching Children about Intimacy

I have taken practical steps to protect my family. With my children, we review together the content of movies before we go. If there is questionable content, we don't go. When my children were younger, I decided where the lines were drawn and what they could see. As my children have matured, they have been able to apply biblical principles and make good decisions on their own. If a television show is inappropriate we turn it off. Recently, when I noticed that a television show aimed at "tween" girls was encouraging casual attitudes about dating, we decided it would no longer be watched in our home. My twelve-year-old daughter was in total agreement with the decision.

I have worked to teach my children morality in their personal lives as well. When it comes to my daughter, I am the "outfit police." I help her understand that there are things a young woman does not need to reveal to others or draw attention to. So much of girls' and women's clothing is designed to be provocative that it can be easy (especially by adding peer pressure) to grow comfortable wearing inappropriate clothing. As a man I can identify provocative clothing better than my wife can, so I make it a point to help my daughter understand what her clothes say about her.

With all of the tangible lessons I try to teach my children about modesty, I have learned that the best way to instruct them about sexual morality is through my relationship with my wife. There is no more powerful example than the one they see every day. I make sure to express my love for my wife in front of my kids. They hear me praise her and tell her she is beautiful. (And they don't hear me praise other women!) I make it clear to her and to them that she is absolutely everything to me, and that no other woman has any chance at all of gaining my affection. Through all of this I teach them what it means to be faithful.

As with all of God's commandments, His imperative against adultery is not punitive. I have seen in my own life the incredible blessing of a healthy marriage. I have experienced the beauty of the intimacy that God desires. A love for God and an appreciation of His gift in marriage drives me to work hard at thinking and acting as faithfully as I can. When God had Moses proclaim, "You shall not commit adultery," He was showing us how to save our families and experience His blessings.

Swallow the Medicine

God's prescription for faithfulness is actually a type of preventative medicine. We need to be immunized against unfaithfulness. As we fill our hearts and minds with love for the spouse God has given us, we are protected from the infection of lust. For those who have fallen victim to the disease of sexual sin, a heart transplant may be necessary. Take the time to give yourself a complete checkup in this area. As you reflect on God's plans for marital intimacy, the following questions may help bring your health condition into focus.

- For those who are married
  - What are the special things that belong to your spouse alone? Make a list, paying attention to intangible things such as attitudes and desires.
  - Are there any words you share with others that rightfully belong to your spouse? Any time? Any attention?
  - Have you polluted your mind with impure thoughts of anyone else? Is pornography an issue?
- For those who are single
  - Are you saving yourself for marriage? Are you diluting God's plan for intimacy by sharing yourself in ways that are reserved for marriage?
  - Are you guarding your mind? Is pornography an issue? Review your media choices. Are you building into your thought life unhealthy attitudes about sexual intimacy?

- For all of us
  - ➤ How do we relate to members of the opposite sex? Are we pure and honorable, or are there moments of flirtation and innuendo?
  - ➤ How do we present ourselves? Consider how you dress and talk to others. Would your actions be described as modest?
  - ➤ What kind of example are we to children? What do we teach them about sexual intimacy? Do we expose them to inappropriate material or do we protect their innocence?

Prescription #8

Work for What You Have

You shall not steal.
Deuteronomy 5:19

*A*lthough she wouldn't want me to tell anyone, my daughter is a thief. She is not a "take a gun and hold up a convenience store" kind of thief, she is more of a "if there is any loose change lying around it's mine" kind of thief. She believes it is her constitutional and God-given right to relocate any unattended change she finds from its place of discovery into her bedroom. She has amended her crime-ridden ways these last few years, but from the age of about five until she was about ten it was remarkable how quickly coins would accumulate in her room. It's not that we waited until the age of ten to tell her not to take other people's loose change, it just took us that long to convince her that all money lying around unattended wasn't hers!

My childhood was different. Perhaps out of fear of being mercilessly beaten, I never intentionally took anything from anyone. A profound sense that stealing was wrong combined with an overwhelming fear that I might get caught effectively rendered theft impossible for me. This is not to say I never took something that did not belong to me. Like many others, there have been a few times when I discovered that I had accidentally "stolen" something,

My wife and I laugh about a time a few years ago when she made such an accidental thief out of me. She was unpacking groceries one day when she discovered that a few items were missing from the bags. The missing goods included a half gallon of ice cream, some canned desserts, and a six-pack of Kool-Aid cartons. After conducting a brief search of the car and finding no evidence of the missing goods I went back to the store, convinced we had left the items behind. I boldly took the receipt to the store manager, who courteously replaced the missing items. I returned home in victory and helped my wife finish the unpacking of the groceries, not giving it another thought.

Several days later I was getting something out of the back of our van when I noticed a small cardboard box shoved up against the back seat. Not knowing what was in it I pulled it toward me and looked inside. To my horror I discovered the missing items (including the rather soggy carton of ice cream!) I grabbed the plastic grocery bag, showed it to my wife to make sure she was aware of her complicity in the crime, and then quickly disposed of the evidence. I was a thief!

These stories are humorous for my family, but I do not think that when God included "Do not steal" on His list of commandments it was to address five-year-old girls with a penchant for collecting loose change or to assign guilt for overlooking a few grocery items. God had something else in mind. Just as doctors don't prescribe powerful medications for minor ailments that will go away on their own but reserve such treatments for serious diseases, God's prescriptions for healthy living are designed to address real sins that cause real harm in the lives of God's people. The commandments weren't designed to blame innocent children for naïve mistakes or to condemn well-intentioned adults who accidentally accumulated a few free groceries. They address serious sin.

When I think about the type of theft that God had in mind I think about my old Jeep Wrangler. I never personally took the Wrangler on a crime spree, but it was involved in what was to me a particularly heinous crime. The Wrangler was a special car for me. On my 35th birthday I was feeling especially old, so I splurged and bought myself a soft-topped Jeep Wrangler. It was a silly car with no practical purpose, but it was inexpensive, it was mine, and I liked it. I liked it a lot, until the day several years ago when—in the middle of the night while parked in my driveway—thieves stole parts of it.

I was leaving the house one morning when I realized the Jeep didn't look quite right. What should have been instantly obvious to me wasn't obvious at all, as my brain was unprepared for what I was seeing and had a difficult time processing the information. As I walked up to the Jeep my brain engaged and it hit me—both doors and the left front fender were missing, gone! A closer look revealed that a few parts had been stolen off the engine as well. My car had been stripped right in my driveway!

I called the police and reported the incident. When the police arrived they laughed at the pathetic sight of my undriveable, door-less, and fenderless car. The policemen's laughter was based on a combination of the fact that it was the first time they had ever seen a car stripped in a driveway, and the fact that my dog, a German shepherd, had managed to sleep through the noise of the theft! I was not nearly as amused as they were. I felt violated and frightened that such a thing could happen. I never looked at the car in the same way. The Jeep had been stripped not only of its doors but also its joy and I traded it in for another car a few months after it was returned from the repair shop.

The Thief in All of Us

Though stripping a car is an obvious violation of the "You shall not steal" commandment, when I think about my Jeep in the context of God's command against stealing, I think the directive cannot be only about this type of crime. Few people would commit such a crime, and few people are even tempted to do so. It makes no sense for God to devote a slot on the top ten list to a rare sin. I do not think that God would include a commandment that had only limited application. With all of the previous commands we saw that they applied to not just a select few individuals but to all the people of Israel. This wider application must be true of the "do not steal" commandment as well; it must affect all of us.

As we dig deeper into the meaning of the commandment and what it truly means to steal (or to take that which rightfully belongs to another) we see that the commandment is indeed universally applicable. Unfortunately we also see that, as was true with the other commands, many of us are guilty of violating this one as well. It contains principles and applications that apply to everyone.

As we begin exploration of the eighth commandment, it is unnecessary to spend any more time proving that such acts as burglary, armed robbery, and driveway auto parts theft constitute stealing. No one would defend such obvious sin, and most people avoid such blatant crimes. Outside of a single time as a teenager when the ice cream parlor in which I worked was held up, I have never even been a witness to such felonious violations of the command. Witnessing theft just isn't common for most people. Nevertheless, in spite of my limited experience as a witness to crime, on a number of occasions I have seen people take something that wasn't theirs.

How People Steal

When I think of such "noncriminal" violations of the commandment, I think of a time when someone bragged to me about the incredible "deal" he had gotten on a barbecue. The man told me that he had seen the grill on sale for $199.99 at the store. He placed the barbecue in his cart along with several other items and headed for the checkout counter. The clerk wasn't paying close attention and in the course of ringing up the entire order the clerk left off a "9" in the price of the barbecue. Because several items had been purchased, the checker didn't catch the error. The customer was charged only $19.99 for the grill! As he told me the story I realized that the man believed he had experienced extraordinarily good fortune.

I was amazed at the man's ignorance. To his surprise I did not share his joy or his assessment of the situation. He had *not* been blessed by God, he had stolen from the store. He had *not* been fortunate, he had been dishonest. When he took the barbecue from the store, he wasn't lucky, he was wrong.

One may ask how this is true. Understanding the story requires knowledge of what it means to steal. If we apply the definition "taking for yourself that which rightly belongs to another," it is clear that the man stole his barbecue. He left the store with $180 that wasn't rightfully his. When he decided to buy the item at the posted price, the customer had mentally accepted the store's sale price of $199.99. When walking up to the register, he was fully aware of the correct price and intended to pay it. He understood that ownership of the grill was being transferred to him in exchange for the posted price, and that it was the store owner's expectation to receive that amount for the product. The additional $180, which rightfully should have gone to the store owner, was in effect taken by the customer. Is this not stealing? No amount of rationalizing can escape the truth that the man ended up with money that rightfully belonged to someone else.

I do not sell any barbecues in my office, but I have been the victim of similar theft in the form of financial rationalization many times in my practice. The fact that many people do not pay their bills as they should is an unfortunate reality for physicians. Some patients simply refuse to pay what they owe. This is not a small problem. When I joined a private medical group several years ago two of the doctors had over $150,000 of uncollected fees on their books.

I have often wondered why it is that so many people don't pay their medical bills. For some it may be that they believe the small amount already paid means they have paid "enough," and that they shouldn't have to pay any more. For others I think that difficult financial circumstances lead them to believe they are entitled to breaks on their bills. Whatever the underlying cause, the fact always remains that they agreed to pay for services and then didn't. In essence, they stole time and expertise from their doctor.

One particular instance of a patient's refusal to pay was especially sad to me. The patient and her husband were members of my church and attended the same adult Sunday School class as my wife and me. The woman was pregnant and came to me for prenatal care and delivery. The couple told me they were struggling financially. They confided that their financial worries were compounded by the fact that they had an insurance plan with a very high deductible, leaving them responsible for the first $500 of medical bills. To help them out, I made sure my charges were submitted immediately and would go against their deductible. I then told my staff to forgive whatever the insurance did not pay, essentially giving them a $500 discount on my services. They seemed genuinely appreciative and thanked me repeatedly.

After their baby was born they brought the child to my office for a checkup and immunizations. They made no mention of inability to pay for the baby's care, and never told me they did not have insurance coverage for the child. Over the course of a few visits they accumulated over $400 in charges for the examinations and shots. After receiving bills for the amount they owed, they simply disappeared from my practice! Letters and calls from my billing service were ignored. I even sent them a personal letter expressing my sadness for what had happened. They never responded.

Looking back on the situation, I believe they stole from me. It wasn't just a matter of uncompensated time. The vaccines their baby received cost me over $200 alone. When I realized how much I had spent, I was deeply hurt that they would take from me in this way. They were regular attendees and members of a Christian church and they called me their friend. Although they did not hold me up at gunpoint, break into my office, or take parts from my jeep, they stole.

Whether it be nonpaying patients, ice cream parlor holdup men, or driveway Jeep thieves, there is a thought process and attitude that underlies all stealing. Thieves feel they are somehow entitled to take from the victim. It seems that thieves have an altered perception of belongings and possessions, that they do not see theft as inherently immoral. To them not all stealing is wrong—there are times and places where stealing is acceptable.

The most extreme example of such corrupt thinking can be found in sociopathic criminals who have no sense of right and wrong, thieves who take simply because they want to. I seriously doubt anyone reading this book falls into this category. Far more common is the thief who believes it is wrong to steal in some circumstances and appropriate to take in others. For these people it seems wrong only to take from someone (or not pay) if the result of such theft is serious harm to the other individual. It is considered acceptable to steal either when the money is *more* needed by the thief or not truly needed by the victim.

I believe the latter attitude characterizes patients who do not pay their bills. They view doctors as well-off and not "needing" the money. To them, difficult financial circumstances justify their behavior. In their view if a patient "needs" the money more than the doctor does, they shouldn't have to pay. This type of thinking illustrates the concept that to some the wrongness of stealing is not inherent in the act but instead proportional to its harm. This attitude lies at the root of all kinds of theft. Insurance fraud, bank fraud, shoplifting, and even software piracy arise from an attitude that declares it acceptable to take from those who are more wealthy and powerful or less needy.

Stealing from the wealthy is so acceptable that it is often glorified in our culture. The story of Robin Hood stealing from the rich and giving to the poor is well known. Robin Hood and his Merry Men are portrayed as heroes in books and movies. In stories such as these being wealthy is considered to be a sign of evil and injustice, rather than of hard work and success. It is up to men such as Robin Hood to remedy the injustices.

Legends such as Robin Hood further illustrate another wrong attitude toward possessions that underlies theft. It is natural to think that all people are equal and, thus, equally entitled to wealth, and to view unequal distribution of wealth as a wrong that must be fixed. The truth that God blesses people unequally is easily ignored.

God Blesses Unequally

Although all people are created equal, the words of Scripture and the reality of life argue against the view that everyone receives equal blessing and wealth. Although it may be common to question why it is that some people struggle to survive while others have more than they could ever spend, the answer remains a mystery. The truth is that God, in His infinite sovereignty, has blessed people unequally. Strange as it may seem to us, inequality in this sense is part of God's plan. Scripture is filled with stories of God giving disproportionately.

The inequality of God's choosing is seen in the origin of the nation of Israel. God chose Abraham to be the father of His chosen people. No other person, no other people group was chosen. Alone among his relatives, Abraham was uniquely blessed by God. Scripture makes it clear that the choosing was God's doing and not Abraham's. Abraham was chosen not because he was the most honest or best behaved man alive. In fact, Scripture tells us that Abraham was on various occasions deceitful and disobedient! Reading through Genesis, we see Abraham committing such sins as lying about his marriage and fathering a child with his wife's handmaid. In spite of his human failings, God chose this man and blessed him. By human standards, this selection of Abraham over others seems unfair, yet it was God's sovereign plan.

Jacob—a Chosen Thief

The apparent "unfairness" of God's choosing continued with Abraham's grandson Jacob. God chose to bless Jacob and make him the father of the nation of Israel (in fact "Israel" was another name for Jacob). The story of Jacob, his twin brother Esau, and their father Isaac is given in the book of Genesis chapter 27. In the story we see that Jacob was chosen not because he was a good man. Jacob was a liar and a thief. He stole the birthright of his older twin brother. From this story we learn a lot about the nature of theft and the sovereignty with which God chooses whom to bless.

Jacob was in the unfortunate position of being his father's second-favorite son. Esau, his twin, was loved dearly by their father Isaac. As the oldest son, Esau, at the end of Isaac's life, would be given a special blessing from his father. As Moses relates the story, when Isaac was nearing death—and probably blind or nearly blind—he called Esau to his side and asked Esau to prepare a favorite meal for him. After the meal Esau would receive the special blessing from his father, one promised to the firstborn.

This blessing was to be a special and private ceremony, a father and eldest son sharing an intimate meal and passing of the torch. One gets the sense that Esau had prepared this type of meal for his father before, as Esau apparently knew exactly what his father was requesting. The purpose of the meal was clearly understood as well. In all likelihood Esau hunted the game and prepared the meal with a great sense of anticipation. He must have been excited as he went about his task. And surely he sensed a love for his father.

Isaac's love for Esau is clear from the text as well. Note Isaac's words as he blessed the son he mistakenly thought was Esau (Jacob had tricked Isaac into thinking he was Esau):

> Then his father Isaac said to him, "Come here, my son, and kiss me." So he went to him and kissed him. When Isaac caught the smell of his clothes, he blessed him and said, "Ah, the smell of my son is like the smell of a field that the LORD has blessed. May God give you of heaven's dew and of earth's richness—an abundance of grain and new wine. May nations serve you and peoples bow down to you. Be lord over your brothers, and may the sons of your mother bow down to you. May those who curse you be cursed and those who bless you be blessed." (Gen 27:26–29)

As Isaac held Jacob, he smelled Esau. The smell of outdoors that came from the clothes Jacob had taken from his brother brought comforting memories to Isaac. That aroma brought to mind happy reminisces of walks in the field with his favorite boy. Out of those reflections overflowed a joy that poured out as a blessing upon his son: "May God Himself give you richness." With the knowledge that he was the promised seed of his father Abraham, specifically chosen by God to be a great nation, Isaac asked God to fulfill that promise in this son (thought to be Esau), repeating to him the words that God had spoken to his own father Abraham:

> I will bless those who bless you, and whoever curses you I will curse; and all peoples on earth will be blessed through you. (Gen 12:3)

These words, this blessing, belonged to Esau. Yet it was not Esau who heard the words and received the gift. It was Jacob, whose name means "supplanter," (one who takes the place of someone else) who was kneeling at his father's bedside and being held in his father's arms as the dying Isaac spoke. No other conclusion can be reached than to say that Jacob stole the blessing from Esau.

Why did Jacob do this? Why would he take from his brother in this way? It isn't clearly stated in the passage, but we can make some guesses. Jacob undoubtedly wasn't happy about Esau's favored position. Jacob and his mother questioned why Esau should get all of the attention and the blessing. They surely thought it unfair that the blessing was based on birth order instead of merit. Jacob believed that the blessing should be his and would not accept things as they were. He felt entitled to change things in his own favor. The result was a rationalization process that culminated in a profound deception and ultimately the theft of his brother's blessing.

Jacob's behavior illustrates something seen in each of the examples of stealing we have discussed so far. In Jacob's case and in the others, stealing resulted when a person concluded he was justified in doing so. Whether because of deeply felt need, perceived economic injustice, or a misplaced sense of entitlement, the reasoning involved in theft represents wrong thinking about God, people, and the world.

God's Sovereign Choice

Jacob's story demonstrates the heart attitude of those who steal, but it says much more about the sovereignty of God. God, who knows everything, was fully aware of Jacob's deceit and sin. In spite of the obvious flaws in Jacob's character made evident by his theft, God chose Jacob to be the father of His chosen people! Unrighteous Jacob was magnificently blessed.

The Apostle Paul bluntly describes God's dealings with Jacob and Esau.

Yet, before the twins were born or had done anything good or bad—in order that God's purpose in election might stand: not by works but by him who calls—she was told, "The older will serve the younger." Just as it is written: "Jacob I loved, but Esau I hated." What then shall we say? Is God unjust? Not at all! For he says to Moses, "I will have mercy on whom I have mercy, and I will have compassion on whom I have compassion." (Rom 9:11–15)

It is pretty clear from Paul's words that God can do anything He wants, and can bless anyone He wants. Aligning ourselves completely with God's purposes and plans requires us to acknowledge this sovereignty. God often exercises His sovereignty by choosing to bless people in ways that appear unjust to us. At its core, stealing is an attempt to "undo" God's unequal distribution of blessing, mercy, and wealth, and is therefore a rejection of God's sovereignty. It is man's way of saying to God, "You got it wrong. You should have given that to me!"

Yet God never gets it wrong. God has determined to give—whether it be material blessing or health—unequally to mankind, and He does so to achieve His purposes. We don't like it (especially if we have gotten the short end of the stick!). If we are honest, most of us don't understand it either. Why should someone else be blessed with more than us, especially if that person is lazy, dishonest, unethical, or evil? We have all seen circumstances where ungodly people seem to prosper. Accepting God's sovereignty requires accepting such inequity in this life. When we arrogantly determine that God has acted unjustly, it is easy to think that we deserve something that belongs to someone else. When we think in this way we are declaring our belief that God is unjust or unfair. Since it arises from this attitude, stealing is more than a material act, it is an attack on the very character of God.

Affirming God's Right to Choose

Just as stealing represents an attack on God's character, accepting the circumstances in which we find ourselves affirms God's character. A review of Scripture shows that God's "unfair" choosing always results in His glory and ultimately accomplishes His perfect purpose. There are innumerable examples of such choosing: God chose David over Saul, David over Jonathan, David over his older brothers, and Solomon over his brothers to be King. God chose to honor such dishonorable people as a prostitute named Rahab and a Moabite woman named Ruth. For his disciples Jesus ignored the religious elite and instead chose tax collectors and fishermen. In the ultimate display of choosing the undeserving, God chose us! In each circumstance man's rules of fairness and justice were and are ignored, yet in every circumstance God was glorified and His purposes accomplished.

Though stealing constitutes a rejection of God's sovereign choosing, the ramifications of the commandment to not steal extend far beyond our attitudes on God's right to give whatever He wants, in whatever manner He chooses, to whomever He chooses to give it. In addition to challenging God's sovereignty, people who steal are demonstrating poor attitudes about work, responsibility, and eternity.

Work as Part of God's Plan

People's attitudes about work say much about their view of God. As much as I dislike it and as much as I complain about it, work is a part of God's plan. Only moments after the fall in the Garden of Eden, God pronounced hard work as a consequence of Adam's sin.

> "Because you listened to your wife and ate from the tree about which I commanded you, 'You must not eat of it,' "Cursed is the ground because of you; through painful toil you will eat of it all the days of your life. It will produce thorns and thistles for you, and you will eat the plants of the field. By the sweat of your brow you will eat your food until you return to the ground, since from it you were taken; for dust you are and to dust you will return." (Gen 3:17–19)

God's words to Adam indicate that harder, less-fulfilling work was intended to be a constant reminder of man's sinfulness. Until the end of time, work is designed to draw our thoughts to our mortality and our need for God. When we work, when we sweat and struggle, the desire for an end of work should turn our thoughts to that time when work was fulfilling. When Christians reflect on the pre-fall condition of man when work was blessed and rewarding, we are reminded that we can take comfort in the hope that a day is coming when hard work will cease. When believers enter into the rest that God has promised we will be freed from the curse of sin and the need to work. But any effort to get by in *this* life without working or to make our way by living off the work of others, goes against God's plan and is a rejection of His will for us. (So much for trying to win the lottery!)

While work is a part of God's plan, our sinful natures lead us to try to avoid it! This is not to say it is wrong to want time off or a vacation. We have seen that God's Sabbath rests were established for a reason, that periods of rest are necessary. But when Christians avoid work altogether they disobey God. The Apostle Paul addressed this tendency in his letter to the church at Thessalonica:

> For even when we were with you, we gave you this rule: "If a man will not work, he shall not eat." We hear that some among you are idle. They are not busy; they are busybodies. Such people we command and urge in the Lord Jesus Christ to settle down and earn the bread they eat. And as for you, brothers, never tire of doing what is right. If anyone does not obey our instruction in this letter, take special note of him. Do not associate with him, in order that he may feel ashamed. (2 Thess 3:10–14)

Paul declares that when believers work for what they have, they honor God. Stealing—trying to succeed without effort or at someone else's expense—is a rejection of this truth. Stealing reflects not just an evil act, but an evil attitude. This evil attitude is not only limited to how we look at work, but also to how we view earthly goods as a whole.

Working for What Lasts

Stealing comprises the greatest evidence of an erroneous view of material wealth. Stealing makes material gain the primary purpose of human existence. A proper view of earthly goods is the direct

opposite of such a view. A correct view of earthly goods is simple—
it requires us to view them as God-given, yet earthly! Earthly blessings are not eternal. The pleasure they bring is brief.

The reality of fleeting pleasure is all too familiar to those who
have ever bought a new car. People are so happy to drive their new
cars, to look at them, clean them, show them off, even to smell
them. They wash and wax them more than they ever did the beat-up
clunker they just got rid of. But before long the smell is gone, the
perfect finish is dented, and the once-beautiful treasure has become
just another clunker. Months, even years of wages sit rusting at the
curb, or worse, are discovered stripped of their fenders and doors in
the driveway!

All material goods are the same. Whether it is the biggest house,
the most luxurious car, or the most beautiful artwork, the joy derived
is only temporary. All of these things do not last. Their worth is
nothing compared to that of things that do last—people, God's
kingdom, and God Himself. When people steal, they confirm that
they value material goods more than the things that last. Thieves
reveal an incredibly flawed perspective on life and its purpose.

Jesus knew how easy it was for people to get their priorities
mixed up in this regard. He specifically addressed this flaw in the
sermon on the Mount of Olives:

> Do not store up for yourselves treasures on earth, where
> moth and rust destroy, and where thieves break in and steal.
> But store up for yourselves treasures in heaven, where moth
> and rust do not destroy, and where thieves do not break in
> and steal. For where your treasure is, there your heart will be
> also. (Matt 6:19–21)

Jesus painted a sharp contrast between earthly goods and eternal
reward. When people have the proper attitude regarding God's
kingdom, they will gladly forego the material treasures of this life
in the pursuit of godliness. Conversely, when people intentionally
violate the law of God by stealing, they are forcefully declaring
their belief that there is no eternal reward and all that matters is this

earthly life. Too many people are willing to risk friendships and a good relationship with God to get what they want and get it now!

It is a foundational truth of the Christian faith that if Christians are to serve God they cannot pursue worldly wealth as a primary goal. Jesus explained in the same Sermon on the Mount:

> No one can serve two masters. Either he will hate the one and love the other, or he will be devoted to the one and despise the other. You cannot serve both God and Money. Therefore I tell you, do not worry about your life, what you will eat or drink; or about your body, what you will wear. Is not life more important than food, and the body more important than clothes? (Matt 6:24–25)

It seems remarkable that, just as He did with the commandment on adultery, Jesus here showed how we are all guilty. Any sense of security we may have in thinking that because we haven't stolen from another person we have not violated this commandment is shattered by Jesus' words. He says that the heart of God's prescription against sin isn't just about whether or not we take from others, but about how we view earthly wealth and God's kingdom.

Jesus revisited this theme later when He said, "For whoever wants to save his life will lose it, but whoever loses his life for me will find it. What good will it be for a man if he gains the whole world, yet forfeits his soul? Or what can a man give in exchange for his soul?" (Matt 16:25–26)

One's view of wealth and possessions says much about the heart. If we stop and think about the godliest people we know, the most spiritual people we have met, we will see as a common thread in their lives an appropriate attitude about material possessions. These people are not always poor, in fact they may have significant wealth. Yet even when blessed in that manner they are not consumed with money and things or their accumulation. They are concerned with people, relationships, and building God's kingdom.

We have repeatedly established the truth that all sin begins with corrupt thinking, which is affirmed by New Testament teaching (James 1:14–15). It is true of adultery, of idolatry, and of stealing. If believers are to combat sin, we must strive to win the battle in our minds. We must think correctly about material wealth and place it in the context of God's eternal plans. When we think rightly about goods and about God, stealing will have no place in our lives.

Training Children about "Things"

Christians must also train children to think correctly about God and possessions. As parents, if we want to raise children who grow up to honor God we must teach them how to think, not just how to act. In fact, if we can get them to think correctly about God and His kingdom, they are well on their way to lives of obedience. If parents are going to do this, they need to focus not just on their actions, but on their attitudes and motives as well.

When it comes to stealing, parents would do well to get to the heart of the matter when a child takes what is not theirs. When a five-year-old sneaks money out of his mother's purse, the instruction shouldn't just be "don't steal," but should include a reminder that God wants every person to earn things, and that by stealing, the child showed that he valued money more than he or she valued his mother.

Parents need to model correct attitudes as well. Think about the lesson we would be teaching our children if we carefully checked our store receipts not only to make sure we were not overcharged, but also to make sure we had not been undercharged! Can you imagine the impact on our children's thinking as we returned to the store and asked if we could please pay more? What lessons will be learned when we intentionally make sure to tell the person at the theater ticket window that our child is now twelve years old and an "adult" so we can make sure we pay enough?

My daughter knows paying correctly is important to me, because she has seen me bring attention to her age to ensure we pay full price. Not too long ago she even corrected me when I did not notice the age cutoff posted in a store. As we walked away she reminded me that we should have paid more! We had gone to "Color me Mine," a place where you purchase ceramics to paint. The store charges a fee to use their paints and brushes to design your purchase in the store.

Adults pay more than children do. As we left the store that day my daughter said to me, "Daddy just so you know, I am an adult now. Children are eleven and under!" She knew that I would want to pay the correct amount because I had taught her that it was the right thing to do.

Every day Christians have similar opportunities to show their children and the people with whom they come in contact that they value people and God more than things. As an employer I make sure to pay my employees fairly for what they do. I check to see how much other doctors pay and make sure what I pay is competitive. I never allow anyone to work off the clock, even if they ask. I try to communicate to them that they are valuable and that I would never take their time for nothing. It is important not only to not intentionally take from others, but to intentionally avoid even taking by accident!

Whether it is by faithfully paying our taxes, our credit card bills, or our mortgage, believers can model what it means to not take from others, and to value and respect other people's possessions. When we do this we honor and respect the God who has given all gifts to all human beings. We acknowledge His sovereignty, and we call attention to the truth that life is about storing up treasures that will last into eternity.

Swallow the Medicine

Most prescriptions simply require patients to take a medication as directed. Some medications such as antibiotics are taken for a short period, while others need to be taken on an ongoing basis. Still other prescriptions, such as orders for physical therapy or losing weight, require patients to actually do something, to exert effort. God's prescription against stealing is such a prescription. The cure for stealing is to work for what we have, and to do so with acceptance of God's eternal plan. As you meditate on God's commandment to not steal, ask yourself these questions to aid in evaluating your heart.

- Do you always make sure you pay what you should, or do you try to get away with what you can? Do you look for opportunities to pay others fairly, or do you look for ways to take whatever advantage you can? Think about a time when you realized you hadn't been charged enough for something. How did you respond?
- Is there anyone you haven't paid? Is there anyone you could have paid, but instead found a loophole to relieve you of responsibility? Consider making amends if you have wronged someone in this way.
- When you have the option or responsibility to pay others, do you pay fairly? Review your habits with regards to tipping and gratuities. Are you stingy with your money, or do you tip generously? What do your actions say about how you value people?
- What are the primary goals of your life? Are they material or spiritual? What does your checkbook say about your heart?
- What is your attitude about work? Do you do your best? Do you try to get out of work when you can, or do you see it as your God-given duty? What would others say about your work ethic?
- How do you respond when other people have more than you? Do you come across as someone who accepts or resists God's sovereignty in this regard?

Remember, we all have a tendency to want more and to justify getting more. We need to lay our hearts before God and allow Him to transform us into people who would never, in any form, steal.

Prescription #9

Speak Truth When It Matters Most

You shall not give false testimony against your neighbor.
Deuteronomy 5:20

*W*ords are dangerous things. Negative information and gossip seem to travel at light speed. As Mark Twain said, "a lie is halfway around the world before truth has its boots on." Although lies of all sorts are terrible, none are as reprehensible as those that damage a person's character. Reputations years in the making can be eroded overnight by a lie. I can say from experience that false attacks on my character are among the most hurtful things I have had to deal with in life. I have been amazed at the lengths to which some people have gone in their efforts to harm my reputation through gossip and slander.

Hurtful Lies

Several years ago I was a victim of a rather ludicrous assault on my character. A mother brought her son in for a checkup when he was eight years old. The child was in perfect health and did not need an examination, as he had been thoroughly examined a year earlier. As I frequently did at the beginning of such visits, I asked the mom why she had brought her child in to see me.

"For a check-up," she replied.

"Is there any particular thing you wanted checked?" I asked.

"No, I just want everything checked," was her answer.

I proceeded to explain that while I was happy to examine her child annually (it was financially beneficial to me) there was no real need for a child his age to be seen every year. I told her that coming in every two to three years was more than enough.

For reasons that I still do not completely understand she took offense at my words. She apparently felt I thought her foolish for coming in so often. After she left the office she went home and told her husband that I had disrespected her and treated her poorly. A few hours later the husband was in my office yelling at me and my staff for our "bad care." After he left, he taped a note to the entrance of the building. On a piece of brown packing paper he wrote in large letters, "STAY AWAY FROM DOCTOR BARRETT HE IS A DANGER TO YOUR CHILDREN!" The wife's false report led to the husband's anger, resulting in a ridiculous attempt to malign my character.

As silly as the man's actions were, they demonstrate a truth about false testimony. False testimony is designed to either benefit the liar or harm the victim. It has at its core the intent to change the course of things. Spreaders of false testimony desire to achieve an outcome to which the truth would never lead. The angry husband wanted to do harm to my practice, causing people to change doctors and to thereby cause me financial loss. His "false testimony" took the form of a handwritten sign on the entrance of my office building. It was brutally obvious and therefore easily ignored, but most false testimony is much more insidious than that of the sign-posting husband, and much more harmful.

When I think of false testimony I think of a situation in which I found myself shortly after entering private medical practice. After a very brief tenure as an employed physician I joined a practice of two experienced family doctors. Although I was the least experienced physician, within three months I was named the physician manager of the group. I was given complete oversight of the six employees as well as responsibility for every aspect of the office. I soon discovered that the other two doctors, although wonderful people and great clinicians, were terrible business managers. The office was disorganized and inefficient. Employee performance was inconsistent, and it seemed that each employee had created her own way of doing things. Although they were inefficient, the employees were content and happy, mostly because they were allowed to do whatever they liked. My attempts to improve productivity and service were met with formidable resistance.

The greatest resistance to my efforts at improving the practice came from the office manager. When I first met her I thought she was sweet, kind, and helpful, and it seemed that patients genuinely liked her. My favorable impression of her was enhanced by the fact that she professed a Christian faith and was initially very warm and receptive to me when I joined the practice. That warmth quickly disappeared when I began to look closely at her performance. I encountered evidence of an overwhelming amount of negligence and error. Although she was personable, she was not competent. The mistakes and intentional oversights I discovered made it clear that if the practice was to succeed, there was no way she could be allowed to continue as the manager of the office.

I thought about firing her for poor performance but was afraid to. In addition to being terrible at her job, she was also pregnant and a member of a minority group. I was afraid that if I fired her she would accuse my partners and me of discrimination. My fears were compounded by the knowledge that my partners had previously given her glowing performance reviews. An outsider might think that I was falsely maligning her work performance as a means of hiding discriminatory motives. Although I carefully documented all of the mistakes I found and it was common knowledge that I was neither racist nor discriminatory toward pregnant women (I delivered babies!) I was fearful that if I let her go I would be accused of wrongdoing.

In consultation with people who had human resources experience I decided that instead of terminating the manager's employment I would keep her on in a diminished role. By maintaining her at the same level of pay I thought I was protecting the practice from any accusations of wrongdoing. It was my hope that she would appreciate that I was trying to save her job and give her a chance at succeeding. Unfortunately, her poor work performance continued and I was forced to counsel her repeatedly. To my relief she eventually quit.

A few months later I received a notice from the Department of Fair Housing and Employment. Although she had quit, the former manager had filed a formal complaint against me in which she accused me of harassing her because of her race. She stated in a legal document that I had intentionally forced her to quit because of her ethnicity. I was being accused of racism and bigotry by someone who claimed to share my Christian faith! I had never made any comments or any actions to suggest that I was biased against her, yet she made sworn statements saying I had discriminated.

I was incredibly discouraged when I received the Fair Employment complaint. For the days and weeks leading up to the scheduled interview with the Fair Employment Investigator I could think of little else. I was fearful that my reputation would be forever damaged. What if they believed her charges? In addition to my concerns about my future in the practice I was hurt by the thought that she would say such things about me. She had to know they weren't true, yet she had sworn them to be so! How could someone do such a thing?

The answer is simple. She wanted to achieve an outcome that could not be achieved if she told the truth. She wanted to hurt me, and she wanted to get additional financial compensation. The only way she could do this was to give false testimony in her affidavit.

I remember thinking at the time that she was obviously violating the ninth commandment against giving false testimony. But was she? Is this false testimony? What exactly does it mean to give false testimony? What illness of the heart was this commandment prescribed for? I was taught as a child that "not giving false testimony" meant never lying. Is that true? To answer these questions requires that we know exactly what the commandment means and exactly what it was that God said through Moses. God had a specific problem in mind when He warned against the disease of false testimony.

Meaning of the Commandment

In trying to understand what the commandment says we need to recognize what it *doesn't* say. The commandment doesn't just say that no one should *ever* give false testimony (although that argument can be made), it says that no one should give false testimony *against a neighbor*. To properly understand the commandment requires an answer to two questions. What does it mean to give false testimony? And, who are our neighbors? Only when we have answered these questions can we understand and apply the commandment. When we do we will discover that there is more to the commandment than just telling the truth. As with the other commands, this one speaks to the nature of God. It tells us about God's heart for justice and His desire that we act justly in our dealings with others.

In defining what it means to give testimony or witness, Vine's Expository Dictionary provides a good start.[1] In the section on the Hebrew word "ed" translated as "testimony" (witness in the KJV) Vine writes:

> This word has to do with the legal or judicial sphere. First, in the area of civil affairs the word can mean someone who is present at a legal transaction and can confirm it if necessary. Such people worked as notaries, e. g., for an oral transfer of property:

> At a later time the "witnesses" not only acted to attest the transaction and to confirm it orally, but they signed a document or deed of purchase. Thus "witness" takes on the new nuance of those able and willing to affirm the truth of a transaction by affixing their signatures:

Thus, from Vine's research the word "testimony" transcends mere gossip or lying. It appears that the word specifically refers to circumstances that have lasting legal ramifications. It is for this reason that the word "testimony" is used in modern translations. The word carries with it a sense of legal importance. The term implies that a person is standing in front of a court or legal representative under circumstances in which what is being said has an impact on someone else's life. It implies circumstances in which words should be chosen carefully and where misspeaking has severe consequences.

Words of a Witness Matter!

I have personally been called to testify in circumstances where my words had a profound impact on someone's life. Not long ago I was called as a witness in a civil lawsuit filed by one of my patients. Both sides were trying to use my testimony to establish their side of the case. Several hundred thousand dollars were at stake, and the patient's medical history was a crucial part of the story.

During the course of an initial deposition, and later before an arbitration judge, I was subjected to almost three hours of questioning regarding the care she had received. I was repeatedly asked to recall statements she had made during medical visits over the years. The experience was exhausting and required an extreme level of concentration. Truthfulness at times hinged on a single word, and it would have been easy to accidentally give a false impression.

The deposition was filled with questions in which if I had not been careful I would have inadvertently given false testimony. It was amazingly stressful, in part because truthfulness was very important to me and more so because in this circumstance a mistake could have changed the entire course of someone's life. In such an instance as this, where so much was at stake, willfully giving false testimony, particularly in order to harm someone or gain advantage, would have been blatantly evil. It is easy to envision how God would hate such an act.

As concerned as I was about my testimony in that civil lawsuit, I do not believe an accidental misstatement in a deposition ranks as a violation of the ninth commandment. There is an aspect of intent in God's admonition against testifying falsely. It is when someone *knowingly* gives false testimony that trouble arises. Anyone who knowingly lies under oath is showing a total lack of concern for the adverse consequences that might befall the person against whom he is testifying.

Why would anyone deliberately do this? There are only a few possible motivations for such a reprehensible act. Either the person giving the false testimony is doing so for personal gain, or to intentionally harm someone else, or both! Regardless of the underlying motivation, the behavior signifies either extreme greed and selfishness or incredible malice. False testimony reveals that the person values personal gain or revenge above all else. Truth and justice are irrelevant and of no value to such a person. All that matters is getting what one desires.

Narrower Scope of the Command

It is simply not possible to love God and one's neighbor and act in such a fashion. Such behavior doesn't just violate the ninth commandment. An argument can be made that it violates the two greatest commandments, loving God with all of your being and loving your neighbor as yourself.

As bad as it is to give false testimony for personal gain, the commandment specifically addresses an even greater evil. God added something to the instruction beyond commanding the people to simply avoid false testimony; He specified the object of such sinful testimony as well. The words "against your neighbor" are especially significant. The admonition is not simply "Do not give false testimony," but rather to not give false testimony "against your neighbor." As we consider what this means it is hard to escape the fact that the phrase "against your neighbor" seems to limit the scope of the command.

In view of the apparently narrower scope of the commandment, it is natural to ask: Does God mean to say that it is acceptable to give false witness against strangers? I do not think so, but the commandment is probably narrower in scope than we have been taught. The broader and more common interpretation of the commandment— that it means we should never speak falsely about anyone—does not seem accurate.

I was reminded of how many people accept the broader application of the commandment just one day prior to writing the first draft of this chapter. I was having lunch with a pastor friend of mine and we were discussing various lessons and sermons we had each taught. He shared with me a recent message in which he had taught on Colossians 3:9. "Do not lie to each other, since you have taken off your old self with its practices." He said that he had told his congregation how sad it was that hundreds of years after the Ten Commandments Paul needed to remind the church not to violate the command against lying.

As I listened to his words the thought occurred to me that as wrong as lying to each other is, it is not a true violation of the commandment! If this was what God intended, He would most likely have said just that. If the ninth commandment simply said, "Do not lie," the interpretation would be pretty straightforward. We know God is not averse to using simple language, for He did so in other instances. God used pretty simple language in the previous commandments, "Do not steal" and "Do not murder."

The extra words and qualifiers used for the ninth commandment cannot then be overlooked. The words "against your neighbor" must be considered. God added these words, so they must be important. Although the commandment specifically addresses false testimony, it also specifically refers to such testimony being given against neighbors. An accurate interpretation and application of the commandment must address why God specifically mentioned neighbors in the commandment.

Who's My Neighbor?

Earlier in the chapter we noted how serious it is when someone gives false testimony in legal matters. As serious as it is today, it was especially weighty under Old Testament law. False testimony could lead to loss of reputation, loss of property, and even loss of life. Although the argument can be made that it is wrong to give false testimony in all circumstances, God intentionally admonishes against harming one's neighbors in this way. We have no choice but to ask ourselves, Who is our neighbor? Many people believe that all people are our neighbors yet this common perception is not correct. The term neighbor does not refer to everyone. If it did, there would be no reason to include the term!

That all men are not our neighbors may come as a surprise to some. Many Christians have been taught that Jesus in His parable of the Good Samaritan specifically taught that all people are our neighbors. A close reading of the parable reveals that this is not what Jesus intended. Jesus told the parable in response to a teacher of the law who asked Jesus the question, "Who is my neighbor?" with specific motivation. The text says that the teacher was "seeking to justify himself." It was this belief in self-justification that Jesus addressed.

The Pharisees had developed interpretations of the law that justified self-righteous thinking. The man to whom the parable was addressed believed that it was possible to gain righteousness through fulfilling the law. He claimed to love his neighbor, and supported his claim by limiting his definition of what and who a neighbor was.

In the parable a Samaritan helped an injured Jew, a man who would meet anyone's definition of neighbor, yet was not aided by other religious Jews described in the parable. It was commonly understood that religious leaders placed a premium on being ceremonially clean. Since the victim in the parable appeared dead, and touching a corpse rendered a man unclean, there was a chance that anyone rendering aid would become unclean. The teacher of the law believed that the obligation to help a Jew in need was trumped by the need to remain ceremonially clean. It was therefore not only justifiable, but appropriate, to not touch the injured man.

The Samaritan in the story valued the injured man more than he valued ceremonial cleanliness. For the teacher to act as the Samaritan did would require him to give up his belief that he must keep himself clean at all costs. The problem for the teacher of the law was his belief that such cleanness was crucial for a man to gain eternal life. When Jesus told the teacher to act as the Samaritan did he was not instructing the teacher to love all people or to view all men as his neighbor. For the man to be like the Samaritan in the story would require that he be willing to risk ceremonial uncleanness in certain circumstances. As such cleanness was the basis for his self-justification, this would represent a dramatic attitude shift. It was this attitude that Jesus addressed in the parable. Any attempt to make the parable about defining "neighbor" as everyone in need is a poor interpretation of the passage. This is not what Jesus intended.

So the question, "Who is my neighbor?" remains. The usage here and throughout Scripture seems to indicate that it is a person with whom one has a relationship. According to W. E. Vine the Hebrew word translated "neighbor" refers to a friend or associate.[2] It describes someone with whom there is a reciprocal relationship. It is someone who is close enough for one to have developed some degree of trust, and someone who would, as a result, expect the other person to care about them and their welfare. A neighbor is someone who would be especially hurt if, as a friend and someone whom they could trust, we were to betray them.

Putting it all together, the admonition against false testimony and the qualification of "against our neighbors," one gets a clearer picture of what God intended by the commandment. When believers knowingly and willingly give false statements about someone we know, someone who trusts us, we commit serious sin. We do more than merely lie. We betray trust and cause deep and lasting hurt and harm. It is a heinous act with dark and terrible motivation. When Christians understand this wickedness it makes sense that God would hate such a grievous sin. Only someone who values things over people, someone whose word means nothing and who has no concern for God's righteous judgment could act in such a way.

Lying is bad enough, but betraying the trust of a friend for personal gain or to cause harm undermines the foundations of a society. If there is no truth among friends in a situation with lasting consequences, what truth is there at all? If the people of Israel would not testify truthfully about one another there was no hope for them as a culture.

Application of this definition of the commandment may lead to Bible readers' universal self-confidence that they are not guilty of violating it. But just as with all of the other commands we have discussed, there is more here than first meets the eye. Underlying the command is not just a need to tell the truth, but something more important, something that applies to everyone. The meaning is found in the concept of "neighborness" we have been discussing.

Fellow Believers as Neighbors

What's really at issue in this command is the concept of relationship. Human beings are supposed to care about our neighbors. We are supposed to value relationships more than we do things, more than we do our own needs and desires. When we apply the idea that our neighbors are those with whom we have significant interaction, it doesn't take a stretch of thinking to realize that for us today the term "neighbor" best applies to our fellow believers. We should treat all people well, but we should take special care of our fellow servants of Christ.

In his letters the Apostle Paul frequently addressed the importance of believers treating each other well. Here's one example in the letter to the church at Philippi:

Do nothing out of selfish ambition or vain conceit, but in humility consider others better than yourselves. Each of you should look not only to your own interests, but also to the interests of others. Your attitude should be the same as that of Christ Jesus. (Phil 2:3–5)

According to Paul, putting others ahead of ourselves is a hallmark of the Christian life. If believers are to be like Jesus there will be times when we have to deny ourselves. Conversely, putting our own interests ahead of those of our brothers and sisters in Christ, in front of our neighbors, is evidence of an unredeemed life. The ultimate expression of such selfishness can be seen in bearing false witness—the violation of the ninth commandment. Perhaps there's no greater harm (other than murder) to a brother or sister in Christ than to testify untruthfully against them!

Paul gets to the heart of this truth about testifying against brothers and sisters in Christ in his letter to the church at Corinth.

If any of you has a dispute with another, dare he take it before the ungodly for judgment instead of before the saints? I say this to shame you. Is it possible that there is nobody among you wise enough to judge a dispute between believers? But instead, one brother goes to law against another—and this in front of unbelievers! The very fact that you have lawsuits among you means you have been completely defeated already. Why not rather be wronged? Why not rather be cheated? Instead, you yourselves cheat and do wrong, and you do this to your brothers. Do you not know that the wicked will not inherit the kingdom of God? (1 Cor 6:1, 5–9)

According to Paul even truthful testimony, when uttered against a fellow believer on our own behalf, is wrong! Paul didn't merely attack the "win at all costs," materialistic, "this life is all there is" attitude that underlies all false testimony, he went even further. The apostle stresses that instead of working to preserve our wealth and position, when it comes to disagreements with believers we are to forfeit our rights and accept wrong! Simply put, if relationship is what matters, then winning doesn't! When Christians model these values we declare our faith in Christ, and our love for the people He gave his life to save. We live out the words of our Savior who said men will "Know us by our love." Our love for one another should be so strong that we will not only avoid doing wrong to each other, but we will accept wrong from each other in order to preserve relationship and further godliness. (There are limits for sin—see Matt 18:15–17.)

People who love in this self-sacrificing way come closest to not violating the command. People who don't love in this way, people who must win and get their way, are moving down the sinful road whose destination is false testimony. Lest anyone think this is an exaggeration look at what Paul says immediately after his admonition: "Do you not know that the wicked will not inherit the kingdom of God?" To Paul, taking a brother or sister in Christ to court was a sign of wickedness and was inconsistent with being redeemed. Instead of seeking legal recourse, when believers have right attitudes toward one another, and have a proper eternal perspective, we will accept harm graciously.

Exercising Restraint When Wronged

In the previous chapter I shared about a family who refused to pay me for the medical care I had provided. Under civil law I was entitled to compensation. I could have taken them to court and almost certainly would have won a legal judgment, but I didn't. Why? Because it would have embarrassed them and it would have damaged their Christian witness. How could I carry through with the legal recourse and yet follow Paul's instruction? I realized I couldn't. I accepted the wrong and wrote off the money.

Not too long ago I experienced another circumstance where the truth of treating a fellow believer differently than I would a nonbeliever came into play. I have a Christian friend who is a general contractor. He is a godly man, and I hired him to remodel our kitchen for us. For understandable reasons the job ran way over the time he had set forth in his contract. The homeowner's frustration that is inherent in all remodeling projects was compounded by these delays and our relationship grew strained. I was convinced that he had failed to live up to his promises. Had he been a nonbeliever, I would have considered reducing payment, filing a complaint with the state, or pursuing some legal remedy. (The desire to maintain a Christian witness may have deterred me, but I would have felt no biblical obligation to let things go.) But because the contractor was a brother in Christ, I believed legal recourse wasn't an option.

Instead of making threats or taking legal action, I called my contractor friend and arranged a meeting. We sat and talked things out. Being a godly man, he accepted responsibility and took action to get the job done quickly. Because he respected me as a fellow believer, he acted in kindness in return. A situation that between unbelievers would have resulted in anger and a loss of relationship did nothing to harm our friendship in Christ. In fact our friendship has continued, and he has done additional work on my home. I believe the attitude that "relationship was more important than finances" was what saved our friendship. It is that mindset that Paul was encouraging, an attitude that makes false testimony against a fellow Christian next to impossible. It flows from a heart striving to be perfectly in line with the commandment.

As with many of the commandments, the attitude that people are more important than things, and that neighbors (or members of our faith community) are most important of all, lies at the very core of the ninth commandment. If we are honest, we will admit that acting in accordance with the command is unnatural. It is hard for believers to set our own desires aside and put other people first. There is no way that—on our own—we can consistently follow this commandment.

Help from the Great Physician

Fortunately, we are not left alone in the struggle to act unselfishly. The Great Physician, who specializes in damaged hearts and minds, comes to our aid. The ability to obey God in this fashion and to put others first, is brought about by the transforming power of God in our lives. If we do not allow God to change us and instead follow our natural inclinations, we will bend the rules and twist the truth to achieve our goals. If we follow those inclinations to their ultimate outcome we will see false testimony and mortally wounded relationships.

Not too long ago I had a young boy in my office who was struggling with precisely these issues. The thirteen-year-old was brought in by his mother. He was doing poorly in school and had developed a habit of lying to get out of trouble.

I asked the mom to step out so he and I could talk freely. I asked him about lying, and about the last time he had lied. He told me that some of his friends at school had told him that an eraser would explode if cooked in the microwave. Like any self-respecting adolescent boy, he determined to test the theory himself. Apparently his friends were right, and the eraser exploded gloriously. Afterwards, he foolishly forgot to dispose of the evidence. When his mother discovered the mess, she confronted him. Fearful of punishment, he lied and blamed his sisters. In essence he gave false testimony against his sisters. He testified in the court of mom that his sisters had committed the crime of which he was guilty!

When the boy finished telling me the story, I pointed out to him that the issue wasn't just that he had lied—there was something much deeper going on. The problem with what he had done was that he showed that he valued his own safety, his own escaping of punishment, more than he did his sisters.

I knew the boy had Christian parents and regularly attended church, so I talked to him about what it meant to put others before ourselves, and how we are to accept negative consequences rather than harm others. I shared with him the truth that the problem wasn't primarily that he had lied, but that he had chosen to save his guilty self at his innocent sisters' expense.

This boy's ethical struggle demonstrates for all of us how easy it is to give false testimony. Self-preservation and self-promotion are powerful motivators. I have observed this many times over the years. I have seen employees mislead their bosses about a fellow employee's actions in order to achieve a promotion. I have seen church workers malign a church volunteer's name in order to further their personal agenda. I have even seen pastors speak ill of other pastors in an effort to promote their own church. In all of these circumstances the person in the wrong valued their desires and plans more than the person who was being harmed by their words. They displayed the unscrupulous thinking that underlies all false testimony.

Avoiding false testimony against our neighbors is not always as easy as we might like, but it is simple. It involves valuing others more than we value ourselves, and valuing our fellow believers most of all. It involves speaking the truth regardless of the personal cost and trusting God to reward us for our obedience. Ultimately, it involves acknowledging our tendencies to be selfish and hurtful and allowing God to transform us.

Swallow the Medicine

Most prescriptions are given solely to benefit the patient suffering the disease. Medication for conditions such as high blood pressure and diabetes help the patient but have no impact on others around them. On occasion, as with antibiotics for contagious diseases, taking a prescription protects others from catching what we have. This prescription is such a medication. False testimony is a disease that hurts us and those with whom we have relationships—

treating it effectively helps others as well. As you ponder the concept of false testimony, think about the friendships God has given you as you answer the following questions.

- Have you ever lied to protect yourself? Look back on the situation. Reflect on what was at stake. Were you appropriately valuing another person? What were the consequences of your lie?
- Have you ever had false testimony given about you? What happened? Consider the consequences. What can you learn from that time?
- How do you treat your neighbors, the people with whom God has placed you in community? Do you treat them differently? Are you more forgiving? Why not?
- Consider a time when you were wronged by a neighbor, by a brother or sister in faith. How did you respond? What was more important to you, your neighbor or justice? Were you willing to accept wrong?

In thinking about accepting wrong from those we have trusted and loved, we have no greater example of upright behavior than that shown by Jesus. Paul tells us that "While we were yet sinners, Christ died for us." We need to learn and live His example.

Prescription #10

Be Content with What You Have

You shall not covet your neighbor's wife. You shall not set
your desire on your neighbor's house or land, his manservant
or maidservant, his ox or donkey, or anything that belongs
to your neighbor.
Deuteronomy 5:21

Being the Lesser Twin

*W*hen I was younger I was particularly jealous of my twin
brother. It is a sad fact, but it is true. Because we are identical, most people think that we had identical childhoods. Well, most
people are wrong. His childhood was better. He had the better name
(There are no easy-to-discover insults that rhyme with "Bret"), he
was the better athlete (once he beat me in a game of one-on-one
basketball, with a *cast* on his leg), and he wasn't as clumsy as I
was. Although we were both abused by our parents, for some reason
I seemed to be singled out for a little bit more. (This is not sour
grapes, all of these facts are readily acknowledged by my brother.)

The inequity in our lives reached a peak in high school. He was
far more successful than I was. Although almost all high school kids
must deal with failure, it's a little more difficult when you are compared to a successful sibling. It is even tougher when that sibling is
your identical twin.

Lest anyone think I am exaggerating the contrast between my twin's and my own high school stories, I will give some of the tragic details. In sports, my twin excelled at running track and cross country. He received his varsity letter as a sophomore, setting a league record in the half-mile run (what is now the 800 meters). He qualified for the sectional championships three years in a row. He was the star of the track team, running on the relay team and occasionally in the quarter mile. The team counted on him, and he almost never lost.

In contrast, my high-school athletic career was a series of failures. Instead of running cross country like my brother, as a freshman I went out for the football team. I was five feet seven inches tall and weighed an unimpressive 117 pounds. For the few weeks I endured tryouts I was little more than a tackling dummy. I was continually pounded by the other players, and spent more time on my back than I did on my feet. When it became obvious that I would never see the playing field in a game I hung up my cleats and quit.

My struggles continued in my sophomore year. I put my football failures behind me and decided to go out for the basketball team. I initially did reasonably well, and in the first few scrimmages played quite a bit. It seemed that I actually had a chance to make the starting lineup, or to at least garner significant playing time. Encouraged by the opportunity before me I gave it my all in practice and the coach considered me to be one of the hardest workers. My hopes for athletic glory came crashing down just before the league season began. I contracted scarlet fever and lost ten pounds in ten days. Along with the weight I lost a lot of strength and stamina. My skills diminished to the point where I spent the rest of the season riding the bench as nothing more than a mop-up player. My playing time was limited to the final few minutes of games in which the outcome was no longer in doubt. Although I lasted the season, I didn't bother trying out the following year.

The following summer between my sophomore and junior years I decided to pursue running. I figured that since my identical twin was successful I stood a decent chance of succeeding as well. I began running at the end of sophomore year and continued working out all summer. That summer I ran every day, frequently twice a day. I worked much harder during that time than my brother did. To me it seemed that my brother was resting on his laurels, as he trained only sporadically. I felt myself improving steadily and I couldn't wait for the first cross country meet of the year, the time when I would display the results of my summer of work. I lined up next to my brother at the start, ready to show the world there was more than one good runner in the Barrett family. Although I ran my heart out, I finished over ninety seconds behind him. (For those unclear on how far that is, it is over a quarter-mile behind in a three-mile race.) Discouragement took hold, and I soon dropped from the team.

My nonathletic life paled in the glow of my brother's successes as well. Bret was far more popular than I was. He was elected as sophomore class vice president and then junior class president. While he was winning, I was losing. I ran for and lost elections for sophomore president and junior class vice president. My junior year saw the greatest possible electoral insult, as I was defeated even in an election for president of the chess club! Bret was friends with athletes and cheerleaders; I had a few friends in the drama department. Although we were identical twins, our lives were vastly different.

It comes then as no surprise that there were a number of times (such as my entire freshman, sophomore, junior, and senior years) when I was envious of what my brother had. I frequently wished I had his confidence, his popularity, his success, and especially his letterman's jacket. I never thought about it back then, but when I look back on my feelings now I have to admit that I was coveting. I didn't want what *I* had, I wanted what *he* had. I didn't want to be *me*, I wanted to be *him*.

Just about everyone can relate to my story in some way. All of us have at one time or another been dissatisfied with our lives and believed things would be better if we could just trade places with someone else. We live in a world of inequality, thus the temptation to want what someone else has is inevitable. Unless you are Bill Gates, there will always be someone who has more money or more stuff than you do. No matter who you are, or what your circumstances are, there will always be someone who seems to have it better than you, at least in some area of life. Whether it is better-behaved kids, a smaller waistline, better complexion, thicker head of hair, faster car, bigger house, or a more attractive spouse—if we are all honest there is at least one part of our lives we wish were different, one area in which we desire what someone else has.

Though wanting what belongs to someone else is common, the tenth commandment seems to warn that such longings can be dangerous, and are sinful in nature. As with conditions such as elevated cholesterol, where too much of a normal substance is harmful, there apparently is a point when wanting what someone else has reaches a level that is harmful to our souls and offensive to God. With this in mind God included an admonition against coveting as the final commandment. It is worthwhile to spend time understanding what it means to covet, and in particular to know what it is about coveting that is wrong. This is a disease to be treated, and we do well to understand its symptoms and treatment.

What Is Coveting?

Growing up I was told that coveting was the same as being envious or jealous of someone. I frequently felt guilty, for jealousy was something I harbored all too often. As an abused child from a modest home, I lacked and was envious of what most kids I knew had. If honest, we will all admit that we have all been similarly jealous of another person at one time or another. Yet childhood jealousy isn't what God is talking about here. There is far more to the commandment than simply avoiding jealousy, because the word "covet" carries a meaning beyond what most people think of when it comes to being jealous.

Covet is a complex word, one that is not used in everyday conversation. In its place people usually use words such as "want" or "desire." Of those synonyms people typically use, *desire* is the word closest in meaning to the Hebrew word translated as "covet." *Desire* is in fact used later in the commandment to clarify and expand on the idea embodied by the word *covet* in the first part of the commandment. It becomes evident from study of the commandment that coveting goes beyond simply thinking in passing, "It would be nice to have that." It indicates a much more intense desire or longing, combined with a dissatisfaction of one's current belongings or situation. In the word "covet," and in the commandment, there is an implication of deep longing, of intensely wishing that one had something else or was someone else.

Coveting a Spouse That's Not Yours

It is not by accident, and is in fact important to note, that the first item or object of covetous desire mentioned in the commandment is not a thing but a person. God through Moses told the people of Israel, and by extension us, not to desire someone else's spouse. "You shall not covet your neighbor's spouse." Not just anyone's spouse, but a neighbor's spouse. There is something particularly egregious in the eyes of God for someone to long for a neighbor's wife or husband.

If we pause and reflect upon it, it doesn't take too long to see how terrible a thing this is. When someone sets his or her heart on wanting a neighbor's spouse, it is tantamount to a rejection of the spouse God has given them, a careless disregard for the needs and happiness of the affected neighbor, and a rejection of the sovereign plan of God who gave spouses to us. There is little more depraved than coveting the wife or husband of a friend.

Not long ago some friends of ours shared a story about their neighbors, a tragedy that illustrates how terrible a sin coveting someone else's spouse truly is. Two couples in their neighborhood had been friends for many years. They regularly spent time together, their kids played together, they even vacationed together on a regular basis. One evening one of the men got his friend's wife alone and confided in her that he had always been attracted to her, and expressed his wish that he could be with her.

With the open expression of that long-held secret desire the once-close friendship was forever destroyed. Understanding how the man's desires destroyed the relationship helps to comprehend the commandment and its importance. There was much more conveyed in the man's desirous words than harmless physical attraction. In his actions and words he communicated serious, dark truths about his perception of reality and about his feelings.

When he told his friend's wife that he wanted to be with her he didn't just express desire for her, he was also openly declaring that he was dissatisfied with the wife he had. He announced that his wife was not enough for him physically or emotionally. He wanted more; he wanted someone else. None of the sacrifices his wife had made over the years, none of the deep emotions that had been shared, none of the moments of physical intimacy mattered. In his eyes his wife was a failure. She was a poor choice and a mistake. It is difficult to suggest another way to interpret what he had said. If he viewed his wife appropriately, as the one woman that God had given Him to share his life, it would have been unthinkable for him to act as he did.

He wasn't merely rejecting his wife with his words. He was also abandoning his role as father, protector, and provider to his children. Although he was his children's father, he now was saying, in effect, that he wished he had never been with their mother in the first place. To be with the new woman was to reject the mother of his children. In so doing he imperiled the family they had built together. The feelings, comfort, and stability of his family were not important enough to him as was his desire to be with someone else. The love and affection of his wife and family were not fulfilling. He wanted more.

Not only did the man reject his wife and children when he expressed his desire for his friend's wife, but also he renounced his friendship with his best friend. Although they had known each other since childhood, his actions now said that those years of friendship meant nothing. His friend's feelings were irrelevant. His friend's love for his own wife was meaningless. All that mattered was what he wanted.

Rejecting God

As deplorable as it was to reject his family and friends, there was an even greater sin. In expressing a desire for his friend's wife he rejected God. If we believe God's word, it is clear that God intended marriage to last a lifetime. God expects marital partners to be completely fulfilled and satisfied by the spouses he gives—not only physically satisfied, but emotionally and relationally as well. The writer of Proverbs perfectly describes this ideal in the counsel he offers a young man in Proverbs 5. Such wisdom also applies to us today.

May your fountain be blessed, and may you rejoice in the wife of your youth. A loving doe, a graceful deer—may her breasts satisfy you always, may you ever be captivated by her love. (Prov 5:18–19)

When a man says that he wants someone else's wife, he is declaring his belief that God made a mistake when He gave him the wife he has. When a woman says she wishes she had someone else's husband, she is saying that God made a mistake when He gave her the husband she has. Instead of "rejoicing in the wife (or husband) of their youth" as God declared His plan to be, they are bemoaning their plight. They are saying that the spouse of their youth may have been good when they were younger, but they need a better companion now.

In considering a rejection of the spouse God provided, very few people go to the extremes as the man who pursued his best friend's wife. Most would not be brazen or foolish enough to act as this man did. Even if we harbored such thoughts, we would most likely be wise enough to keep them to ourselves. Fear of the consequences that would follow helps us restrain ourselves. Unfortunately such restraint does not render anyone innocent. The whole concept of what it means to covet entails that even having such thoughts is a violation of the commandment. Covetousness is a thought or a feeling, not an action. Although all of the commandments attack sinful thinking, the tenth is the only one that is specifically limited to thoughts or unseen desires. It isn't wrong just to take what isn't ours, but also to desire and long for that which we do not have.

Coveting Is Common

If we are honest, covetous thoughts are far more common than we care to admit. I have heard covetous feelings expressed on numerous occasions by patients who did not even realize what they were saying. I could give a very long list of examples, but here are just a few of the common remarks I have heard over the years that revealed a covetous heart:

"My husband doesn't do enough around the house."
"My wife isn't affectionate."
"My wife doesn't support me enough in what I do."
"I wish my husband was more understanding."

At first glance, it seems that these may all be appropriate and valid complaints. There is no clear statement of wrongful desire. But a deeper look at what was being said and a closer examination of the words reveals a common thread. In each case the spouse is failing to meet expectations. The spouse is not doing what the complainer wishes they would do. The covetousness of each complaint is readily exposed by asking a simple question—"Compared to whom?" With this question the problem becomes clear. What is really being said in each instance is "I wish my spouse was more like someone else." Frequently, the person has the husband or wife of someone they know in mind when expressing their dissatisfaction. What is really being said is "I wish my wife supported me as much as Justin's wife supports him" or "I wish my husband was as understanding as Shawna's husband is." Isn't this a violation of the commandment? At the most basic level, isn't there very little difference between wishing your spouse would change, and wishing you could change spouses?

It is not insignificant that God begins the list of what people should not covet with the words "your neighbor's wife." I believe God starts with not coveting our neighbor's spouse for a number of reasons. Since no one has a perfect spouse (a fact that my wife will readily affirm!), and the flaws in our spouses are so well known to us, it is easy for discontent to sneak in. It is easy in our selfishness to focus too much on our spouse's failings. At the same time, the marriage relationship is truly the center, the very heart, of our earthly lives. It is the greatest earthly gift that our Heavenly Father bestows. Therefore we all need to be careful, for while marriage should be a place of great blessing and growth, it often is a place where dissatisfaction arises. Dissatisfaction is only one small step away from coveting.

Learning to Be Content

Undoubtedly, some people who are reading this are in difficult marriages. They may find it very difficult to take joy in their spouse. As I shared in the chapter on honoring one's parents, I am fully aware that not all families are wonderful. Not all spouses are fabulous either. But what was true with parents is also true with marriages and spouses; namely, that God teaches us and shapes us in every circumstance. Our loving Father causes all things to work together for the good of those who love Him (Rom 8:28). All things means, *all* things, and that includes all families, marriages, spouses, hurts, and disappointments. Space does not allow for a full explanation of what this means, but it is sufficient to say that people can take comfort in knowing that God is in control of our lives and has given us exactly what we need and has placed us exactly where we need to be in order to fulfill His plans for good in our lives. True acceptance of this truth brings about contentment in all circumstances. As a result, contentment in all circumstances, even difficult ones, should be a goal for every believer. "All circumstances" includes all marriages!

The latter part of the verse makes it clear that being content in all circumstances is at the heart of the final commandment. Not only are we not to covet our neighbor's wife, we are not to covet anything else he has either! Not property, standing, possessions, or livestock, not job or reputation, not hair, health, or physical condition. We are not to covet letterman's jackets, junior class presidencies, or popularity. Since God has given His children all they need and has promised to bring about good in every situation, there is nothing in this world that someone else has that we should prefer to what we have. Nothing!

How can this be? Isn't it natural to want more? Isn't that the American way? The fact that wanting more is natural and is the American way does not mean that it is God's way. In fact I have become convinced that whenever I feel a natural inclination to do something, I am usually better off not doing it! My natural inclinations and the values of my culture are usually at odds with God's plan.

The perils of desiring more are brought to mind by a conversation I had not too long ago with a young patient. I do not recall why he had come in to see me, but I do remember the conversation. During the "small talk" part of the visit I asked him what his goals in life were. He was twenty-five years old, and his answer showed that he had previously spent significant time thinking about this very question. His life goals were quite similar to those of almost every young person—both Christian and nonbeliever—I have talked to over the years. He wanted a big house, a nice car, a well-paying job that he enjoyed, and a comfortable retirement by his mid-fifties. He was convinced that when he achieved these goals he would be happy and content.

I had to break the news to him that if he was like many fifty-year-old men I had encountered over the years he was in for major disappointment. I had treated far too many men and women who had reached middle age and discovered that even though they had achieved all of their financial goals, they were still unhappy and unsatisfied. They had managed to accumulate everything they thought they needed for happiness and contentment, yet those ideals still eluded them. They had fallen victim to the lie that things bring happiness. The idea that "stuff" satisfies is simply a foolish and false belief. "Stuff" never satisfies.

The final commandment attacks this faulty notion that possessions bring lasting joy. After all, what is the heart attitude underlying all covetousness? Is it not the belief that if we only had *that* we would be truly happy? If not truly happy at least if we had *that* we would be happier than we currently are? Further, doesn't that attitude reflect a deep-seated belief that this life is all there is and that accumulating stuff in this life is therefore man's greatest goal? Isn't that temporal view of life directly contrary to God's eternal plan?

Proper Attitude about Possessions

When we look at what really matters in life, and consider appropriate attitudes toward possessions and other things, the meaning of commandment truly comes into focus. There are a number of foundational truths regarding material possessions embodied by the command to not covet. Here are a few.

1. Love of worldly goods is inconsistent with a love for God. Jesus made this absolutely clear in the Sermon on the Mount: "No one can serve two masters. Either he will hate the one and love the other, or he will be devoted to the one and despise the other. You cannot serve both God and Money" (Matt 6:24). Covetousness is an expression of a love of the world and misplaced priorities.
2. When the pursuit of worldly wealth is our primary goal, we are not pursuing God's kingdom.

Serving God will require a very loose hold on material possessions. The descriptions of the early church found in Acts
reveal men and women who viewed their material wealth not
as an end of their life's work, but as a means of furthering
God's kingdom. Jesus instructed His disciples to not lay up
for themselves treasures on earth but rather treasure in heaven
(Matt 6:19–20).

3. God has promised to give His children everything that they
need. "My God will meet all your needs according to his glorious riches in Christ Jesus" (Phil 4:19). Jesus said that when
we seek God's kingdom first, our earthly needs will be sup-
plied (Matt 6:33). Simply put, if we do not have something,
Scripture strongly suggests that we don't need it!

4. Contentment is an attribute of a godly life. Note how Paul
describes it to his friend Timothy:
But godliness with contentment is great gain. For we brought
nothing into the world, and we can take nothing out of it. But if
we have food and clothing, we will be content with that. People
who want to get rich fall into temptation and a trap and into
many foolish and harmful desires that plunge men into ruin
and destruction. For the love of money is a root of all kinds of
evil. Some people, eager for money, have wandered from the
faith and pierced themselves with many griefs. (1 Tim 6:6–10)

At its core the covetousness forbidden by the commandment
indicates a lack of trust in God and a belief that He is incapable of
providing what His children need. Or worse, it suggests a belief that
He is capable and yet doesn't care enough to intervene! Covetousness
reveals an ungrateful heart and a disregard for others. It challenges
the sovereignty of God and spits on His mercy and grace. It is completely inconsistent with the life of faith.

Remedy for Covetousness

As terrible as the sin of covetousness is, there is an antidote. It
was hinted at earlier. Covetousness is a sign of dissatisfaction and
ingratitude. The cure, or the preventive medicine, is gratitude and

contentment. The solution to covetousness is delighting in God and in all that He has given His loved ones.

I have seen this play out in my own life. Although I live in one of the most materialistic communities in the world, and work in a profession in which I am surrounded by narcissistic and egotistic individuals who want more and more, I truly feel blessed and satisfied. I have achieved this state by practicing the discipline of gratitude. I have learned to make it a habit to thank God regularly for everything in my life. I thank Him for my wife, my children, His love, His grace, for everything He has given me. The more I say "Thank you" to God, the more grateful and content I am. My life isn't perfect from a worldly perspective, but I am embracing the truth that it really couldn't be any better. It is the life God has given me.

Kenton Beshore, Senior Pastor of Mariners Church in Irvine, California, has a wonderful way of teaching this attitude to his church. Each year at Thanksgiving he gives a sermon on gratitude. In it he provides a helpful definition of contentment. Contentment, he says, is in wanting what you have. When you are truly content, you don't need or want anything else in life. His recurrent joke is to ask, "Who is more content, a man with five children or a man with five million dollars?" The answer is "The man with five children, because he doesn't want any more!" In his message he repeatedly stresses how important it is to realize how blessed people are and how much they have in God. Although he doesn't mention the tenth commandment in his sermon, Kenton teaches his congregation contentment and the key to obeying it.

At the end of the sermon, he instructs the congregation to declare how good their lives are. He has them all repeat, "I love my life, it couldn't be better!" He then leads the congregation to declare their contentment in other things by saying, "I love my wife, she couldn't be better!", "I love my husband, he couldn't be better!", and "I love my job, it couldn't be better!" The "I love mys" include bosses, children, beat-up cars, and everything else in our lives. When people are truly content, they will love the life that God has given them. When believers love the lives they have, there will be no reason to covet.

Teaching Contentment to Kids

Parents can model this value for their children on a daily basis. When watching television (admittedly a practice of questionable value!) parents can respond to the barrage of advertising by simply saying, "We don't need that!" How wonderful it would be to tell our children that we are happy with what we have! Parents can resist the temptation to always need the newest and the best. One particular way to teach contentment is by avoiding debt. Buying things we can't afford (and usually don't need) tells our children that having things "now' is all that matters. Teaching contentment with what we have is a great gift to our kids.

We can resist trying to teach our children strictly by our words. I have heard many parents quickly tell their children that they don't "need" a new toy or a new outfit. And yet the same parents rush to get the newest electronic gadget or toy because they just "had to have it!" What does that teach their children? This came to mind a few years ago when my son and I went shopping for a big screen TV. He had built a television stand for the family room, and I had promised that we would eventually buy the TV it was built to hold. A local store advertised a model that seemed to be what we were looking for, so we went to check it out. As we stood in the store looking at the TV I realized that we really could not afford it at that time. I decided we did not really need it then and it would be unwise to buy it. We walked out of the store empty-handed. I believe my son and I learned a valuable lesson that day.

Another way I teach my children to not covet is by continually praising their mother in their presence. I express that I would never want anyone else's wife, because I have the wife God specifically gave me. My children have heard me repeat the truth that although my wife is not perfect, she is the perfect wife for me. God gave me the woman who was and is my perfect partner. There is no reason for me to wish for anyone else. When it comes to my marriage, I am content.

Contentment as a Way of Life

It is a sad truth that in all of my years in practice I have met very few truly content people. People who are truly satisfied and act like they have enough are a rare breed. I have seen men who lived in modest homes in decent neighborhoods work ridiculous hours so they could "provide for their families." By "provide" they meant give each child their own bedroom, designer clothes, big screen TVs, and expensive vacations. Some of these men achieve their stated goals, yet I have never seen one stop the long hours once those goals were achieved. They always end up wanting more.

It is time for believers to heed the advice of Kenton Beshore in his valuable message on contentment. Christians need to stop and thank God for all He has given. People should not limit their gratitude to those things that are obviously wonderful and that bring immediate joy. Married people need to thank God for their spouses, even if they are flawed or difficult to live with. God has a perfect plan. Believers need to thank God for their children, even if they are disobedient and disrespectful. Christians should be thankful for their jobs, even if they are unappreciated and underpaid. Forgiven sinners need to thank God especially for His eternal plan for good in their lives. Believers can be grateful that this life is not all there is. As we do, our desires for "other" things will fade. The temptation to want someone else's life will disappear as we seek to learn and do all that we can in the life God has given us.

In the life of contentment believers escape the dangers that come from coveting. We will not neglect our families in pursuit of material goods. We will maintain an eternal perspective that allows us to seek God's kingdom first. Our joy will increase as we appreciate the beauty of all God has given us.

As I look back on my life, and especially on my high school years, I am truly grateful for the life God gave me. My unpopularity in high school kept me away from temptations to which I might have otherwise succumbed. The humility I learned through all of my failures has balanced the conceit that could have come from later successes. The struggles, tears, and discouragements in life have made me a better parent and doctor than I ever could have been otherwise.

Looking back, I can see now that when I desired my brother's life, I was wrong. The life I had was the perfect life for me, and I am content in that. I do not covet my brother's life any longer. Not because my life is more successful, but because my life is mine, the life God has given me.

Swallow the Medicine

God's prescription against covetousness is perhaps the simplest there is. The cure is summed up in two words: "Thank You." Gratitude cures the disease of covetousness. Your level of contentment is an accurate measure of your health. Read through these questions and see how healthy your heart is in this regard.

- What is there that you want and do not have? Do you need it?
- Are you truly satisfied with the life God has given you? If not, why not?
- Do you truly believe that God will give you all that you need? Don't answer too quickly. Stop and consider how you truly view God's provision in your life.
- Do you regularly thank God for what you have—for *all* of what you have, both good and the seemingly bad?
- If married, do you rejoice in the mate God has given you? Do you ever find yourself wishing your spouse would change? Take time to ask God what He wants you to learn from your spouse's imperfections. Take time to consider what your spouse is learning through yours!

Conclusion

Hopelessly Sick, a Permanent Cure

*S*ome diseases can be cured, many only treated. Dealing with incurable illness is a regular part of my life, as I encounter patients with chronic conditions such as diabetes and elevated cholesterol. I can offer them treatments to protect from complications and perhaps lengthen their life, but the disease remains.

Sin is like that. People can suppress it, occasionally control it, but not overcome it. Sin is always with us. Even when an outward appearance suggests health, it is only an illusion. Our diseased nature is there, waiting for an opportunity to take over our lives. The realization of this burden could easily call us to cry out in despair, "How can I break free?"

The Apostle Paul clearly understood this sentiment, for he wrote in similar fashion in his letter to the church at Rome.

> So I find this law at work: When I want to do good, evil is right there with me ... What a wretched man I am! Who will rescue me from this body of death? (Rom 7:21, 25)

Yet despair over our condition is not the purpose of God's commandments. While each prescription provides treatment for a specific aspect of our infected hearts, they collectively serve a greater purpose—they point us to the cure. As Paul wrote to the church in Galatia:

So the law was put in charge to lead us to Christ that we might be justified by faith. (Gal 3:24)

What an amazing truth. The prescriptions we have reviewed are timeless, reliable guides to spiritually healthy lives—medicine for the soul that when followed produce remarkable blessings—but they don't cure us. Jesus does.

Hope for Bartimaeus

How do humans access that cure? What is involved? The story of Bartimaeus, a blind beggar whose tale is recounted by Luke (18:35–43), Mark (10:46–52), and Matthew (20:29–34), shows how people in need of life-saving treatment can call upon the Great Physician.

As a blind man in first century Israel, life had little hope for Bartimaeus. There were no community resources, no Braille Institute, no work programs, and no government disability benefits. His only hope for survival lay in the generosity of others, frequently that of strangers. Survival was all he dare hope for, since as a blind man he would never be able to provide for a family and was therefore doomed to a lonely existence. Even simple functions such as bathing and elimination required the assistance of others.

He spent each day at the gates of the city of Jericho, a wealthy town with a temperate climate and active trade, which made it an ideal place for a beggar to ply his "trade."[1] Bartimaeus' life was surely miserable, lonely, helpless, and hopeless, a fact perhaps worsened by a cultural assumption that his blindness was his fault (see John 9:1–3).

But his understanding and recognition of his impossible, incurable condition led to the despair that put him in the perfect place to receive a complete and total cure. Bartimaeus believed that Jesus was his one and only hope for life and a future. Scripture tells us that on the day Jesus was departing Jericho, Bartimaeus, aware of who it was that was passing by, called out to Jesus in the midst of the crowd, "Lord, Son of David, have mercy on me!"

The crowd attempted to silence him, but his desperation intensified. Rather than be quieted, he yelled all the more, "Lord, Son of David, have mercy on me!"

And Jesus did. He stopped and asked that Bartimaeus be brought to him. When brought to the Savior, Jesus asked him a simple question, "What would you have me do for you?" Bartimaeus' humble reply, "Lord, I want to see" was more than a request for sight. Embodied in the petition for the ability to see came a request for life itself, for with sight came the freedom to live, to work, and to love.

Confronted with the request, Jesus was moved with compassion. Jesus reached out and touched the beggar's eyes, saying, "Go, your faith has healed you" (Mark 10:52). In saying "Go," it was as if Jesus was saying, "You are normal now, you can live your life, you can go the way you want to go, you have a choice. Live your life."

And what did the newly sighted Bartimaeus choose to do? Suddenly faced with a world of options and possibilities that had long been denied him, perhaps even since birth, Bartimaeus chose to follow Jesus.

Hope for Us

It is no accident that Bartimaeus' story is recounted three times in the New Testament. It is a powerful example of how healing can be received, and of how believers should approach the Great Physician to receive the cure we need.

Healing begins with the recognition of hopelessness and helplessness, the understanding that humans do not have in themselves any chance of breaking free from a diseased state. According to the Apostle Paul, this is the ultimate purpose of God's law, of the ten prescriptions. But Paul makes it clear that the commandments are not intended to lead us to despair, but to a hope in Christ. Paul wrote after his seemingly despairing words earlier in Romans 7:

What a wretched man I am! Who will rescue me from this body of death? **Thanks be to God—through Jesus Christ our Lord!** (Rom 7:24–25, emphasis added)

As with Bartimaeus and Paul, our despair leads us to cry out for mercy from the only One capable of providing it. Bartimaeus' healing required nothing more of him than to call out to Jesus. That same requirement applies to all of us today. Diseased and disabled by the curse of sin, ultimate cure awaits, and all that is needed is for the sick to call out to Jesus and receive it.

Bartimaeus showed not only *how* to call out to Jesus, but also *whom* to call upon. "Lord, Son of David" he cried. Lord, the master, ruler, and ultimate authority. Son of David, the promised Messiah who would deliver all people. When people call out to Jesus in this way, in compassion He reaches out and heals.

The Apostle John, in his gospel, described the healing process:

For God so loved the world that he gave his one and only Son, that whoever believes in him shall not perish but have eternal life. (John 3:16)

What an amazing hope. We have a deadly illness, but we don't have to die! God, in the person of His Son, has provided a way to perfect, eternal health.

While the cure is guaranteed when we come to faith in Christ, the healing process is not without setbacks. These setbacks, however, are no reflection of the effectiveness of the treatment. God's work cannot be stopped.

In fact, Scripture makes it clear that the healing work of Jesus is enduring, that the end is certain, and our efforts to follow His prescriptions should continue.

Dear friends, now we are children of God, and what we will be has not yet been made known. But we know that when he appears, we shall be like him, for we shall see him as he is. Everyone who has this hope in him purifies himself, just as he is pure. (1 John 3:2–3)

So what do we do when we suffer relapses, when we find ourselves struggling with sin? John tells us.

If we confess our sins, he is faithful and just and will forgive us our sins and purify us from all unrighteousness. (1 John 1:9–10)

These words are a blessed hope. For those who do not yet believe, the commandments of God serve as a reminder of our terminal condition and need for a cure. For those who have come to faith they are a means to identify areas where we need the Physician's transforming touch, and to encourage us to call on Him even more.

It is that simple. When confronted with the severity of our sin, with the diseased state of our hearts, believers need not be without hope. Instead, we admit that in recognizing our disease we also recognize our need for the cure that only God provides.

The Apostle Paul spelled it out for the believers in Rome.

So now there is no condemnation for those who belong to Christ Jesus. And because you belong to him, the power of the life-giving Spirit has freed you from the power of sin that leads to death. The law of Moses was unable to save us because of the weakness of our sinful nature. So God did what the law could not do. He sent his own Son in a body like the bodies we sinners have. And in that body God declared an end to sin's control over us by giving his Son as a sacrifice for our sins. He did this so that the just requirement of the law would be fully satisfied for us, who no longer follow our sinful nature but instead follow the Spirit. (Rom 8:1–4, *New Living Translation*)

As we follow the Spirit, we will walk in the health that God desires for his loved ones in this life, confident that the insidious, "incurable" disease of sin has been forever healed.

Endnotes

Finding Motivation

1. W. E. Vine, Merrill F. Unger, and William White Jr, *Vine's Complete Expository Dictionary of Old and New Testament Words* (Nashville: Thomas Nelson, 1996).
2. Religious People Live Longer Than Nonbelievers, http://www.webmd.com/content/article/27/1728_60239, accessed February 2008).
3. R. Bonita, M. A. Ford, and A. W. Stewart, "Predicting Survival After Stroke: A Three-Year Follow-Up," *Stroke*, no. 19, 1988: 669–73.
4. David R. Francis, "It's True: Churchgoers Are Wealthier," http://www.csmonitor.com/2005/1114/p15s02-cogn.html

A Matter of Desire

1. Aish.com, The Jewish Website, http://www.aish.com/.

Prescription #1: Follow the One Road

1. W. E. Vine, Merrill F. Unger, and William White Jr, *Vine's Complete Expository Dictionary of Old and New Testament Words* (Nashville: Thomas Nelson, 1996).

Prescription #2: Understand the Nature of God

1. Shemsu Sesen, "The Rise of Thebes, the Rise of Amun," http://emhotep.net/2010/07/10/periods/first-intermediate/the-rise-of-thebes-the-rise-of-amun/.
2. "Ancient Egypt Temples—Home to the Gods," http://www.ancient-egypt-online.com/ancient-egypt-temples.html.
3. "Ancient Egyptian Temples," http://www.historylink101.net/egypt_1/religion_temples.htm.
4. Wikipedia, "Ennead," http://en.wikipedia.org/wiki/Ennead.
5. "Egyptian Gods: Huh," http://egyptian-gods.org/egyptian-gods-huh/.
6. "Ancient Egypt Temples—Home to the Gods," http://www.ancient-egypt-online.com/ancient-egypt-temples.html.
7. "Ancient Egyptian Temples," http://www.historylink101.net/egypt_1/religion_temples.htm.

Prescription #3: Don't Ask God to Do It Your Way

1. *Nelson's Illustrated Bible Dictionary*, Herbert Lockyer, ed. (Nashville: Thomas Nelson, 1986).

Prescription #4: Remember What God Has Done

1. W. E. Vine, Merrill F. Unger, and William White Jr, *Vine's Complete Expository Dictionary of Old and New Testament Words* (Nashville: Thomas Nelson, 1996).

Prescription #5: Honor the Parents God Gave You

1. W. E. Vine, Merrill F. Unger, and William White Jr, *Vine's Complete Expository Dictionary of Old and New Testament Words* (Nashville: Thomas Nelson, 1996).

Prescription #6: Value Human Life

1. Alfred Dersheim, *The Life and Times of Jesus the Messiah* (Peabody, MA: Hendrickson).

Prescription #7: Be Faithful to Your Spouse

1. "Your Love Amazes Me," Recorded by John Berry, Written by Amanda Hunt-Taylor and Chuck Jones, 1994.
2. "Young Adults and Liberals Struggle with Morality," Barna Group, August 25, 2008; www.barna.org/barna-update/article/16-teensnext-gen/25-young-adults-and-liberals-struggle-with-morality?q=pornography.
3. "Young Adults and Liberals Struggle with Morality," Barna Group.

Prescription #9: Speak Truth When It Matters Most

1. W. E. Vine, Merrill F. Unger, and William White Jr, *Vine's Complete Expository Dictionary of Old and New Testament Words* (Nashville: Thomas Nelson, 1996).
2. Vine, Unger, and White, *Vine's Expository Dictionary*.

Hopelessly Sick, a Permanent Cure

1. *Easton's Bible Dictionary*, PC Study Bible formatted electronic database, © 2003, 2006 Biblesoft, Inc.

CPSIA information can be obtained at www.ICGtesting.com
Printed in the USA
BVOW022312150712

295178BV00001B/5/P